Cleansing the City

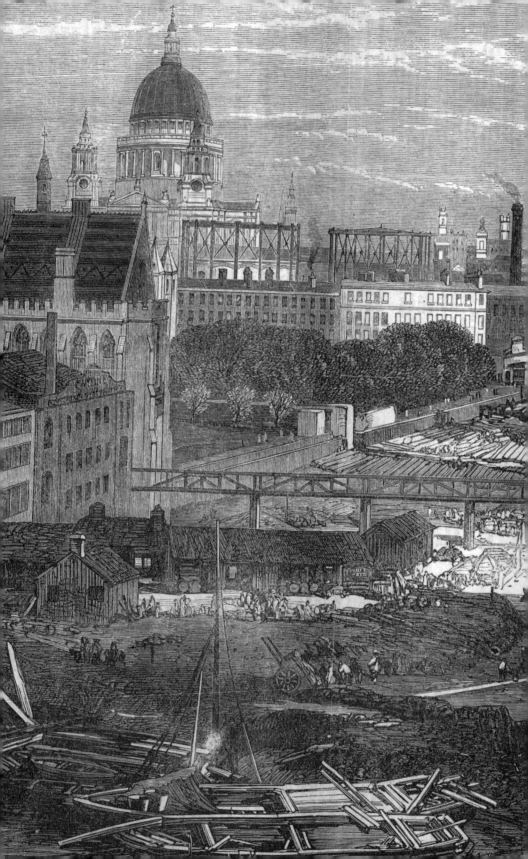

Cleansing the City

Sanitary Geographies in Victorian London

Michelle Allen

Ohio University Press

Athens

Ohio University Press, Athens, Ohio 45701
www.ohioswallow.com
© 2008 by Ohio University Press

Printed in the United States of America
All rights reserved

Ohio University Press books are printed on acid-free paper ⊗ ™

15 14 13 12 11 10 09 08   5 4 3 2 1

Library of Congress Cataloging-in-Publication Data

Allen, Michelle Elizabeth.
   Cleansing the city : sanitary geographies in Victorian London / Michelle Allen.
      p. ; cm.
   Includes bibliographical references and index.
   ISBN-13: 978-0-8214-1770-6 (hc : alk. paper)
   ISBN-10: 0-8214-1770-3 (hc : alk. paper)
   ISBN-13: 978-0-8214-1771-3 (pbk : alk. paper)
   ISBN-10: 0-8214-1771-1 (pbk : alk. paper)
   1. Hygiene—England—London—History—19th century. 2. Public health—England—
London—History—19th century. 3. Urban health—England—London—History—
19th century. 4. Dickens, Charles, 1812–1870. Our mutual friend 5. Gissing, George,
1857–1903. Nether world. I. Title.
   [DNLM: 1. Dickens, Charles, 1812–1870. Our mutual friend. 2. Gissing, George,
1857–1903. Nether world. 3. Public Health—history—London. 4. History, 19th Century—
London. 5. Medicine in Literature—London. 6. Sanitation—history—London. 7. Social
Environment—London. WA 11 FE5 A427ca 2008]
   RA488.L8A45 2008
   362.109421—dc22

2007041299

contents

illustrations

Acknowledgments

Working on a project about sewage over many years has been gratifying in some expected and unexpected ways. I have shared obscure sources and puzzled over nineteenth-century sanitary practices with colleagues, and I have had lively conversations about toilets and plumbing with near-total strangers. I made the requisite pilgrimage to the Paris Sewers Museum, and I received a private tour of the architecturally magnificent Abbey Mills sewage-pumping station in London. More important, I am fortunate to have been inspired and encouraged by many teachers, colleagues, family members, and friends.

Karen Chase and Michael Levenson filled many of these roles as codirectors of this project during its life as a dissertation at the University of Virginia. Their guidance and support were invaluable; likewise, their influence on not just this book but also my thinking about literature, history, and culture has been incalculable. Friends at Virginia vital to my success and my sanity include the remarkable women of the "diss group"—Amanda French, June Griffin, Elizabeth Outka, Lisa Spiro, and Virginia Zimmerman; Dickens seminar participants John Picker and Danny Siegel; and long-time supporters Raphael Shargel and Melissa Stickney. June, especially, talked me through more of this project than either of us probably cares to remember, and Virginia has remained my most trusted critic. Herbert Tucker and Cynthia Wall also read and offered their insights on my work at various junctures.

London, of course, has played a central role in the research and writing of this book. To Michael Levenson and Steve Cushman I owe the opportunity to spend two wonderful summers working with the Culture of London study-abroad program. I have fond memories of walking the city various summers with Margaret Croskery, Sonja Czarnecki, and Rosemary Gould. Ben Nithsdale of Thames Water very generously devoted a day of his work week to showing me the city's drains, at Beckton sewage works and at the aforementioned Abbey Mills. In London, I also first met David Pike, whose expertise in underground spaces continues to amaze, and Joe McLaughlin, who in his roles as reader and advisor more than anyone helped me make the leap from dissertation to book. Institutional support from the University of Virginia, the Locating the Victorians conference, and Lafayette College also made research in London possible.

More recently, the English Department at the U.S. Naval Academy has provided a more congenial and stimulating academic home than I could have ever imagined. Colleagues John Beckman, Allyson Booth, Anne Marie Drew, Fred Fetrow, Bob Madison, Charlie Nolan, Mike Parker, and Christy Stanlake have in their different ways helped keep me afloat. Mark McWilliams and Jason Shaffer (resident Shaw enthusiast) read parts of the manuscript and provided substantive criticism and advice. Ken Sabel helped with digital imaging. The Naval Academy Research Council provided summer funding, which enabled me to bring this project to fruition.

Many more people and institutions have helped make this book a reality. I am grateful to the staff of Alderman Library at the University of Virginia, Nimitz Library at the U.S. Naval Academy (particularly Flo Todd of Interlibrary Loan), the Library of Congress, the British Library, and London Metropolitan Archives. David Sanders at Ohio University Press has been enthusiastic about this project from the start, moving the book through the publication process with grace and efficiency. John Morris as editor and Sally Bennett as copyeditor both provided valuable assistance. I also appreciate the generous comments of the two anonymous readers of the manuscript for the Press; I hope I was able to do justice to their insights and suggestions through my revision. An earlier version of chapter 1 appeared as "From Cesspool to Sewer: Sanitary Reform and the Rhetoric of Resistance" in *Victorian Literature and Culture* 30, no. 2 (2002) and is reprinted with permission of the editors and publishers. I am also indebted to the organizers of and participants in a number of conferences where I was able to present my work, particularly the Middle Atlantic Conference on British Studies, Monuments and Dust, the Nineteenth-Century Studies Association, and the North American Victorian Studies Association.

Finally, I extend my warmest thanks to the Allen and Emerson families, especially Mary and Fred Allen for their love and generosity, Lottie Allen-Emerson for forcing me to stick to my deadlines, and Rob Emerson for his patience, good humor, and unwavering belief in me and my work.

Cleansing the City

The Sanitary City

The "Effacing Fingers" of Reform

*T*he rapid development of London in the nineteenth century brought new challenges not only to the health but also to the social order and cultural identity of the metropolis. Epidemic diseases, such as cholera and typhus, swept through the city. An unprecedented volume of waste matter overflowed from cesspools, rotted in out-of-the-way streets, and flooded the River Thames. Growing numbers of poor residents, who found their house space contracting as the city modernized, took refuge in filthy, overcrowded tenements. And the economic and social divide separating respectable citizens from the debased lower classes grew ever wider. Emerging from these material and social conditions was the movement for sanitary reform. Under this banner, individuals and associations from fields as diverse as medicine, journalism, and engineering campaigned in various ways to improve the health and welfare of the city. They planned sewers and other public works, explored and wrote about the darkest corners of the metropolis, advocated for public health legislation, and generally spread the gospel of sanitation: that cleanliness equals health, while dirt and disease equal death. The message was well received by educated members of the public, who became familiar with sanitary ideas not only through official reports but also through popular periodicals and novels.[1] Part of the explanation for the appeal lies in the sensational nature of much sanitary literature, which offered a titillating glance at sordid places and immoral acts. But sanitary reform also spoke to generations of Victorians because of the confidence of its adherents and the scope of their claims. As the Reverend Charles Girdlestone wrote in 1853, "Health . . . is not the only gain which sanitary reformers aim at."[2] Health was really the most humble claim of sanitary reformers; at their most ambitious, reformers promised to uplift a suffering urban underclass, to moralize the population, and thus to herald in a harmonious social order—they promised the new Jerusalem. Utopian visions aside, the achievements of sanitary reformers over the course of the century were substantial and significant. As a result of improvements in water supply and waste disposal, as well as in personal hygiene and nutrition, the death rate in England declined from 20.5 per thousand in 1861 to 16.9 in 1901.[3] And by most accounts, London was a cleaner and healthier place to live at the end of the century than at the beginning.

What we have yet to recognize, however, is that sanitary reform generated a surprising resistance. The challenge of purification aroused an anxiety perhaps less widespread but certainly no less real than that aroused by filth. Sanitary measures, such as slum clearances, sewer construction, and road improvements, were necessarily disruptive of the routines and sensibilities of urban inhabitants. As we shall see, the disruption associated with purification was far-reaching because in altering the physical space of the city, it altered its social and symbolic meanings, too. This book focuses on sites of filth and sites of purity, both as they were imagined and as they were experienced. In doing so, it highlights some of the difficulties, discomforts, and fears associated not simply with pollution but also with purification—a process we are inclined to see as generally positive. It is concerned less with the aims and accomplishments of sanitary reformers than with the range of responses to and perceptions of what was essentially a new urban phenomenon—the concerted cultivation of cleanliness. How did urban inhabitants understand the reconstruction of the built environment occasioned by sanitary measures? What kinds of imaginative responses were excited by these alterations, which affected both private and public landscapes? What do these often-ambivalent responses reveal about the everyday experience of modernization?

We can enter into these questions by way of a series of four articles titled "Some London Clearings," published in 1884–85 in *All the Year Round,* the weekly magazine begun by Charles Dickens and carried on after his death by his son. In the articles, the narrator acts as a guide, leading his readers through the twists and turns of labyrinthine London in search of relics from the city's past. In one piece he tracks down Milton's burial place, in another the medieval St. John's Gate in Clerkenwell, and in a third the former site of the French Protestant church in Soho. As he wanders, the narrator provides a running commentary on the people and events associated with certain places, many of which have disappeared or will soon disappear from the urban scene. Of course, as the title indicates, the occasion for reminiscence is "some London clearings," that is, the destruction of the old urban fabric to make way for wide thoroughfares, railway lines and stations, warehouses, and the like. Clearances of this sort had convulsed central London since the 1840s and were closely associated with sanitary reform because they destroyed and thus "purified" some of the most densely built, most densely populated, and dirtiest areas of the city. In the context of the series in *All the Year Round,* clearance schemes obviously threaten the historic landscape the narrator seeks to explore. Yet, paradoxically, they also serve as the impetus for urban exploration.

This dynamic plays out clearly in the third article from the series, focused on Eastcheap.[4] The narrator chooses to explore the area for the very reason that it has recently undergone reconstruction. In the early 1880s, the Metropolitan and District Railway companies extended the line of the Underground eastward toward Tower Hill and, in the process, widened and improved some of the affected streets, including Eastcheap itself. The article begins, appropriately enough, with a journey on the new section of the Underground, "at this moment a new and startling experience" ("Eastcheap," 103). As the narrator leads his readers out of the station, he emphasizes the utter unfamiliarity of a scene once quite familiar:

> And now everything is changed. For if you will trust yourself implicitly to some friendly guide . . . when you come out into the

open air . . . it is quite probable that you will fail to guess rightly
where you are. For apart from the novelty of thus coming up to daylight in the very inner recesses of the City, there is a certain strange-
ness and unfamiliarity about the scene. Here is a meeting-place of
great thoroughfares, with a whirl of traffic from the various con-
verging streams; but there is a feeling of space and roominess which
is quite a new sensation in this part of the City. ("Eastcheap," 103)

The narrator takes pleasure in the novelty of open space and wide thoroughfares in such a busy, congested part of the city; however, he passes quickly
from celebration of the new to nostalgic remembrance of the old, specifically,
"the Eastcheap of Shakespeare's times" ("Eastcheap," 104). There follows an
extended reverie on the Old Boar's Head tavern and the fictional characters
—Bardolph, Nym, Pistol, Falstaff—who haunted it, although nothing of the
structure remains. Similarly, entering Seething Lane, the narrator recollects
that Samuel Pepys lived in the area, although literally there is "nothing very
much to remind us of the days of Pepys at the end of this lane" ("Eastcheap,"
107). He finds one link to the past in the shape of a solid red-brick house that
Pepys "may have seen," but this link seems precarious not only because Pepys
may (or may not) have seen it but also because the house sits in the midst of
a ruin, the lone survivor among similar houses only recently destroyed. Ruin
lends itself to reverie and to mildly expressed regret: "[N]ow no more shall
domestic fires burn in those snug fireplaces . . . for here is an end of it all in
a heap of old bricks and some ragged rafters" ("Eastcheap," 108). This is the
shape of the new sanitary city: "space and roominess" on one side, "a heap of
old bricks and some ragged rafters" on the other. The sanitary city is in a state
of flux with destructive and constructive forces working in an uneven rhythm
to yield a landscape never wholly new, yet never entirely old.

Since he focuses so much attention on old London, we might reasonably
expect the narrator to lament its rampant destruction, and at moments he does.
In the article on Clerkenwell, he marvels over the changes effected by the
construction of Clerkenwell Road and regrets the disfigurement of St. John's
Square and some of the smaller streets leading into the square: "At the present
date it is difficult to make out the ancient precincts of the priory, for the
Clerkenwell Road has been driven right through the old streets and courts
which might have given a clue to the former plan; and St. John's Gate seems

to lead from nowhere to chaos."[5] Of the adjacent Red Lion Street, he remarks, "[I]t is rather disappointing to find that the early numbers are missing, have vanished, indeed, into the open clearing, for we had hoped to find Number One still existing, the old Jerusalem tavern" ("Clerkenwell," 125). But as in the article on Eastcheap, the absence of the Jerusalem tavern does not hinder— and may even aid—the author's imaginative rendering of eighteenth-century street life: the recollection of those who once lived in the now-dismantled Red Lion Street seems to afford the writer ample pleasure and ample subject matter.

Across the series, the narrator acknowledges certain negative consequences of urban improvement, including the impact of clearances not only on historic places but also on the urban poor; for those parts of town targeted for destruction by both government bodies and private companies were invariably inhabited by the city's poorest classes. Cutting lines of communication through the slums made good financial sense (because the property was less valuable than most in central London) and good sanitary sense (because the known harbors of filth and disease would be eradicated). At the same time, these clearances displaced thousands of working-class inhabitants, who already had limited housing options. As we shall see, the recognition of the harrowing impact of reform on the working classes had become almost a cliché in journalism of the 1880s. In the articles for *All the Year Round,* the narrator in typical fashion raises the curtain on the often-uncalculated human cost of improvement, noting the forced migration of the urban poor, first, in the context of the Metropolitan and District Railways' expansion in the City, and in a later piece, in the context of the imminent creation of Shaftesbury Road in Soho. Standing near the City boundary, he explains in the first piece that Crippelgate has become "a very Lazarus gate, out of which the privileged City has turned its poor. Clerkenwell, St. Luke's . . . Hoxton, and Shoreditch, with Bethnal Green, form a solid mass of closely packed houses, amongst which the only people who really flourish are the publicans."[6] And in the latter piece on Soho, he notes the sudden exposure of an ordinarily hidden way of life, as clearances penetrate the closely built spaces: "The old street, half of which has been lopped away, has a curious blinking, half-awakened aspect . . . full daylight streaming in where once was convenient gloom and obscurity. Many of the inhabitants are packing up their goods and chattels—the bundles of old rags and old rubbish out of which by some mysterious alchemy they have hitherto contrived to make a living."[7] If only briefly, the narrator reminds us of the human beings who live amidst—and are swept aside with—the old rubbish.

I am not suggesting that the narrator makes a humanitarian argument against slum clearances, but I do think these observations reflect an understanding of the complexity of urban change. If, in any case, he were to make a case against clearances, it would most likely be on aesthetic grounds. He expresses regret over the disappearance of the "dingy old streets" of Soho, as with the old streets of Clerkenwell and Eastcheap, and he laments that "the effacing fingers of the Board of Works are passing over the ancient landmarks" ("Soho," 309). Nevertheless, regret should not be confused with opposition to "the effacing fingers" of progress. Indeed, the narrator admits that as much as he loves the picturesque flavor of Soho, still, "little may be worth preserving" ("Soho," 309). Nowhere in the series does he explicitly advocate preservation or call for a halt to progress. Furthermore, as we have seen, he is as ready to admire the fruits of improvement as he is to lament the lost past. It is with a flush of civic pride that the narrator looks out on the new thoroughfare of Eastcheap: "[A] fine, broad, open way," he calls it, "which now leads as a grand central avenue to the Tower" ("Eastcheap," 104). In addition to affording an impressive view of the Tower of London, the local clearings have opened up a view of the Monument to the Great Fire; the monument is "no longer lost among *dingy courts and lanes,* but looking as if it meant to take its share of what is going on the world, after its long retirement" ("Eastcheap," 104–5; emphasis added). The "dingy old streets" that are appealing in one context are in another merely obstructive; in an interesting twist, clearances made in the name of progress—the railway—also carve a path into the past, in the form of a monument to a defining event in London's history. For one urban observer, improvements entail a loss, but they also provide challenges that are not entirely unwelcome: the challenge to reconstruct an imagined past from small clues remaining in the present and the challenge simply to find one's way in a city defined by change. The narrator concludes the final installment of the series by accepting the inevitability of change but takes a tone that is unmistakably elegiac: "And so the work goes on, and when we come again the once familiar corner is a thing of the past" ("Soho," 312).

This ambivalent, multifaceted response to urban improvement takes us to the heart of this project. For in the pages that follow, I pay particular attention to responses that afford an alternative perspective on the reform question: that is, responses that challenge the widely held belief in the unquestioned efficacy and desirability of sanitary reforms. These responses generally reflect a middle-class perspective; the middle-class bias of the source material consulted for this study prevents us from hearing the unmediated voices of the working classes, even when the fate of the dispossessed is the explicit topic of inquiry. Yet within this limited middle-class register, the responses to reform are surprisingly diverse. They may, for instance, express nostalgic attachment to an urban landscape threatened by progress (as in the case of the pieces from *All the Year Round*); they may express anxiety about the effects that sanitary appliances and techniques have on middle-class family life; or they may express disillusionment with the efficacy of reform in improving the working classes. I do not mean to suggest that responses of this sort are ideologically neutral; on the contrary, expressions of both resistance and support for sanitary reform reveal a range of assumptions about poverty and social class, about the integrity of the individual and of domestic life, and about urban and national identity. One reason for examining the varied responses to sanitary developments is that they tell us a great deal about these assumptions. Still, it is important to recognize the highly imaginative, often idiosyncratic, character of much of the writing on sanitary topics: it cannot be reduced to a single ideological interpretation. It can, however, give us insight into the fears, frustrations, and delights excited by the daily experience of a city in the throes of modernization.

The Danger of Dirt

Exactly why conversations about dirt reflect so many concerns central to the experience of modernity has everything to do with the changed significance of filth and purity in the nineteenth century. In the literature of London life, images of filth are certainly not exclusive to the Victorian period. We need only recall Jonathan Swift's indulgent evocation of waste imagery in "A Description of a City Shower" (1710) for confirmation: "Sweepings from butchers' stalls, dung, guts and blood, / Drowned puppies, stinking sprats, all drenched in mud, / Dead cats, and turnip tops, come tumbling down the flood."[8] The resonant triplet concludes an ambitious catalogue of the animate and inanimate refuse that competes for space in the London streets. Representations of foul water and filthy streets abound in eighteenth-century literature, from Swift's "City Shower" to Defoe's *Tour Thro' the Whole Island of Great Britain* (1724–26) to Smollett's *Humphry Clinker* (1771). But in the nineteenth century, the literary engagement with filth became more urgent, as filth itself took on more challenging material and social meanings.

Consider, for instance, the following passage from Charles Dickens's *Dombey and Son* (1848):

> Those who study the physical sciences, and bring them to bear upon the health of Man, tell us that if the noxious particles that rise from vitiated air were palpable to the sight, we should see them lowering in a dense black cloud above such haunts, and rolling slowly on to corrupt the better portions of a town. But if the moral pestilence that rises with them, and in the eternal laws of outraged Nature, is inseparable from them, could be made discernible too, how terrible the revelation! Then should we see depravity, impiety, drunkenness, theft, murder, and a long train of nameless sins against the natural affections and repulsions of man-kind, overhanging the devoted spots, and creeping on, to blight the innocent and spread contagion among the pure.[9]

The description of the progress of pollution and disease is fully informed by contemporary medical and scientific discourse: according to the miasmic theory of disease, people contracted infectious diseases by breathing the fumes generated by decomposing wastes. "Vitiated air," invisible and diffuse, constituted one of the gravest dangers of urban life. In the passage, however, Dickens uses miasmic theory to its full metaphoric potential, imagining fetid matter and foul air not only as sources of disease but also as sources of the moral and social disorder of the city. In fact, Dickens suggests that "moral pestilence" is "inseparable" from physical corruption and that filth may, after all, be just another name for "depravity, impiety, drunkenness, theft, murder." But the real horror of the passage lies in the idea of social transgression, of the unstoppable communication of a pestilence—moral or otherwise—from the poor to the rich. Miasmas are almost always imagined to travel from low "haunts" to "the better portions of a town." From Dickens's striking representation of urban pollution, we may infer a provisional generalization about the meanings of filth for the educated members of the middle class in mid-Victorian cities: the problem of filth was at once a physical danger (defined as such by an emergent scientific authority), a demoralizing influence, and a social threat; moreover, it was inextricably tied to perceptions and anxieties about the urban poor, who were themselves insufficiently contained.

We can link the newly acquired meanings of filth in the period to the urban environment itself and, more broadly, to the processes of modernization.[10] By the middle of the nineteenth century, Britain had become essentially urban in character, as more people lived in towns than in the country for the first time in its history.[11] London was at the center of this demographic shift and registered its impact at every level of experience. Its population grew from about a million in 1800 to over seven million in 1911.[12] This growth paralleled other social and material changes that were astonishing to many Victorian observers. The city's geographic limits expanded in every direction as speculative builders aggressively developed the surrounding countryside.[13] Ever more invasive railway lines above- and belowground increased Londoners' mobility and made possible the suburban expansion, but they also cut through neighborhoods and destroyed vast amounts of working-class housing. Along with the construction of new streets and docks, warehouses and office blocks, the railway contributed to the overcrowded and degraded living conditions of the poor, who despite demolitions and evictions generally remained within the central districts to be near their work.[14] The social and economic gulf separating the respectable classes from the laboring classes thus found an analogue in increasing spatial segregation.

The rapid and uncontrolled development of London was not without its costs, placing as it did new pressures on urban space and resources. Certainly one of the more offensive costs was the high concentration of filth in the city: human, animal, and industrial wastes of an unprecedented volume flooded the Thames, collected in streets, overfilled cesspools and privies, and impressed themselves on urban consciousness. Historian Anthony Wohl succinctly articulates the urban equation: "[T]he accumulation of excrement . . . was the unavoidable by-product of urban growth."[15] How to dispose of the accumulated waste was a problem that preoccupied the minds of countless reformers, engineers, scientists, and amateur sanitarians, but the problem acquired a particular urgency because the retention of waste in the city was associated with disease and even death. Henry Morley, a regular contributor to Dickens's journals *Household Words* and *All the Year Round,* spoke for his generation when he remarked in 1858, "[W]e have discovered the great danger of dirt."[16] This critical connection derived from the miasmic, or "pythogenic," theory of disease, which held sway in public health circles into the 1880s.[17] Adherents of this theory pitted themselves against "contagionists," who maintained that epidemic diseases were spread by person-to-person contact; the "anticontagionists," in contrast, maintained that disease was transmitted by contact with a corrupt environment, specifically, with the poisoned air generated by decomposing matter. The exact nature of these airborne poisons was unknown and, moreover, of little interest to sanitary reformers, who focused their energies less on medical theory than on practical efforts to reduce the spread of disease.[19] The campaign against dirt and, more specifically, against decomposition was thus based on an incorrect (or at least, incomplete) theory, but experience nevertheless seemed to bear the theory out. Major epidemic diseases, notably cholera, typhus, and typhoid, were on the rise in Victorian England, and these diseases did indeed flourish in filthy environments.[20]

Cholera was especially influential in determining the meaning of filth in the nineteenth century. Reaching England for the first time in 1831, it appeared again in 1848–49, 1853–54, and 1866–67.[21] Part of the reason the disease caused such alarm was that it spread quickly and unpredictably through the population. Its victims were also struck down suddenly and very often with fatal results: during the first outbreak, over five thousand people in London and around thirty-two thousand across England died.[22] As the German researcher Robert Koch discovered in 1884, the source of the disease is the cholera bacillus, which can be transmitted through contaminated water or excrement.[23] Earlier in the century, however, its etiology was still very much debated. In 1854, the physician John Snow famously traced the outbreak of the disease in Soho to a water pump providing contaminated supplies.[24] But this discovery did not prove conclusive for most in the sanitary and medical communities, and more general miasmic explanations continued to prevail. Wohl's finding that over seven hundred studies of cholera were published between 1845 and 1856 illustrates both the intensity of debate about the nature and origins of the disease, and the anxiety surrounding its appearance.[25] In his discussion of cholera,

Bill Luckin makes the point that this kind of attention helped consolidate public opinion about the danger of dirt: "[T]he Victorian obsession with the infection and its causation was central to the full emergence of pollution as a major social problem."[26]

Fully connected with the challenge of excremental accumulation was another distressing "by-product of urban growth": large concentrations of poverty. London may have been the wealthiest city in the world, but as the physician and sanitary reformer Hector Gavin insisted in 1848, "[A] mass of misery . . . fester[ed] beneath the affluence of London."[27] While many middle-class residents had the luxury of open space in the suburbs, the poorest of the working classes found themselves ever more crowded in the increasingly less residential central parts of the city. The living conditions of these inhabitants were notoriously wretched. Throughout the century, parish officers, doctors, reformers, and journalists obsessively described and redescribed the scene of urban poverty. Bare, dark, and filthy rooms with decaying walls and broken windowpanes; interiors crowded with ragged and ill-nourished human beings; putrid waste matter, fetid cesspools, and piles of reeking garbage in the courts and alleys—all figure prominently in these accounts. Not surprisingly, conditions of this sort were attended by a high incidence of disease and mortality, reinforcing stereotypical perceptions of the poor as both dirty and —in an age when dirt meant disease—dangerous. In *Town Swamps and Social Bridges* (1859), George Godwin, the committed social reformer and long-time editor of the architectural journal the *Builder,* traces the links in the chain connecting poverty, filth, and disease: "[W]here human beings are crowded to-gether in ill-arranged dwellings; where the drainage is bad and the cesspool lurks; where refuse rots, the air is vitiated, or the water impure and scanty,—there cholera and fever . . . reign and slay."[28] The grammatical alignment of "human beings" with "drainage," "cesspool," and "refuse" is worth noting here, not only because correlations of this sort were frequent in writing about the urban condition but also because they indicate the difficulty of isolating the perceived dangers of urban life. Which was more troubling, cesspools or human degradation? Pollution itself or what it represented?

Sanitary reform emerged within this context as both an outgrowth of urbanization and a constituent part of it. The cholera epidemic was critical in the move to institutionalize sanitary reform in the 1830s and 1840s, and the earliest efforts of reformers were directed toward the challenge of preventing the disease. In Roy Porter's phrase, "Cholera concentrated the mind."[29] At the heart of the sanitary movement was the conviction that such diseases were indeed preventable and that their prevention lay in the rational organization of the environment. The titles of two early documents of the movement—both published in 1838—indicate the philosophy quite clearly, if not succinctly: the physicians Neil Arnott and James Kay (later Kay-Shuttleworth) produced the "Report on the Prevalence of Certain Physical Causes of Fever in the Metropolis, which Might Be Removed by Proper Sanatory Measures," and Dr. Thomas Southwood Smith contributed the "Report on Some of the Physical Causes of Sickness and Mortality to Which the Poor Are Particularly Exposed; and Which Are Capable of Removal by Sanatory Regulations." The reports were initiated by Edwin Chadwick in his capacity as secretary to the Poor Law Commission, and according to Francis Sheppard, they "provided the blue-prints for the mid-nineteenth-century sanitary movement."[30] For Chadwick, the most visible figure of the sanitary movement in its formative years, the environmentalist principle and, more specifically, the miasmic theory of disease helped shape a systematic approach to waste disposal in the metropolis. With the threat of cholera again imminent at the end of 1847, the Royal Commission on the Health of the Metropolis, headed by Chadwick, asserted that the best recourse against the spread of the disease was "sanitary arrangements . . . such as will secure the purity of the atmosphere, particularly by the immediate and complete removal of all filth and refuse."[31] Removing waste from the city as quickly as it was produced and before the dreaded decomposition was allowed to begin was the imperative around which Chadwick's sanitary program was organized; the pipe sewer would be his central tool. Chadwick's technical approach to waste removal was in fact comprehensive. "Its central conception," according to his biographer S. E. Finer, "was that of an articulated service where water supply, house drainage, street drainage, and the main sewerage and the cleansing of streets should form a circle in which the motive power and mode of cleansing depended upon *Hydraulic Power*."[32] We see in Chadwick's commitment to an integrated system of sewerage and to the removal of wastes by water the prototype of modern sanitation.

As technologically and administratively oriented as sanitary reform was, it was still a highly moralistic discourse with one eye trained steadily on the urban poor. Indeed, the problem of poverty was central to Chadwick's sanitary program, originating as it did in his work for the Poor Law Commission. According to Chadwick's reasoning, since disease was a burden on the poor rates and a threat to productive labor, prevention of disease made good economic sense.[33] The inquiries into prevention directed by Chadwick and undertaken by Arnott, Kay, and Southwood Smith focused on the most impoverished neighborhoods in London's East End. The theory and practice of sanitary science were thus fully shaped by prevailing social assumptions about the poor. As Gerry Kearns has argued, "[T]he environmental approach did not completely displace other conceptions of disease in scientific or popular works. Disease, filth, and contagion retained moral and class-based connotations."[34] We see, for instance, in the thought of Southwood Smith a full investment in the moral dimension of public health reform—an investment that is not surprising given his dual roles as physician and Unitarian minister. It is worth reproducing here a relevant portion from his testimony before the Royal Commission on the State of Large Towns and Populous Districts (1844):

> A clean, fresh, and well-ordered house exercises over its inmates a moral, no less than a physical, influence, and has a direct tendency to make the members of the family sober, peaceable, and considerate of the feelings and happiness of each other; nor is it difficult to trace a connection between habitual feelings of this sort and the formation of habits of respect for property, for the laws in general, and even for those higher duties and obligations, the observance of which no laws can enforce: whereas, a filthy, squalid, unwholesome dwelling, in which none of the decencies common to society, even in the lowest stage of civilization, are or can be observed, tends directly to make every dweller in such a hovel regardless of the feelings and happiness of each other, selfish and sensual; and the connection is obvious between the constant indulgence of appetites and passions of this class, and the formation of habits of idleness, dishonesty, debauchery, and violence; in a word, the training to every kind and degree of brutality and ruffianism.[35]

In the passage, Southwood Smith forges a causal link between the environment and morality: while a clean house "has a direct tendency" to produce righteous minds, a filthy house "tends directly" to turn people into brutes. But the environmental argument is overshadowed by the litany of stereotypical descriptors applied to the urban poor: sensual, idle, improvident, dishonest, animalistic. The (bad) habits of the poor eclipse the unsanitary conditions that are Southwood Smith's ostensible subject. The result is a near collapse of causality, and instead we get something closer to identification: filth, disease, poverty, and immorality are so closely bound that each term could easily serve as a metonym for all the others. Southwood Smith races from filth to brutality in the span of a single sentence, obscuring along the way the distinction between physical and moral disease and suggesting the expanded purview of the urban physician.

The passage articulates more directly some of the possibilities that Dickens suggests in *Dombey and Son*. Together the two passages reveal the heightened symbolism of filth in the period and, more specifically, the way filth embodied the challenges of the urban condition. Indeed, sanitary discourse became an important vehicle for expressing concerns about the disorder associated with the Victorian city. As we have seen, urban disorder took many shapes, ranging from disease to immoral behavior to social subversion. All these problems were imaginatively traced to the massing together of a degraded population—the "great unwashed"—in an insalubrious environment. The city thus served as a breeding ground for dangerous people and activities, such as crime, alcoholism, prostitution, and political radicalism; moreover, because the city encouraged mobility, these dangers could not be easily isolated. To use a metaphor drawn from miasmic theory, quarantine was an ineffective stay against the pervasive epidemic atmosphere of the town. The anxiety excited by filth owed much to its association with the dangers of urban life. At the same time, this association must have served a useful imaginative function, since filth—unlike less tangible urban threats—could be collected and removed. Filth could be flushed.

Following anthropologist Mary Douglas's important work on the symbolic function of pollution behaviors, we can recognize the dialectical relationship between filth and purity. As Douglas argues, dirt is "matter out of place" and, thus, part of a larger symbolic system of the "ordering and classification of matter."[36] David Trotter similarly associates waste with system (although in his study of nineteenth-century art and fiction, *Cooking with Mud*, he imagines an

alternative to waste in the decidedly unsystematic phenomenon of "mess").
For Trotter, waste is always symptomatic, signifying a failure of the system that
produced it: "It testifies, in its very dereliction, to the power which cast it
down and out."[37] This understanding of filth and purity as system—what
William Cohen identifies as a "structural argument"[38]—underpins my discussion of sanitary reform in the chapters that follow. Applying this approach
to the Victorian context helps us understand how the specific and, at the same
time, capacious definition of filth in the period gave rise to an equally specific
and capacious definition of purity. Victorian filth, we might say, created sanitary reform; that is, the particular way in which the Victorians imagined filth
lent itself to a way of imagining purity that took shape as sanitary reform.
Filth signified urban disease in its widest sense—a failure of the urban system.
In providing the cure, sanitation had to address itself equally to the urban system, to the entire spectrum of material and social disorders associated with
the Victorian city. Sanitary measures, such as ridding the city of decomposing
matter, eliminated filth figured as disease, but these same measures, by providing a "clean, fresh, and well-ordered" living environment, were imagined
to eliminate filth figured as the improvident slum dweller. Sanitary reform was
thus uniquely suited both to conditions on the ground and to the metaphoric
meanings that had accrued to filth in the nineteenth century.

This idea of sanitary reform as a comprehensive solution to the multiply constituted problem of filth finds its fullest expression in the writings of Charles
Kingsley, novelist, social reformer, and Anglican priest. Like Chadwick waging
a war against accumulated waste, Kingsley conducted a lifelong campaign
to redeem the social and spiritual condition of the poor by improving their
physical condition. For Kingsley, the deplorable state of modern urban life—
characterized by a demoralized working class increasingly alienated from a
prosperous ruling class—was directly traceable to its sanitary condition. In
the lecture "Great Cities and Their Influence for Good and Evil" (1857),
Kingsley emphasizes this interdependence: "[T]he social state of a city depends
directly on its moral state, and . . . on the physical state of that city; on the
food, water, air, and lodging of its inhabitants."[39] What lends additional force
to this otherwise-familiar argument is the context in which Kingsley expresses
it: he draws this sanitary "lesson" from his boyhood experience of the Bristol
Riots in 1831. The rather amazing implication is that clean air would have

prevented such an uprising in Bristol, as it would in all such cities where the degraded population has "nothing to lose and all to gain by anarchy."[40] The proposition accords to sanitary reform tremendous social power.

But if reform was able to promote the political and social health of the community, it was no less capable of fostering its spiritual health. As a clergyman, Kingsley made it his mission to foreground what had been traditionally repudiated by the church: the material conditions of life and the physical condition of individual bodies.[41] In the introduction to his collection of sermons, *Who Causes Pestilence?* (1854), Kingsley maintains that it is a "sacred duty" to minister to the people's physical needs and "to go forth on a crusade against filth."[42] Only by attending to the needs of the body can the needs of the mind and the soul be met. Yet sanitary reform was not merely an act of duty to one's fellow men and women; it was an act of righteousness demanded by God. Kingsley was not alone in this providential interpretation of reform. In fact, as Graeme Davison and Christopher Hamlin have shown, the sanitary movement was grounded in a natural theology that had been reframed in the early nineteenth century to address urban life.[43] According to this view, the city, like nature, was a carefully contrived system, reflecting the providential order of the universe. Outbreaks of disease, the prevalence of slums, river pollution, and such were merely anomalies that could—and must—be rectified to restore the divine order (and divine favor). In "Charles Kingsley: The Rector in the City," Marc Reboul describes Kingsley's faith in the possibilities of reform as "the providential—if slightly utopian—means that could be used to by-pass social antagonisms and to create God's Kingdom on earth."[44] For Kingsley and other Victorian sanitary reformers, the aphorism that cleanliness was next to godliness had taken on new meaning in an urbanized world.

In the comprehensive vision of sanitary reform drawn by Kingsley, we find a clue to the movement's cultural and literary resonance. Sanitary reform gained a hold on the public imagination because while it addressed (and often cultivated) people's anxieties about the dangers of the city, it also offered a plan for alleviating these dangers. To return to Trotter's idea of waste as system, sanitary reform made a chaotic world intelligible: "Waste-theory makes it possible to understand the most intractable phenomena—ooze and slush, a prostitute—as the outcome of system: as malfunction, or surplus function, rather than random perversity or bad luck."[45] In other words, sanitary reform served as a kind of framework for making sense of urban problems and urban change, from the spread of disease to the growth of a suffering underclass, from the profusion of filth to the decline of religious observance. These were failings, but with the right adjustments to the urban system—the draining of cesspools, the clearing of slums—they could be resolved. Moreover, as Davison contends, sanitary reform succeeded as an idea because it had an "intellectual coherence": this coherence can be attributed to its grounding in natural theology, which cast human and divine, material and spiritual elements in a unified narrative of progressive change.[46] Unlike educational, religious, or even political reforms, sanitary reform provided a clear and comprehensive vision of the city in a time of great change. It offered the comfort that comes from certitude.

As compelling as this ideal vision of reform was and is, this book directs critical attention to very different, often antagonistic, visions of and responses to sanitary progress. These significant alternative perspectives have been largely overlooked in historical and literary studies. Scholars have tended, rather, to emphasize the power and reach of the sanitary movement, implicitly regarding Kingsley's, Chadwick's, and others' dedication to the cause of cleanliness as characteristic of liberal Victorian attitudes.[47] This emphasis reflects the still-pervasive idea of the Victorian period as an age of reform, but perhaps it also reflects a more fundamental conviction about the universal desirability of modern sanitation and hygiene.[48] Looking backward from a (Western) sanitary landscape happily provided with flush toilets and waterborne sewage, we are more likely to appreciate the exertions of a Chadwick than the protestations of an unknown pamphleteer who, for example, warns of the danger of sewer gases infiltrating the home. It is one of the guiding assumptions of this study, however, that the cry of the unknown pamphleteer has much to teach us about the contested process of change in the Victorian city.

Matter in Place

As I have already suggested, the initiatives of the sanitary movement were inevitably bound up with ideas about the city and, more specifically, with ideas about the organization and meaning of urban space. However else it manifested itself in the culture, sanitary reform was necessarily a spatial phenomenon. The problem of filth was conceived primarily in spatial terms: waste matter accumulated in the city's streets, alleys, and courts; sewage fouled the river Thames in the geographical heart of the city; and the poor crowded to-gether in disease-ridden tenements, which were a blight on the urban land-scape. The solutions reformers sought were likewise conceived in spatial terms: the construction of sewers and embankments would channel waste out of the city; model dwellings would provide healthful accommodation for the working classes; and slum clearances would create a more commodious city. What reform demanded was a fundamental reconfiguration and, hence, respatialization of the city. One of the aims of the chapters that follow is to demonstrate how in changing the shape of the city, sanitary reform altered the cultural meanings and human experience of it. For as the insights of cultural geography have taught us, space is *meaningful*: that is, spatial formations reflect and instantiate a range of meanings and values, from the cultural to the social to the political. As significant as the spatial dimension of reform is, however, few studies of the movement have looked seriously at the actual spaces of re-form, at the impact of reform on the ground level. Literary critics have un-derstandably privileged the textual and discursive in their work on sanitary reform. Joseph Childers and Nancy Metz, for instance, have contributed important work on the shared rhetoric and representational strategies of literature and sanitary reports, and Mary Poovey has explored the similar ideological commitments of the sanitary movement and domesticity.[49] In this book, I provide a more comprehensive view of sanitary reform and its relation to the social and material life of the city by reconceiving the subject in terms of geography. A critical geography of reform encompasses at once the textual, the social, and the spatial, allowing us to see interplay among discourse, the social order, and the built environment.

In this emphasis on the significance of space, I have been influenced by the turn toward geography seen in recent literary and cultural criticism.[50] The recognition now of the importance of bringing a spatial perspective to social and cultural analysis has its foundation in the work of Henri Lefebvre, Michel Foucault, and Edward Soja, among others. In *The Production of Space,* Lefebvre brings the insights of Marx to bear on the sustained study of space, which (like Marx's commodities) has a story to tell about social life. "Space," argues Lefebvre, "implies, contains and dissimulates social relations."[51] It does so be-cause it is at once the product, or outcome, of social life and the constraining medium through which social life takes shape. As Soja explains in *Postmodern*

Geographies, the idea of space as socially produced and, in turn, productive of social life and action runs counter to deeply held assumptions about the neutrality, or naturalness, of space.[52] But, as he insists elsewhere, society cannot really be imagined outside of a spatial matrix (and vice versa): the process of spatial reproduction "gives form not only to the grand movements of societal development but also to the recursive practice of day-to-day activity."[53] Space is thus not merely reflective but also constitutive of social experience. Foucault tends to imagine these spatial operations in terms of a disciplinary power. In remarks on Bentham's Panopticon, a technology of power that clearly operates through a specific architectural form, he describes space as an expression of might and an enforcer of moral behavior.[54] While certainly one should recognize that the interests of the powerful are expressed and reproduced through space, postpositivist geographers have also been careful to allow for limited human agency. According to Trevor Barnes and Derek Gregory, "People can't make places be whatever they want them to be. . . . At the same time, the wider social structure is not all-determining, immutably fixing people and places."[55]

The insights of humanist geographer Yi-Fu Tuan are particularly relevant to this problem of the individual's relation to social space. In *Topophilia,* Tuan emphasizes the experiential aspect of geography, that is, the way people perceive and experience place—a phenomenon he calls "topophilia."[56] Tuan's sustained engagement with questions of feeling and value, enjoyment and attachment, in relation to the environment has encouraged me to focus on the experiential dimension of Victorian sanitary history, to describe that elusive area where public works and private feelings meet. If Tuan's work reminds us to take seriously feelings about space, then the work of spatial theorists helps explain why such feelings can run so hot: there is a great deal at stake in the disposition of space. As Soja conceives it, the process of social reproduction is continual but not seamless. He describes lived space as a "competitive arena . . . for social practices aimed either at the maintenance and reinforcement of existing spatiality or at significant restructuring and/or radical transformation."[57] This claim helps us make sense of the competing responses to sanitary reform, expressions both of support and of resistance. These responses, which center on the organization of urban space, ultimately express competing visions of social life and competing cultural values.

As part of the emphasis on the spatial dimension of reform, the pages that follow also reflect a commitment to the particularity of place. Many literary critical discussions of the city treat urban experience in general terms, often privileging certain theoretical concepts, such as the crowd, the flaneur, or urban spectacle.[58] As useful as these discussions may be, we can achieve a more nuanced understanding of city life by recognizing the multiplicity of places that constitute the city and by approaching each place with a respect for its singularity. As Joseph McLaughlin explains in the context of his analysis of Joseph Conrad's novel *The Secret Agent,* "While it is certainly not incorrect to think in terms of a somewhat abstract opposition between *the* office and *the* street, we must also remember that for Conrad these were not mythic abstractions; instead they were specific buildings (Scotland Yard and Charing Cross Station) and streetscapes (the Strand)."[59] Preferring the specific to the abstract when writing about the city requires us to take seriously the minutiae of history, literature, and geography, such as the precise route that a character takes in a novel or the material and symbolic significance of being upriver versus downriver. When we attend to particular places and to the ideas and conceptions of such places, we come closer to understanding the felt experience of the city at a given moment. We also begin to appreciate that the process of urban change—or, in this case, sanitary development—affected people in very different ways depending on their spatial and social locations.

Critical to this textual and experiential study of London's sanitary life is the joining together of a rich variety of documentary materials, from the archival records of the Metropolitan Board of Works to the cartoons of *Punch* magazine, from special-interest periodicals such as the *Builder* to illustrated weeklies such as the *Graphic* and *Illustrated London News.* At the same time, the Victorian novel plays a central role in the book. We can understand this role by invoking once again the language and insights of cultural geography. From this perspective, literature is not exempt from the processes of social and spatial formation; on the contrary, literary productions continually emerge from and re-enter the social and material field. At the same time, literature is capable of critiquing these very processes by creating new visions of space and society that may challenge prevailing ideas. In other words, these new conceptions of space, or imagined geographies, can be important sites of resistance. These assumptions inform the extended discussions of Dickens's *Our*

Mutual Friend and George Gissing's *Nether World* in chapters 3 and 5. Both novels are expressly concerned with the problem of filth and the pursuit of cleanliness in London; both explore the possibilities and limits of social, moral, and spatial regeneration; and both engage with these issues through the representation of urban space. As attuned as they are to material conditions, the novels offer imagined geographies that privilege the human experience of urban improvement and that recognize the emotional resonance of urban space. These and other novelistic reconceptions of space, then, afford an alternative way of seeing and perhaps redefining the city. They may reflect a felt disorientation, they may restore the integrity of a devalued place, or they may imagine a place not yet created.

From Resistance to Disillusion

Each chapter addresses the social challenge and imaginative resonance of filth and purification within the context of one of several key sanitary initiatives: waste disposal, river purification, and housing reform. The first chapter reveals the surprising resistance to reform excited by the London sewer. Although the developing sewerage technology seemed to exemplify sanitary progress, many social observers represented the underground network of pipes as an instrument of social chaos, threatening the ideals of spatial division and social hierarchy in the urban context. In the second chapter, centered on debates about the pollution and purification of the Thames in the 1850s and 1860s, I focus on expressions of resistance to the Thames Embankment, one of Victorian London's most celebrated engineering achievements. Despite the wide support the Embankment received, many observers lamented the loss of an eccentric and vital riverside culture that the Embankment was imagined to displace. Chapter 3 continues the discussion of the polluted river in the context of the imagined geography of the Thames in Dickens's *Our Mutual Friend*. In his great novel of the period, Dickens unsettles the prevailing negative perceptions of the river: although the novel places a high value on moral and material purification, it also deliberately exploits the imaginative energy of filth. While the first three chapters highlight moments of resistance to reform, chapters 4 and 5 record a more pervasive disillusionment with reform that

was characteristic of attitudes later in the century. Chapter 4 traces this disillusionment to the perceived failure of housing reform policies and initiatives
in the 1870s and 1880s, as well as to more pessimistic ideas about poverty and
social change, influenced by social Darwinism. We find a similar pessimism
about the capacity of reform to reclaim the lives of the urban poor in Gissing's
Nether World, the central text of chapter 5. Although Gissing's views about
reform have often been dismissed for their conservatism, they are significant
because they represent an important cultural shift: by the 1880s, even committed reformers had begun to recognize that the aims of improvement did
not always achieve the desired ends.

This point about the shift in attitude toward sanitary reform, from optimism to pessimism, from idealism to disillusionment, requires qualification.
Certainly, resistance to sanitary measures in the middle decades of the century
was real enough, but it is fair to say that apocalyptic visions of the sewer or
loving evocations of the filthy Thames reflected a minority view. Despite recurrent expressions of resistance, the sanitary movement inspired considerable optimism during the period roughly from the 1840s through the 1860s.
Reformers from Chadwick to Kingsley unequivocally affirmed the far-reaching
and beneficent influence of sanitary improvements on the health and welfare
of the populace, and to a greater or lesser degree, their lay audience accepted
the redemptive powers of purification. After about the 1860s, however, doubts
about the efficacy of sanitary reform to do more than cleanse the streets had
begun to enter the debate with greater frequency and insistence. Interventions in the built environment had a dramatic effect, but did they produce
the desired effect? Slums were cleared, streets widened, and sewers built, but
were the poor better off physically and morally than they had been? One of
the defining principles of sanitary reform and the source of much of its imaginative resonance was the understanding that urban improvement and human
improvement were complementary processes. Indeed, purifying the environment and uplifting a potentially dangerous underclass were conceived as a
unitary mission. But in the latter decades of the century, the mission began
to seem less coherent. Public health reform was still important, but it was not
seen as the only, or even necessarily the best, means to help a poor family escape the demoralizing influence of the slums: emigration, suburban relocation, and a host of other schemes were advocated by social reformers. At the

same time, reformers were carving out new limits concerning the kinds of people they felt they could help: the upper strata of the working classes could benefit from better-quality housing equipped with sanitary appliances, but the abject poor were perhaps beyond the reach of such help. These changing attitudes marked the end of the sanitary state and the beginning of the welfare state.

Sanitary reform did not by any means disappear from British social life. Its achievements, especially in terms of urban infrastructure, were too significant and its program and approach had become too institutionalized to be discounted. Moreover, social reformers did not simply give up. As Wohl explains in *Endangered Lives,* the "reform impulse" was as strong as ever at the turn of the century, in part because of the perceived failures I have mentioned.[60] But the character of the sanitary reform movement had forever changed. At the material level, this change was marked by increasing specialization, as sanitation developed into a highly technical field requiring the expertise of scientists and municipal engineers. At the imaginative level, the change was marked by a loss of the coherent vision that sanitary reform in its early decades had so satisfactorily supplied. As I state at the outset of the introduction, sanitary reform comprehended the challenges of the Victorian city. It brought the authority of science and religion to bear on these challenges, and it used the tools provided by engineering, medicine, government, and literature to imagine and to build a healthier city. Such a comprehensive vision of social and spatial life also bore the seeds of its own resistance, and the story of that resistance is what *Cleansing the City* seeks to tell.

chapter 1

The London Sewer

Purification and the Experience of Urban Disorder

There are more ways than one of looking at sewers, especially
at old London sewers.

John Hollingshead, *Underground London* (1862)

A pivotal point in London's sanitary history is the substitution of the sewer for the cesspool as the principal means of waste removal in the metropolis. Until the mid-nineteenth century, domestic refuse was generally collected in cesspools (enclosed pits sunk into the ground), which were periodically emptied by manual labor. As London became more densely populated, this method of waste disposal began to seem increasingly inefficient and unsafe. Leaders of the public health movement helped turn public and legislative opinion against the practice of collection and cartage, promoting instead the removal of waste by water-carriage through sewers. A relatively new idea in 1848, the reliance on water to wash away both surface debris and household wastes has clearly proven to be an influential sanitary innovation (so much so that it may come as a surprise to us that sewers were not always used for human waste). Yet when sewerage was first implemented in the nineteenth-century metropolis, it provoked considerable opposition and anxiety.

The sewer was perceived by many as disruptive and potentially dangerous because it inevitably altered the city's geography—in terms of both material environment and social structure. The subversive potential of the sewer was figured in multiple ways: for some, the sewer seemed to jeopardize individual and local autonomy because it took waste removal out of the hands of house-holders and parishes and invested it in a newly consolidated drainage author-ity; for others, the sewer posed a threat to the ideals of domestic privacy and enclosure because it connected the home to a vast drainage system; and for others still, the sewer seemed to weaken the spatial and social barriers sepa-rating the healthy bourgeoisie from a corrupt working class. In this chapter, I recover these and other visions of social relations in a changing city by exam-ining expressions of resistance to the sewer. Opening with Henry Mayhew's account of metropolitan disposal practices in *London Labour and the London Poor* (1861–62), the chapter goes on to explore resistant responses to sewerage registered in numerous periodicals and pamphlets. These underanalyzed rep-resentations of resistance deepen our understanding of the felt experience of urban development in nineteenth-century London. Although the sewer, as the embodiment and exemplar of sanitary progress, was intended to order the environment and cleanse the atmosphere, it was frequently seen as an instru-ment of social chaos, threatening the ideals of spatial division and social hier-archy in the Victorian urban context.

From Cesspool to Sewer

Mayhew's *London Labour and the London Poor* stands in ambiguous relation to the sanitary reform movement. The document is of course suffused with filth: old rags, bones, metal scraps, the blood from slaughterhouses, dog dung, and sewer rats are each taken up in turn as Mayhew catalogues the peculiar and multifarious occupations of the street people of London. Moreover, the multi-volume *London Labour* had its origins in the cholera epidemic of 1848–49. As Gertrude Himmelfarb explains, the publication in September 1849 of Mayhew's article "A Visit to the Cholera Districts of Bermondsey" in the *Morning Chroni-cle* was so well received that it inspired Mayhew to produce for the paper the series "Labour and the Poor" (1849–50); this series was the precursor to *London*

Labour and the London Poor, published first in weekly parts (1850–52) and then in volume form (1851–52; 1861–62).[1] For Himmelfarb, the imagery of decay and disease in *London Labour* was instrumental in defining the poverty of the street laborers not as "an economic condition [but] as a pathological one."[2] But while *London Labour* may have taken shape in the context of the sanitary movement, it seems at times disconnected from the discourse of reform so identifiable with that movement. Anne Humpherys notes the paradox in her study of Mayhew: his discussion of refuse removal in the metropolis is dependent on the statistics and reports amassed by sanitarians, yet "it is curious that in the long discussion in *London Labour,* Mayhew did not describe directly the sanitary problems connected with refuse disposal which most concerned his contemporaries and which resulted in the limited reform at the time."[3] It is true that Mayhew does devote considerable space to the topic of sewage "recycling"—a favorite idea in sanitary circles involving the export of town sewage into the country for use as fertilizer.[4] It is also true that Mayhew occasionally conflates environmental and moral "obscenity" when describing the habitations of his laborers, a conventional practice in sanitary writing. But the overall picture created by *London Labour* is of a sanitary economy that is remarkably functional, with every type of waste finding a correspondent laborer to collect it. Prefacing his description of the city's dustmen, nightmen, chimney sweepers, and scavengers, Mayhew marvels, "These men constitute a large body, and are a class who . . . do their work silently and efficiently. Almost without the cognizance of the mass of the people, the refuse is removed from our streets and houses; and London, as if in the care of a tidy housewife, is *always* being cleaned" (2:159; italics in original). Such a remark is decidedly out of step with the sanitary discourse at midcentury, when the mounting volume of refuse in streets and slums and cesspools was identified as a major urban crisis and when a series of legislative acts had just been passed to try to resolve this crisis.

So it is perhaps not surprising that Mayhew's discussion of the cesspool, the especial target of sanitary reformers, is marked more by absorbed interest than by any kind of condemnation. Mayhew closes his lengthy account of the patterns of waste removal in the metropolis with a first-person narrative describing one night spent with a gang of London nightmen. It was the task of these men to excavate and cart off the human excreta deposited in cesspools, labor referred to as "nightwork" because by law it could only be performed after twelve o'clock at night. As Mayhew acknowledges, the work of emptying cesspools was "sometimes severe" (2:451). The "ropeman" of the gang would lower a tub down into the reeking pit of refuse, where the "holeman" waited to fill it; two "tubmen" then carried the load to a cart, destined for one of the city's dust yards, laystalls, or manure wharves that accepted deposits of human waste (fig. 1.1). Not only was the work necessarily strenuous, but it was also dangerous, since the noxious fumes generated by decomposing refuse could cause instantaneous death by asphyxiation. In his 1842 *Report on the Sanitary Condition of the Labouring Population of Great Britain,* Edwin Chadwick inveighs against the cesspool on these and other grounds: "It is proved that the present mode of retaining refuse in the house in cesspools and privies is injurious to the health and often extremely dangerous. The process of emptying them by hand labour, and removing the contents by cartage, is very offensive, and often the occasion of serious accidents."[5] Add to these drawbacks the fact that cleaning cesspools was expensive (and so, in poorer quarters, rarely done), and Chadwick's case against the cesspool is complete.

In Mayhew's sketch of the nightmen at work, however, he minimizes or omits altogether the more grim details of cesspool labor. The opening sentences set the tone for a slightly romanticized representation: "The scene was peculiar enough. The artificial light, shining into the dark filthy-looking cavern or cesspool, threw the adjacent houses into a deep shade. All around was perfectly still" (2:451). The filthiness of the cesspool, while acknowledged, is offset by the hushed atmosphere and the contrast of light and dark, which evoke a sense of mystery more than revulsion. The description continues:

> There was not an incident to interrupt the labour, except that at one time the window of a neighbouring house was thrown up, a night-capped head was protruded, and then down was banged the sash with an impatient curse. It appeared as if a gentleman's slumbers had been disturbed, though the nightmen laughed and declared it was a lady's voice! The smell, although the air was frosty, was for some little time, perhaps ten minutes, literally sickening; after that period the chief sensation experienced was a slight headache; the unpleasantness of the odour still continuing, though without any sickening effect. The nightmen, however, pronounced the stench

1.1. Emptying a London cesspool by night—a labor-intensive practice forced into obsolescence by sanitary reformers. Drawing, "London Nightmen," from a daguerreotype by Richard Beard, in Henry Mayhew, *London Labour and the London Poor,* 4 vols. (London: Griffin, Bohn, and Co., 1861–62), 2:433.

> 'nothing at all'; and one even declared it was refreshing! . . . The nightmen whom I saw evidently enjoyed a bottle of gin, which had been provided for them by the master of the house, as well as some bread and cheese, and two pots of beer. (2:451–52)

Throughout the account, Mayhew vacillates between emphasizing the mysterious, alien quality of the labor and normalizing it. In other words, he is both an outsider, who is at first sickened by the odor of the cesspool, and an insider, who can share in the nightmen's laughter at the expense of the respectable householder with "a lady's voice." At no point, however, does he worry about the cesspool's alleged role in producing an epidemic atmosphere or suggest the nightmen themselves posed some kind of moral danger, despite the heavy drinking associated with the job.

One reason for Mayhew's indulgence may be his awareness that at the time of writing, nightwork was no longer the primary mode of refuse removal in the metropolis. The middle decades of the nineteenth century brought with them radical changes in the sanitary practice of London's inhabitants, who began to rely increasingly on a vast and rapidly expanding network of sewers to wash refuse out of the city. Until this time, London's sewers, which have their origins in the natural watercourses draining into the Thames, were regarded as conduits for surface water only; household waste in both solid and liquid forms was—at least theoretically—deposited in cesspools, rather than in sewers.[6] In fact, as Mayhew explains, "until somewhere about 1830 no cesspool matter could, without an indictable offence being committed, be drained into a sewer!" (2:438). In the first half of the century, however, the function of sewers began to change as a result of multiple pressures: the impracticability of the cesspool in areas of increasing population density; the rising popularity of the water closet, especially in affluent neighborhoods; and the early sanitary campaigns of Chadwick and others, who decried the collection of filth in cesspools as a threat to the public health.[7] Many of London's wealthier inhabitants had begun to sluice their domestic wastewater into the main sewers as early as the first decades of the century. Rather than suppress these unregulated connections altogether, several of the eight Commissions of Sewers in the metropolis began to allow the construction of private drains upon petition and the payment of a fee. As early as 1807, the Westminster Commission was granted powers to oversee the connection of any new drain to a main sewer within its jurisdiction.[8] According to the official literature of the London County Council, it had become permissible to drain refuse into the sewers by 1815.[9]

What was permissive sanitary practice soon became compulsory for all of London's inhabitants, largely through the exertions of Chadwick. Proceeding from the widely held conviction that miasmas generated by decomposing waste were responsible for the spread of infectious diseases, Chadwick advocated removing filth from the city as quickly as possible, before decomposition could begin. Drainage with an ample water supply was, he believed, the most effective way to achieve this goal. Chadwick's innovation was to envision house drainage, public sewerage, street cleansing, and water supply as interdependent parts of an integrated sanitary system.[10] The cesspool, arch-symbol of an inefficient and disaggregated sanitary regime, clearly had no place in such a system. Chadwick's vision, developed in a series of government reports through the 1840s, helped shape the influential body of sanitary legislation passed in 1848, including the Public Health Act, the Nuisances Removal and Diseases Prevention Act, and the Metropolitan and City Sewers Acts.[11] Of particular significance here is the Metropolitan Sewers Act, which replaced seven of London's independently administered sewer commissions with a single Metropolitan Commission of Sewers.[12] The consolidation of the commissions marked an important step in standardizing London's drainage, from both an administrative and a technological perspective. And although the new commission was hampered in some key ways—the City of London was allowed to retain its own Commission of Sewers, for instance—it nonetheless was invested with a range of powers and met many of Chadwick's goals. Under the act, the Metropolitan Commission was charged with executing a survey of London in preparation for an extension of water and sewer services. It was also granted authority over all the drains, sewers, water closets, cesspools, and privies in the city, with the express power to compel owners of newly built houses to drain them into the sewers. The act thus marks the first time in London's history that citizens were legally obligated to use the public sewers to dispose of their private waste.

The Metropolitan Commission of Sewers (1848–55) was dissolved before it had even finalized the plan for its much-vaunted comprehensive sewerage system for London. The task was left to the city's succeeding drainage authority, the Metropolitan Board of Works (1855–89). But the influence of Chadwick and the Metropolitan Commission on London's sanitary landscape was unmatched. Starting in 1848, they pursued an aggressive course aimed at flushing all the accumulated filth of the city into the sewers and thence into the river.[13] They used vast quantities of water to cleanse courts and alleys and to clear the old sewers of deposits. They also launched a vigorous assault on cesspools, emptying them by pumping their contents into the sewers and whenever possible filling them in and laying down pipe drains instead. According to Joseph Bazalgette, engineer to the Board of Works and architect of the board's main drainage scheme, as many as thirty thousand cesspools were abolished during the six years of the Metropolitan Commission's existence.[14] By the end of the commission's tenure in 1855, the application of water to waste management had become accepted practice, and the very function of the sewer had been reconceived. In Bazalgette's estimation, the Metropolitan Commission of Sewers effected a sanitary revolution: "That Commission entertained opposite views respecting the use of sewers to those which had been previously held, and directed its energies mainly to the introduction of pipe-sewers of small dimensions . . . to the abolition of cesspools, and to the diversion of all house drainage . . . into the sewers, making the adoption of the new system compulsory."[15] The cesspool did not disappear overnight, but after 1848 its obsolescence was ensured.

When Mayhew witnessed a gang of nightmen engaged in their secret labor, he knew that he was recording a dying mode of work; he knew that—to use his words—the cesspool system had been "abolished" by the "newer system" of drainage (2:387). As Richard Maxwell has shown, the imminent extinction of many street trades that Mayhew describes is a recurrent theme of *London Labour:* "[S]ocial and economic pressures of a new intensity were threatening the street-folk. The people Mayhew interviewed often mention that they had made more money ten or twenty years previously. Furthermore, many of the principal occupations seemed to be disappearing by mid-century."[16] Mayhew's attitude toward the changes associated with modernization is not always easy to determine. In respect to the development of London's sewerage, he seems to recognize the advantages of a consolidated Metropolitan Commission of Sewers, for instance, noting that the earlier independent commissions had made a chaos of underground London (2:415). He also recognizes the noxiousness of the cesspool system and the advantages of removing excrement from a household immediately rather than retaining it through all the stages of decomposition (2:446). Still, Mayhew's sympathy seems to lie with the man over the machine, with the plight of the cesspool laborer in a changing urban order. This sympathy is reflected in the statement obtained from a "cesspool-sewerman," a man whose job it was to pump cesspool refuse into the sewers with the new technology of the pump and hose, a hybrid method suited to the transitional character of waste disposal in London at the time.

The cesspool-sewerman recognizes both the role his own work has played in displacing the nightmen and, more generally, the precarious position of all workers in the modernizing city: "In time the nightmen'll disappear; in course they must, there's so many new dodges comes up, always some one of the working classes is a being ruined. If it ain't steam, it's something else knocks the bread out of their mouths quite as quick" (2:448–49). Through the voice of the laborer, Mayhew reveals his concern over the negative effects that industrialization and sanitary progress, in particular, have on individual workers.

While reform might entail the loss of wages and of certain kinds of labor, it also brings with it the loss of something more difficult to define. Maxwell makes the point that for Mayhew the street laborers represented an image of discontinuity, of freedom and mobility, that was both important to him imaginatively and emblematic of London life.[17] To lose the nightman, the "tosher" (sewer hunter), or the rat catcher is to lose something of the spirit of the city itself. This attitude is most evident in Mayhew's description of the toshers, for him the most daring and canny of the city's workers in filth, who risked their lives in searching the labyrinthine sewers for treasure or, at least, saleable bits of refuse. Reflecting on Mayhew's attitude toward the toshers, we find that Maxwell's discontinuity is not so much at issue as is the romanticization of a dangerous and utterly alien way of life: "Many wondrous tales are still told among the people of men having lost their way in the sewers, and of having wandered among the filthy passages . . . till, faint and overpowered, they dropped down and died on the spot. Other stories are told of sewer-hunters beset by myriads of enormous rats, and slaying thousands of them in their struggle for life, till at length the swarms of the savage things overpowered them, and in a few days afterwards their skeletons were discovered picked to the very bones" (Mayhew, 2:150). Such thrilling, if gruesome, adventures were becoming more rare just as Mayhew was recording them because the Metropolitan Commission had closed the entrances to the sewers opening out into the Thames and forbidden unauthorized entrance. The intrepid sewer hunters were certainly displeased with the new regulations, as Mayhew makes clear, but then Mayhew himself seems also to regret the passing of this curious mode of making a living and almost to root for the toshers who managed "to evade the vigilance of the sewer officials" (2:152). This vigilance must certainly have put an end to the "wondrous" tales and stories that made London such a vital and rich place.

But even the decidedly unromantic aspects of the city's outmoded waste disposal practices seem to have been valuable to Mayhew, if only because they were familiar and quickly disappearing. The night yards and manure wharves where night soil was deposited were surely among the worst nuisances suppressed by the new sanitary legislation. There, great pools of excrement were mixed with other refuse and allowed to dry out as part of the process of making manure. Mayhew devotes a section to these places, titled "Of the Present Disposal of the Night-Soil," yet he repeats no less than four times that with the sanitary legislation of 1848, such places were banned from operating in the city. One reason that Mayhew may devote so much space to sanitary practices that were essentially obsolete—such as emptying cesspools and making manure—is that this work is scaled to human comprehension and capacities. Although Mayhew estimates the amount of cesspool refuse annually deposited in night yards to be in the millions of cubic feet, these millions arrived in wagonloads in the tens and twenties. The scale changed dramatically with the implementation of an integrated system of sewerage relying on steam to move the waste. Referring to the Metropolitan Commission of Sewers' ambitious (and unrealized) new plan for constructing intercepting sewers to link with the existing lines, Mayhew writes, "It is difficult to convey to a reader . . . any adequate notion of the largeness . . . of this undertaking. Even a map conveys no sufficient idea of it" (2:413). Against this statement of the essentially unrepresentable character of the new sewerage we can place the image of the older mode of refuse removal by cartage: "The purchaser nearer home conveyed it [night soil manure] away in his own cart, and with his own horses, which had perhaps come up to town laden with cabbages to Covent Garden, or hay to Cumberland-market" (2:450). The image conveys an idea of London not as a modern, million-peopled metropolis, but as a traditional community made up of recognizable individuals—the farmer who sells cabbages at Covent Garden. It suggests that the city, for all its stink, is still an essentially knowable place.

Mayhew's ambivalence toward the rationalizing project of sewerage in London becomes more pronounced when seen in the context of Chadwick's determined attack on older, inefficient modes of refuse removal. In arguing the superiority of drainage over hand cartage of waste, Chadwick offers many reasons for his position—the prevention of dangerous accumulations and cost-effectiveness chief among them. But he also sees sewerage as a means to rid the city of the obscure, independent workers in filth, whom he regards as no better than criminals: "Conceiving it probable that the amount of filth left by defective cleansing had its corresponding description of persons, I made inquiries of the Commissioners of Metropolitan Police. From returns which they obtained from their superintendents, it appears that of the class of bone-pickers, mud-rakers, people living on the produce of dung-heaps in mews, courts, yards, and bye lanes insufficient cleansed, 598 are known to the police."[18] These are Mayhew's marginal laborers, but the difference between the two investigators' approaches is significant. For Chadwick, these workers are another species of refuse, and he establishes their danger to the community by linking them to the "chiffoniers" (rag gatherers) of Paris, who were "conspicuous actors in the revolution of 1830."[19] There is no room for nostalgia for the nightmen in a document that so staunchly advocates the application of "capital and machinery" to waste removal.[20] Mayhew, in contrast, while he might follow Chadwick in condemning the immorality of the laborers, nonetheless is drawn to them and to the irrational, eccentric underworld they populate. As David Pike explains, the modern sewer systems of London and Paris "represented the rational control of the archaic underground, the essence of modern society."[21] Writing just at the moment when this control was being imposed, Mayhew registers his resistance to a reforming process that seems to devalue the individual laborer and to rob London of its familiar vitality.

The "Underground Labyrinth"

Mayhew's ambivalent response to the new technological approach to sanitation may not be representative, but it does reflect an uncertainty about the place of the individual in the modern city that is echoed by many other writers on metropolitan sewerage. The journalist John Hollingshead addresses just this uncertainty in his book *Underground London* (1862), parts of which appeared originally in *All the Year Round*. Hollingshead opens his account of the main drainage system then under construction (1859–65) with a gesture toward the resistance and anxiety it provoked: "The sewerage scheme now being rapidly carried out is so vast, that it has naturally driven many people almost mad who have grappled with it and opposed it."[22] He goes on to describe some of the more fantastic delusions inspired by the sewers in terms more likely to arouse concerns than allay them: "Some people cannot be brought to believe that any tunnels have been constructed anywhere, and they look upon the thick-ribbed shore-cuttings, the houses on wheels, and the excavators' spades and lanterns, scattered about in different parts of London, as mere surface decoys, set up to satisfy a few inquisitive rate-payers. Others regard the tunnels as only too real and substantial; volcanoes of filth; gorged veins of putridity; ready to explode at any moment in a whirlwind of foul gas, and poison all those whom they fail to smother."[23] As different as these two imagined responses are, both reflect a perception of disorder that attends the loss of individual control. The modern sanitary landscape is a world away from Mayhew's picturesque representation of sanitation by cesspool. Under the earlier system, residents might witness for themselves the contents of a cesspool flooding an adjacent street or yard, or they might catch sight of a receding cart full of excrement, fruits of the nightmen's labor. Put simply, the cesspool allowed the (dis)comfort of ocular proof. The sewerage system of waste disposal, however, formed a vast underground network radiating across London: its sheer size and inaccessibility placed it beyond the comprehension of ordinary citizens (fig. 1.2). Furthermore, the authority over this network was not vested in private householders or local boards but in a newly created metropolitan administration (first the Metropolitan Commission of Sewers, then the Metropolitan Board of Works). Sewerage limited the individual's ability to affect or control the urban environment.

In his discussion of the sanitary movement, Richard L. Schoenwald emphasizes its disciplinary character, arguing that sanitary technologies trained people to live in an increasingly complex and ordered world: "If a man could be forced to yield to interference in such a sensitive domain, he could be made to acquiesce in any kind of control."[24] H. J. Dyos makes a similar point in the context of urbanization, of which sanitary reform and administrative centralization were assuredly a part: with urban living came "the psychological challenge of delivering up full personal freedom of action."[25] Dyos and Schoenwald insist quite rightly that the conditions of modern life, exemplified in the sewer, placed new restrictions on the urban inhabitant's "freedom of action." What this analysis overlooks, however, are the terms in which resistance to reform was most frequently expressed. Although the sewer may have

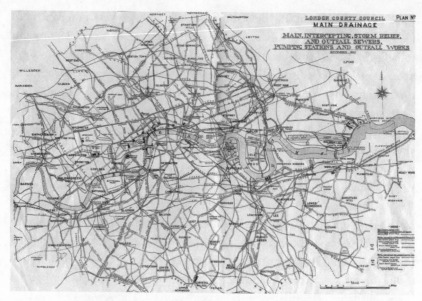

1.2. The "underground labyrinth" made visible in a plan of London's main drainage from 1930, prepared by the London County Council. Plan courtesy of Thames Water plc.

served (and may still serve) a regulatory function, it was perceived by many Victorians, paradoxically, as an instrument of disorder, of overwhelming environmental and social confusion. These perceptions of the fundamentally disruptive character of the sewer found imaginative expression in visions of chaos—Hollingshead's vision, for instance, of underground "volcanoes of filth" threatening to transform London into a modern Pompeii. The apocalyptic rhetoric, which seems by any measure to exceed the reality it describes, in fact expresses a profound sense of individual impotence in the face of material and social change.

The idea of sewerage as a chaotic and unwieldy system of waste management owes something to the growing awareness of the detrimental effect sewers had on the environment. For the aggressive assault on filth launched by the Metropolitan Commission of Sewers in 1848 ironically contributed to the unprecedented pollution of the Thames in the 1850s. The energies of the Metropolitan Commission, as we have seen, were directed toward flushing the city's accumulated waste into the sewers, sewers that discharged their contents directly into the river. A surveyor for the commission was able to report satisfactorily that over 290 miles of sewers had been flushed by February of 1849: "From these," he goes on to explain, "about 79,483 cube [*sic*] yards of deposit have been removed. . . . [T]his, with few exceptions, has been sent into the River Thames."[26] The sudden and intensive discharge of the city's domestic refuse into the river resulted in the rapid physical deterioration of the Thames. Although it was by no means pristine in the first decades of the century, the condition of the Thames at midcentury was demonstrably worse. The river quickly became notorious for its filth, as reflected in the numerous epithets attached to it: it was "a great tidal sewer,"[27] a "*cloaca maxima*,"[28] a "hotbed of infection and the nursery of epidemics."[29] The nuisance reached a crisis point in the unusually hot summer of 1858, when the stench from the river and its oozy banks was so offensive that the episode became thereafter known as the "Great Stink." Chapter 2 examines the crisis of Thames pollution at length; what is relevant in this context is the way environmental degradation was associated with the functional transformation of the sewer.

In an article for *Household Words* from July 1858, Henry Morley makes this point when he notes the glaring deficiency of sewerage: "We get rid of [filth] from about houses, concentrate it in a mass, and then—not knowing what else to do with it—pour it into our water-courses. We have discovered one half of a wholesome principle of drainage; of the other half we are in search."[30] How to dispose of the city's sewage was a question that plagued sanitary reformers and engineers for much of the nineteenth century. Chadwick's pet solution of piping it out to agricultural districts for use as fertilizer reflected the hopes of many in the field, who dreamed of converting "valuable" sewage into agricultural gold.[31] This part of his drainage plan, however, was never developed and ultimately proved unworkable. The decision to discharge waste into the Thames was thus not conceived as a solution to the problem of waste disposal; rather, it was a consciously adopted strategy with recognized limitations. According to Christopher Hamlin, "For Chadwick, ridding towns of decaying organic refuse was the first priority"; polluting a town's river was merely the lesser of two evils.[32]

The physical deterioration of the Thames surely provided the stimulus for much of the resistance to sewerage. This protest often took the form of an unfavorable comparison of the sewer to an imaginatively sanitized version of the cesspool. In a pamphlet of 1858, John Wiggins laments the impact that the abolition of cesspools had on the condition of the river: "[W]hen in an evil hour, they were voted, by scientific men, too great a nuisance, to be borne, or tolerated, any longer . . . and all cesspools, present and future, were prohibited by law, the whole sewage of this vast metropolis, was at once, precipitated into the Thames, and the river side of London, in dry and hot summers, is well nigh rendered uninhabitable."[33] Nearly twenty years later, the tendency to remember the cesspool approvingly persists: "Under the cesspool system our rivers, streamlets, wells and water tanks were free from the pollution which has been gradually accruing since the substitution of water closets," writes Robert Pulling in 1875.[34] Discussing more generally the environmental impact of a waterborne waste disposal system, the author of *The Sewage Difficulty* (1866) contends that "the whole system of the hydraulic disposal of the excreta of town populations is nothing else than an ingenious method of polluting enormous quantities of water."[35] The deplorably filthy condition of the Thames provided an occasion for objecting to the prevailing, but still relatively new, function of sewers.

The environmental explanation, however, does not fully account for the sometimes hostile reception of sewerage in the period. Negative reactions seem to have resulted in some cases from fear and distrust of the enlarged role of government demanded by the new sanitary program. In London, the vestries, the water companies, and the Corporation of the City of London vehemently resisted the centralizing tendencies of the Chadwickian public health agenda.[36] For these groups, sanitary reform represented nothing less than an effort to create and control a single government authority responsible for the entire metropolis. Joshua Toulmin Smith, noted advocate of local self-government, advanced this view in his 1848 attack on the Metropolitan Sanitary Commission, whose "real end would appear to have been to forward the ceaseless attempts of a liberal government towards the engrossing under one central patronage the actual control over all local institutions, works, and arrangements, small as well as great."[37] Although the *Times* had supported the public health legislation of 1848, by October of that year it began to criticize the Metropolitan Commission of Sewers and to denounce centralization.[38] The paper makes what is essentially a political point by invoking the perceptible problem of Thames pollution: "Not a single cesspool to be found in the city,—except one, reaching from Richmond to Gravesend, with an exposed surface averaging a quarter of a mile in breadth! No filth in the sewers,—all in the river! What a magnificent application of centralization to cleanliness!"[39] By equating centralization with defective sewerage, the *Times* suggests that government interference only exacerbates sanitary problems. Here, the polluted river reflects a distorted political order. A slightly different statement of the same problem appears in Wiggins's aforementioned pamphlet on Thames pollution. If the sewer is an emblem for centralization, then the cesspool must embody a more efficient local authority: "[C]esspools, dealt with the enemy [i.e., excrement] in detail, cut him off in detachments, and prevented that concentration of his forces, which now, taxes to the utmost, all our energies and resources."[40] As the reference to "concentration" and the play on the word "taxes" seem to indicate, Wiggins objects to the centralization of government authority necessitated by comprehensive sanitary measures. The passage also darkly hints that the expansion of government influence results in a correspondent inflation of filth: sewage, like the agency responsible for it, has become bloated and intractable and thus threatens to overwhelm the disempowered urban inhabitant.

The second appearance of cholera in London in 1848–49 ironically served as a catalyst for intensified attacks on the Metropolitan Commission of Sewers and on centralization. Even in the face of fourteen thousand deaths from the epidemic, an article in the conservative *Economist* published in October 1849 complains of "A Greater Plague than Cholera": sanitary legislation.[41] The article argues that anxiety about cholera has led to undue "interference," including the harassment of such "useful workmen" as the "tallow melter or catgut manufacturer, or bone crusher or soap boiler."[42] One of the most notable and outspoken critics of sanitary reform, Herbert Spencer, expressed similar concerns about the threat posed to individual and local interests by sanitary legislation. His first book, *Social Statics* (1851), was also shaped by the cholera epidemic of 1848–49. In it, Spencer argues that government intervention in matters of health and cleanliness represents a violation of privacy and domestic autonomy. He reasons that sanitary legislation not only encourages but also requires government interference in private life and that once this precedent is established, limiting the government's sphere of action becomes impossible:

If, therefore, it is the duty of the State to protect the health of its subjects, it is its duty to see that all the conditions to health are fulfilled by them. The legislature must prescribe so many meals a day for each individual; fix the quantities and qualities of food for men, women, and children; state the proportion of fluids, when to be taken, and of what kind; specify the amount of exercise, and define its character; describe the clothing to be employed; determine the hours of sleep; and to enforce these regulations it must employ officials *to oversee every one's domestic arrangements.* [43]

Although this vision of the hyperregulated sanitary state is deliberately exaggerated, it reflects very real fears about the loss of control over one's home and body that systematic sanitation seemed to promise. Indeed, this control, or oversight, is exactly what reformers hoped to gain in respect to the working class. In his study of Chadwick's *Sanitary Report* and the role it played in defining the working-class body, Peter Logan notes "the centrality of middle-class inspection to working-class reform." [44] This inspection may have taken the form of a "friendly" cottage visitation on the part of a middle-class woman or of a professional call from a Medical Officer of Health. Surveillance could be achieved on a larger scale by means of urban reconstruction: the clearance of slums, the creation of wide-open streets, and the construction of model dwellings. In all cases, this exposure was understood to impart a moralizing influence. The Reverend George Lewis voiced a familiar sentiment when he asserted in *Lectures on the Social and Physical Condition of the People* (1842), "Domestic cleanliness is a social virtue, and to be practised must have eyes upon it." [45] What Spencer recognized was that the regulatory gaze of the reformer was potentially self-reflexive. Whereas the surveillance of the urban poor might be an effective tool for social control, the surveillance of the middle class produced social disorder—a confusion of the boundaries between the bourgeois subject and the working-class object, between private and public life.

Sewerage did redraw the boundaries of urban life in the nineteenth century, creating what Joel Tarr refers to as the "networked city." As Tarr discusses in the context of developing sewer systems in the United States, sewerage is a large technological system, and as such its implementation implied a new conception of the city as a comprehensively planned but also administratively and technically complex space. [46] This very new sense of the city emerges in another of Morley's articles for *Household Words,* suggestively titled "A Foe under Foot" (1852). The piece is overtly critical of the Metropolitan Commission of Sewers' inability to provide the system of waste disposal that London so desperately needed, but for Morley this inability stems from the very nature of systems—they are large, comprehensive, and complex. Referring to the ordnance survey executed by the commission, Morley laments the commission's commitment to large-scale reforms that are too sweeping to be practicable: "We have had a crow's nest on the top of St. Paul's, and a tremendous trigonometrical survey of the whole town, preparatory to a grand measure of universal sewerage reform; useful local measures have been discouraged, in anticipation of the coming universal measure that has never come, and never can come in our day, simply because there is no door large enough for it to enter by."[47] The image that Morley uses to represent administrative inefficiency and a failed reform effort is the "foe under foot"—in other words, sewage. He warns, "There is a lake of filth under London, large enough to swallow the whole population."[48] The familiar apocalyptic rhetoric reflects anxiety not just about the volume of sewage in the city but about who is controlling the sewage: the individual has been replaced by a central authority, which induces a feeling of bewildered impotence.

A similar feeling is described in G. Rochfort Clarke's sensationally titled pamphlet of 1860, *The Reform of the Sewers: Where Shall We Bathe? What Shall We Drink?* As the title makes clear, Clarke regards sewerage with suspicion and urges a return to the simpler method of the cesspool system. He contends that "it will be easier for London to empty a million of such small things [i.e., cesspools] than to find its way through the underground labyrinth, or know what to do when it arrives at the far end."[49] While the mazelike course of the labyrinth appropriately suggests the form of the sewer, it also reflects the sewer's technical complexity, which places it beyond the comprehension of ordinary citizens. Clarke pursues this point in his mockery of those who might reject the cesspool as old-fashioned: "The objections are, it is a plan as old as Adam, it is too straightforward and simple, it does not sufficiently inflate the mind with the grand idea of a network of sewers, carrying rivers of slops, all floating in dismal pomp towards one point, and then radiating back again through another network of pipes."[50] We must be careful not to dismiss Clarke's rhetorically florid argument as the ranting of an eccentric. On some level, Clarke, like Mayhew, intuited that the shift from cesspool to sewer was about more than just waste disposal. The city was changing into a complex urban system, and with it the role of the individual was changing too. The representation of the sewer as an "underground labyrinth" or a "lake of filth" was one way to dramatize these changes—to express both their magnitude and one's own vulnerability.

The Smell of Subversion

The turn toward sewerage at midcentury certainly marked the beginning of an aggressive modernization of underground space, but as Pike argues, alternative associations of the sewer with the archaic and the irrational persisted.[51] This duality helps explain the often-contradictory responses to the sewer. Expressions of resistance in some cases seem to derive from fears of modernity —of the complexity introduced by sanitary technology and administration. In other cases, resistance seems to derive from the sewer's imaginative tie to the primitive—whether figured as human waste or humans *as* waste. Despite the claims for the sewer's superiority to the cesspool from a sanitary point of view, it was still quite obviously a conduit for excrement and a site, imaginatively speaking, of social rejection and abjection. These two very challenging aspects of sewerage—its simultaneous modernity and primitivism—come into greater focus when we consider one of the Victorian householder's chief complaints about the sewer: sewer gas. Although the water closet linked to a domestic drainpipe had been heralded by sanitary science as the safest and most efficient means of disposal, in practice the appliance gave off its share of foul smells and, it was believed, enteric disease. Because the city's oldest sewers had not been designed to accommodate and carry house refuse, the accumulation of waste within them was a common occurrence. The noxious vapors generated by these deposits, rather than dissipating within the sewers, tended to escape through any available outlet, usually into the street or into those houses with connecting drains. In *A Lay Lecture on Sanitary Matters* (1873), S. S. Brown explains the potential danger of sanitary modernization: "You may abolish cesspits . . . from the neighborhood of your houses by proper sewerage, but unless you are guarded against the return into your dwellings of the gases of decomposition from the sewers, you may be worse off than before."[52] Paradoxically, the sewer exposed the home to the very dangers it was intended to combat—the fatal odors of decomposition. The inability of householders to prevent the noxious fumes of the sewer from entering their homes reinforced their loss of control even as it suggested the difficulty of achieving healthy isolation from a physically and morally tainted underclass. For the infiltration of foul smells signaled the threat not only of disease but also of moral corruption, embodied in the figure of the working-class other.

While the cesspool could be invoked as an image of containment and segregation, the sewer served as an image of connection, drawing together the individual and the mass, the poor and the rich, the diseased and the healthy. This vision of the sewer as an instrument of connection and, thus, social transgression finds expression in an undated pamphlet by G. R. Booth objecting to the plan for main drainage developed by the Metropolitan Board of Works in the late 1850s. Booth warns against the construction of what he calls "monster sewers," seeing in them a source of material and moral contagion: "It therefore becomes a point of the utmost importance that the seeds of disease should at once be arrested: that they should not be carried from house to house, from street to street, from unhealthy parts to salubrious districts, by the construction of monster sewers, impregnated with the feculent matter of each locality, and sowing it again broadcast, not only over the suburbs, but over whole districts further removed, equally entitled, nevertheless, to protection in the eye of common humanity."[53] The cause for alarm lies not simply in the idea of waste circulating throughout the metropolis, but in the idea of waste from "unhealthy," or impoverished, areas infiltrating "salubrious districts," such as the suburbs. Booth is ostensibly concerned with diseased sewage, but his rhetoric also implies a concern with boundaries and the difficulty of separating oneself from the urban poor (that other filthy mass). The problem with the sewer was that it threatened to erode social distinctions, to thrust everyone into the primordial muck. Hollingshead makes this very point in the context of a descriptive tour of one of London's main sewers. Although the sewer he inspects runs underneath the aristocratic neighborhood of Berkeley Square, Hollingshead concludes that "there was nothing in the construction of our main sewer, or in the quality of our black flood, to tell us that we were so near the abodes of the blest."[54] The "black flood" of the sewer represents the common denominator of human civilization, what Peter Stallybrass and Allon White have called "the ultimate truth of the social."[55] Sewer gases served as a powerful sensory reminder of this secret truth, of the risk of connection and dissolution imposed by the sewer.

Although the problem of sewer gases was discussed periodically through-out the middle decades of the century, one event turned public attention to the problem with a heightened intensity. In November 1871, the Prince of Wales contracted typhoid fever, a disease which at the time was linked to ex-posure to emanations from the sewer: the prince was poisoned by sewer gas.[56] His illness, from which he recovered early in 1872, inspired "a national anxi-ety," in the words of the *Times*.[57] In addition to prompting an outpouring of sympathetic interest in the royal family, the prince's ill health precipitated a period of agitation over the perils of sewer gas. A leading article from the *Times* simultaneously reported and fed the frenzy: "It is a more terrible, more constant, and far more insidious danger which now occupies the foreground in public anxiety. It is the pestilence that walketh in darkness—that is to say, in the darkness of drains, traps, pipes, close fittings, abstruse mechanisms, out of reach and sight altogether."[58] Here again the anxiety excited by the sewer is linked to its complexity and inaccessibility. The "darkness of drains" and "abstruse mechanisms" prevent the householder from asserting control, in-deed, from taking any action at all. But the prince's illness lent a particular urgency to the problem of sewer gas, suggesting as it did that rank or class provided no insurance against exposure.

In fact, the middle and upper classes were most vulnerable to this affliction; sewer gases generally infiltrated homes equipped with modern sanitary con-veniences, and these tended to be the homes of the affluent. Despite efforts to make sewerage universal in London, the new suburban housing developments, as well as the fashionable districts in town, were more extensively drained and sewered than working-class neighborhoods. Moreover, the adoption of the water closet remained a prerogative of the wealthier classes throughout most of the century.[59] As a result, middle- and upper-class families experienced the sewer-gas scourge more intimately than any other social group. The sewer-gas phenomenon thus shifted the discursive focus of reform away from the fever dens of the poor to the bedchambers of princes and, more frequently, to "ordinary middle-class houses" as sites of disease and death.[60] The architect Henry Collins, in a pamphlet from 1875 concerning sanitary defects "in the dwellings of the upper and middle classes," makes the rather strange assertion that since the living conditions of the poor had been amply addressed, "we can afford to pause, to consider whether in many instances the middle and upper strata of society are not so reduced as to require assistance, whether in point of fact it is not *they* who cannot help themselves."[61] Collins seems close to proposing exactly what Spencer had feared—the establishment of a sanitary police to look after everyone's "domestic arrangements."

Indeed, the problem of sewer gases highlights the threat that sewerage posed to domesticity. In its coverage of the Prince of Wales's illness, the *Times* sounds a pessimistic note on the subject of domestic autonomy: "The Prince's fever warns us how little reason there is to rely on the perfection of the domestic arrangements of the most carefully-watched houses; and, moreover, we know that, do what we may, there are subtle influences of life and death which penetrate from the outer air into the most jealously-guarded chambers."[62] By opening a channel of communication between the "outer air" and the interior chamber and by allowing fatal fumes to "penetrate" this chamber, the sewer posed a threat to the ideals of privacy and social segregation embodied in the home. The phenomenon suggests the vulnerability of a domestic ideology that posited the home as a protected space, divorced both physically and symbolically from the public sphere. Leonore Davidoff and Catherine Hall and also Elizabeth Langland have complicated our understanding of the Victorian myth of separate spheres by insisting on the key roles played by middle-class women in ensuring both the material and the social success of their families and hence the political stability of their social class.[63] Focusing on the spatial aspects of domesticity in the urban context, Karen Chase and Michael Levenson would have us recognize that the literal and figurative walls separating home life from public life were far more permeable than either we might think, or the middle-class Victorian family would have liked.[64] By considering the sensory dimension of middle-class domestic life, we gain a clearer understanding of the gap between the rhetorical ideal and lived experience.[65] How could the home truly be private and separate when a single drainpipe linked it to a network of pipes and sewers radiating across London?

The tension between the ideal of home as a shelter removed from the dangers of urban life and the experience of home as vulnerable to those dangers emerges from a comparison of two very different applications of the same metaphor: the home as castle. In *Great Expectations* (1860–61), Dickens participates in and sustains the myth of home as a place exempt from the pressures of the city through his representation of Wemmick's unique approach to domestic life. Although Jaggers's clerk moves daily between suburban Walworth and legal London, he erects a clear and impenetrable barrier between the two: "No; the office is one thing, and private life is another. When I go into the office, I leave the Castle behind me, and when I come into the Castle, I leave the office behind me."[66] Wemmick's self-styled residential "Castle" functions as a retreat from the calculating, amoral professional world. Within the Castle barricades, Wemmick pursues an active emotional life, cultivating relationships with the Aged P. and Miss Skiffins. There he is able to sustain the illusion of domestic self-sufficiency by managing a miniature farm and garden on his freehold property. When he claims, "I am my own engineer, and my own carpenter, and my own plumber, and my own gardener, and my own Jack of all Trades,"[67] Wemmick expresses a pride in his independence and his capacity for self-governance—qualities that he is not free to exercise in the employ of Jaggers. The domestic ideal of *Great Expectations* is not without its complications. The difficult conditions under which the sanctity of the Castle is maintained—Wemmick's necessary silence about his home life and his adoption of what Garrett Stewart has called "emotional schizophrenia"[68]—suggest that domesticity is a hard-won social and psychological construction. Dickens nevertheless wants his readers to believe it can be won.

The success of the Dickensian Castle relies on its imagined disconnection not only from the public realm but also quite literally from the network of sewers: Wemmick is his "own plumber." The sewer must be excluded from the idealized fortress because it would challenge the clarity of Wemmick's distinction between home and office, between "out there" and "in here." A pamphlet warning against sewer gases, written in 1871 in the wake of the prince's illness, allows us to see what happens to the domestic ideal when the sewer is not excluded. In the piece, the redolently named author, "Captain Flower," invokes the myth of the home as castle in order to suggest that sewerage has destroyed it: "No longer then can an Englishman boast that 'his house is his castle.' Why? Because he has ignorantly constructed for himself a cumbrous machinery by which his enemy enters; and though none 'of mortal mould' may make him afraid, a secret enemy 'holds' his approaches, and his castle is no longer his."[69] The passage contrasts the ignorance of the householder with the "cumbrous machinery" of water closet and drainpipe to suggest the vulnerability of individuals to dangerous technological innovation. The enemy is really twofold—sanitary science and the smell that kills. At stake is not only the material condition of the home but also the comforting idea one has about home: that it is an autonomous sphere free from outside influence and modern pressures.

In light of the association of the sewer with domestic instability, it is not surprising that women were imagined to be especially susceptible to sewer-gas poisoning. The *Times* claimed that those most frequently afflicted were "the delicate mothers and children of well-to-do people [who] often spend all their day indoors."[70] In his handbook *Dangers to Health: A Pictorial Guide to Domestic Sanitary Defects* (1883), T. Pridgin Teale provides an illustration of the literal threat to women caused by faulty sanitary appliances (fig. 1.3). The drawing provides a cutaway view of a lady's bedroom and the adjacent lavatory with an untrapped waste pipe. A series of lightly shaded arrows indicates the path of escaping sewer gas, which leads from the drain and into the bedroom, finally concentrating in a swirl over the bed. Accompanying text informs us that the room belonged to a woman who not only had been "dangerously ill" from a fever but also was nearing her confinement. The status of the victim as wife and mother lends additional force to the already disturbing prospect of the exposed home. Following Elizabeth Wilson's contention that in the Victorian city "the condition of women became the touchstone for judgments on city life,"[71] we can interpret concerns about women falling ill from sewer gases as an expression of anxiety about the indiscriminate connections that seemed to be a condition of modernity.

The emphasis on women's exposure to danger in the urban context also inevitably raises the specter of fallen female sexuality. According to Deborah Nord, in the mid-Victorian literature of reform, the threat of epidemic disease —of miasmic connections—merges with the threat of unregulated female sexuality.[72] The prostitute and even "the bourgeois wife with a past" were imaginatively linked with filth and disease; moreover, these sexually suspect women were figured as agents of contamination, much like the sewer.[73] The suggestion that a woman was vulnerable or that she might be "contaminated" (if only by sewer gas) evoked the threat of not only social but also sexual subversion—the destruction of the home from within. A vivid example of the

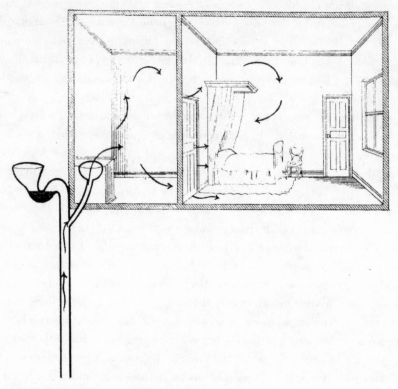

1.3. A silent and invisible interloper—sewer gas—threatens the purity of a lady's boudoir. Illustration from T. Pridgin Teale, *Dangers to Health: A Pictorial Guide to Domestic Sanitary Defects,* 4th ed. (London: Churchill, 1883), plate 11.

deliberate staging of the confrontation between the Victorian "angel in the house" and her subterranean "other" appears in a passage from *Facts and Fallacies of the Sewerage System of London* (1857):

> But there is one thing they [men] forget—which all London seems to "forget"—that is, that beneath that home there is eternally bubbling up a foul and fearful poison, which reaches those they love, wherever they may be within their domicile; and that, almost from morning till night, they breathe it, and from night till morning, too. The strong in body, fitted to bear the greater hardship, permit the weaker to inhale that poison, perhaps some 18 or 20 hours a

day, the average period that the majority of women remain in their homes, and which they cannot or will not leave because of their duties and of their domestic love; whilst man in his strength goes forth and breathes the purer air, perhaps, for 12 or 14 hours of every day.[74]

The passage reverses the meanings typically attached to the separate spheres of home and work: here, home is a site of contagion, while the public sphere of work and the city circulates with "purer air." The sexual threat implicit in the association of the "weaker" sex with this contagion—with "a foul and fearful poison"—is further strengthened by the reminder that men are often long absent from home. What men may "forget" are the perils to the sanctity of home life embodied in the fallen woman. In the social imagination, the sewer exposed the drawing room to the destabilizing forces of the city, including disease, poverty, moral degradation, and—more troubling still—illicit sexuality. The diffusion of sewer gases in even the best-regulated homes seemed to jeopardize the very existence of domestic purity in the urban context.

"Look to Your Drains!"

Despite the challenge represented by the new sanitary technology, the idea of the home as protected retreat remained a powerful cultural construct. As householders struggled to maintain a sense of control over their private lives, they began to renegotiate their roles within the sanitary landscape and to assume new sanitary duties. The anxiety surrounding sewer gases, brought to a head in 1871 by the prince's illness, generated a public discourse focused not only on the dangers but also on the prevention of sewer gas poisoning. With characteristic directness, *Punch* comments on the role the royal infirmity played in generating interest in small-scale preventive measures: "Most of our contemporaries have lately improved an alarming occasion with many monitory observations on typhoid fever. The whole of these, however . . . may be pretty well summed up in the caution,—Look to your drains!"[75] In this imperative lay the promise that looking to, or at, one's drains might restore a threatened social stability. But how might the darkness of the drain be illuminated? How could one train the gaze on an underground labyrinth?

The answer, at least in part, came in the form of a new kind of publication that began to appear with some frequency in the 1870s: the domestic drainage manual.[76] These books promised to educate the concerned layperson in the science of drainage and offered practical advice on preventing sewer gases from entering the home. In the preface to the representative *Sewer Gas, and How to Keep It out of Houses* (1872), Osborne Reynolds describes the gap that his book seeks to fill: "What appears to be wanted is a book of approved scientific merit, and of such a practical character that a householder or any unscientific person can learn from it how to ascertain if drains are safe, and, if not, how to get them put right."[77] These guides almost certainly exploited people's fears of sewerage to sell books and to promote drain traps. Many of them conclude their discussion of the dangers of sewer gas and the ease with which it infiltrates the home by recommending a particular kind of drain trap, often mentioned by brand name. For instance, whereas Reynolds encourages the use of a single trap outside the confines of the home, another writer advocates the "double check trap,"[78] and still another recommends "Buchan's Patent Ventilating Sewage Gas Trap."[79] The arguably manipulative aspect of the drainage manuals comes to the fore in *An Architect's Letter about Sewer Gas and House Drainage* (1876), in which the architect Henry Masters counsels a father who has purportedly lost his daughter to drain poisoning: "The very severe affliction that has befallen your family must naturally make you feel anxious for the future. . . . [T]he only course I can advise is that all the old drains be taken out and a new system of draining and ventilating be substituted."[80] Masters's advice, suggesting that one can prevent further suffering and anxiety by taking enlightened action, must have instilled in readers a sense of power and control denied them by earlier apocalyptic accounts of the sewer. These guides, whether exploitative or not, encouraged householders to take a participatory role in the process of waste removal and thus helped to demystify modern sewerage.

In addition to repairing faulty drains, the drainage manuals also recommended adopting a rigorous program of sewer surveillance. Reynolds suggests beginning with a simple orientation: "The first thing for the anxious householder to do is to get a clear conception of what the drains in his house are for, and whereabouts he may expect to find them."[81] More extensive inquiries might have been inspired by Teale's *Dangers to Health*. In the introduction, Teale projects a vision of his ideal reader, the householder who, "aided by the diagrams[,] . . . may test every sanitary point, one by one, and as he goes round book in hand, may catechise his plumber, his mason, or his joiner."[82] Examining all the drains of a house became a way to familiarize them, that is, to redefine them as an integral part of the home, rather than belonging to the urban network. In *Woman as a Sanitary Reformer* (1880), Benjamin Ward Richardson adapts the ideology of separate spheres to the demands of sanitary modernization: women must oversee the domestic sanitary arrangements because, after all, he asks rhetorically, "What does a man know about a house?"[83] Drain inspection is imagined simply as another household duty to be performed by the dedicated materfamilias: "She would demand to have marked for her on a map or plan the precise position of every drainpipe in the establishment, and would insist, with intelligent skill, on having every drain kept as systematically clean as the china in the housemaid's cupboard."[84] This vision of the middle-class woman as accomplished overseer, rather than beleaguered victim, of sanitary technology reflects a renewed confidence in the ability of city dwellers to control their environment.

Richardson and his colleagues were certainly in earnest when they advised responsible householders to sniff out their faulty drains, but the opportunity for parody was not lost on *Punch*. The cartoon titled "Utile cum dulce" (fig. 1.4) takes as its theme the desire to bring drainage within sight and thus within the realm of personal control. The scene transpires at a dining table shared by two men, the "inquisitive gent" and the "fastidious host," but table and meal are completely overshadowed by an elaborate complex of drainpipes that snakes across the room. When asked "what this elaborately-carved and curiously-ramified structure is for," the host replies with perfect aplomb, "O, it's the drains! I like to have 'em where I can look after 'em myself." By offering a comic version of the newly developing sewage-conscious householder, *Punch* parodies the contemporary rage for domestic drainage management, while simultaneously offering a fantasy of high-style sewer surveillance.

Although it was clearly not possible to inspect every aspect of the vast metropolitan sewerage system or even to look very deeply into one's own drains, the authors of the drainage guides realized the importance of at least the illusion of visibility in demystifying sewerage. In this respect, they follow in the tradition of Mayhew, Hollingshead, and others who sought to expose the

1.4. Sanitary technology meets Arts and Crafts style in this parody of domestic drain surveillance from *Punch*. "Utile cum dulce," *Punch,* 6 January 1872, 2.

urban underworld for the edification (and delight) of readers. Hollingshead claims to provide "a panorama of underground London" and to that end lists all the main sewers under the jurisdiction of the Metropolitan Board of Works.[85] Similarly, Mayhew invites readers to "peruse the following accounts [of the course of the sewers] with the assistance of a map of the environs" (2:406).

Armchair explorations of this sort were admittedly limited: only a few pages after he makes the above suggestion, Mayhew expresses doubts about comprehending London's main drainage even with the help of a map. Still, written accounts of subterranean London responded to fears of an urban system that was becoming more difficult to control, or even to see, by verbally showing readers this system.[86] The domestic drainage manual went further by investing individuals with the authority and responsibility to superintend their own plumbing, and in this way it may have helped householders adapt to the new conditions of urban living. A testament to the empowering effects of private drain surveillance appears in the *Times* in October 1874. In a letter to the editor, a correspondent writes to advertise his success in securing his home from sewer gas, but not without first qualifying his claim: "I am not competent to discuss the great sewerage question, but I can confidently assert that, so far as the interior of each house is concerned, the adoption of the above plan is an effectual safeguard against the danger of sewer gas."[87] The letter reflects the achievement of a difficult balance. Rather than resisting the vast metropolitan drainage system, the enlightened householder learned to compromise, relinquishing control of the urban mass, while maintaining order within a newly circumscribed private sphere.

chapter 2

"Thames Fever"

The Contest for the River in the Metropolitan Imagination

Bake, bake, bake,
  O Thames, on thy way to the sea!
But the appetite which thy stink strikes dead
  Will never come back to me.

"To the Thames (After Tennyson)," Punch (1858)

Why is it that so many imperfect and decayed objects are admittedly more beautiful . . . than the same objects when complete and sound? . . . What, in a word, is the source, the
meaning, the reason of that strange and exquisite picturesque
charm and eye-delight so habitually clinging round decadence and ruin . . . ?

W. R. Greg, "The Special Beauty Conferred by
Imperfection and Decay," Contemporary Review (1872)

*T*his chapter explores competing visions of the river Thames during the
1850s and 1860s. Concerns about the state of the river were stimulated in part by its material condition, which had degenerated in the
first part of the century, but anxiety about the Thames was further cultivated
by popular representations, which helped determine the prevailing view of
the river as a polluted waste space. Within this context, the Thames Embankment was heralded both as a sure means of cleansing the river and as a guarantor
of urban purity. Not only would the structure house a major new sewer line,
but it would also replace a squalid, irregularly disposed shore with an imposing
granite facade, stretching from Westminster to Blackfriars bridges. Although

many regarded the Embankment as a major sanitary achievement, some few observers of the urban scene objected to the "improvement" of the Thames. Instead, they celebrated the very features of the river that the Embankment promised to destroy: the variety of industrial activities, the chaotic assortment of structural forms, and the eccentric appearance of the shore. Where others saw "pollution," they saw an aesthetically vital and culturally valuable riverfront. We see in these conflicting responses to the physical condition of the Thames a contest for control of the river's social and cultural meanings. What the Thames looked like, how it was visually perceived, was a significant social question, not least because of its geographic and symbolic centrality to the capital. Ultimately, the river served as a stage on which the identity and aspirations of the metropolis were contested. But the meanings of the river were shaped equally by physical alterations, cultural representations, and human behavior. This last was perhaps the feature of the river most difficult to control.

Constructions of Pollution

Public perceptions of the Thames in the mid-nineteenth century were significantly shaped—if not permanently altered—by events on the river in 1858. In June of that year, high temperatures coupled with a period of drought transformed the filthy river and its foul banks into a stinking pit. The "Great Stink" was the name given to the most notorious pollution crisis in the nineteenth century.[1] Those working in and visiting the neighborhood of the Thames at this time, including dockworkers, steamboat passengers, Templars, members of Parliament, and the queen herself, complained of the sickening effects of the river's stench and feared it as a source of disease. One inmate of the Temple lamented to the *Times*, "If I open my windows in rushes the stench, and I imbibe large draughts of poisonous matter; if I close them the heat is so great that I am almost suffocated and get poisoned all the same."[2] The situation upriver at the Houses of Parliament was not much improved; there, according to a "hard-worked and nearly-stifled MP" writing to the *Times*, the fumes escaping up from the river into the building were so offensive that the members of Parliament "might have just as well stood over a filthy cesspool or a putrid drain."[3] On several occasions during the summer of 1858,

MPs were seen fleeing from committee rooms clutching their papers and shielding their noses.[4] In the previous chapter, I discussed the role the extension of sewerage played in the rapid physical degradation of the Thames. The reliance on sewers and, in turn, the river to remove human waste from the city was still a relatively new phenomenon by the late 1850s, but its impact was quickly felt. The consensus, registered in the reformist journal the *Builder,* was that the sanitary changes implemented around 1848 were essentially to blame for the river's foul state: "Fifteen or sixteen years ago the Thames water was not so bad, and persons on the river did not hesitate at dipping in a vessel and drinking the contents. Such a thing now [i.e., in 1858] would be like an act of insanity."[5]

This moment in the life of the Thames is significant for the following discussion of the river's social meanings for two reasons: not only did the predominantly negative perceptions of the river circulating in 1858 have a remarkable staying power in the public imagination, but also examining these perceptions allows us to see the way in which "pollution" was constructed out of a nexus of cultural representations, material conditions, and social values. That the Victorians themselves recognized the Great Stink as a social construction is suggested by a quotation from the *Times.* In an interesting moment of self-reflexivity, the paper reports, "Thames fever is now at its height. . . . People are afraid to travel by the steamboats, afraid not only of prospective disease but of immediate nausea, head-ache, and giddiness."[6] As described here, "Thames fever" is not a medical condition but a perceptual one: to be seized by this fever is to be seized with pervasive feelings of anxiety about the appalling state of the river. The phrase suggests the ease with which Victorian commentators shifted from the medical to the cultural register and back again when addressing the problem of Thames pollution.

As the quotation also indicates, the stink on the Thames was a favorite topic of Londoners in 1858. While the intricacies of the main drainage plan for London were debated on the floor of the House, the danger and disgrace of the river became a staple of the periodical press. *Punch* found in the river's stench a nearly inexhaustible source of grim satire and scatological humor: silly poems such as "Piff-Piff! An Ode to the Thames," "Slow but Sewer," and "A Sonnet upon a Scent" crowded its pages.[7] The tone assumed in the serious journals was consistently urgent, although here, too, hyperbolic prophesies of doom proliferated. The *Builder* saw in the polluted Thames "an evil . . . which may in August, or earlier, repeat the horrors of the Great Plague"; while the *Times* warned its readers, "Our indignant British river . . . makes his presence felt like a forgotten corpse. . . . We, in the very focus of the miasma, shall perhaps be making our chronicle of nightly deaths."[8] As these descriptions suggest, in the process of reporting the crisis on the river the press undoubt-edly cultivated it. Luckin, focusing on the relation of the Great Stink to political discourse, justly characterizes representations of the Thames in the late 1850s as "intensely pessimistic, bordering at times on the cataclysmic."[9] Writers seem to have vied with one another to produce the most chilling account of the Thames and to heighten public anxiety about the potential dangers of its condition. In his timely pamphlet *The Polluted Thames* (1858), John Wiggins warns that the mud banks serve as "repositories and stores of malaria."[10] In a letter to the *Times* (also in 1858), the chemist Alfred Smee draws attention to the "putrid fermentation" transpiring on the river and "liable in the highest degree to communicate its death-producing influence."[11] The physician John Spurgin asserts in *Drainage of Cities* (1858) that pouring sewage into the river is calculated "to turn salubrity into disease, a ventilating current into pesti-lence, refreshing water into poison; and, in short, life into death."[12]

Exaggerated they may have been, but these sensationalized representations shaped the dominant meanings of the river in the period. Assertions from some in the scientific community that the state of the Thames was not ac-companied by a rising incidence of disease were largely ignored by a Victorian public who embraced the rhetoric of filth. Articles published in the *Sanitary Review, and Journal of Public Health* in 1858, for instance, dismiss the popular perceptions of the river as a source of mass destruction. While the sanitary and medical authorities writing in the *Review* insist that the sewage in the river is a problem and that alternative arrangements should be made for its disposal, they nevertheless object to rampant unsubstantiated claims that the river is murdering the inhabitants of London. One article counters these rumors di-rectly, charging, "There have been strange stories flying of men struck down with the stench, and of all kinds of fatal diseases upspringing on the river's banks. There has been much exaggeration as to the amount of mischief done to the health of the community by the foul river, and much absurd speculation as to the necessary consequences to be expected from it."[13] Luckin's research into the records of mortality for the metropolis and his conclusion that "1858 was a relatively healthy year" confirm this more cautious assessment.[14] Statistics and microscopy, however, could not compete for the public attention with graphic descriptions and personal experience of the river's material horrors. Thomas Wood makes this very point in his treatise *London Health and London Traffic* (1859), when he appeals to the common sense, as well as the olfactory sense, of his readers in making his case against the Thames: "There is little occasion for minute chemical analysis or the advice of the great medical authorities in a matter such as this. An odour so offensive and so depressing, so faint and so fetid, speaks in a language which can scarcely be misunderstood."[15] Within Wood's text, medical authority is displaced not by sensory experience per se but by rhetorical authority—the writer's ability to "speak in a language [of filth] which can scarcely be misunderstood."

The sensory experience nevertheless holds an important place in any account of the nineteenth-century Thames. For the highly sensationalized representations of the river in the 1850s gained a hold on the public imagination for the very reason that the material condition of the river had visibly deteriorated. In the several decades leading up to the Great Stink, the Thames became the depository for an ever-greater volume of waste associated not only with sewerage but also with the accelerated development of commerce, transport, and industry in Victorian London. Industrial pollution, although more severe in the northern manufacturing towns, took its toll on the Thames: paper mills, tanneries, dye-works, and breweries all used the river as both water source and waste basin.[16] Also active on the river and contributing to its degradation were the coal trade, gas works, and passenger steamship companies, which began operating in 1815.[17] On the low-tech side, the reeking by-products of slaughterhouses and cattle yards continued to drain into the Thames, as they had for centuries. And, of course, London's surging population made its messy mark. As Wohl's research indicates, approximately 250 tons of sewage were discharged daily into the river in the 1850s.[18] Because the Thames is a tidal river, most of this mass of refuse remained in London instead of flowing out to sea as had been hoped. The tides also contributed to one of the great scourges of the metropolis—the mudflats. Running along the river's margins, these vast muddy banks measured as much as 700 feet in width at Waterloo Bridge and averaged a depth of six feet.[19] They also harbored deposits of reeking sewage, which were primarily responsible for the horrid stench associated with the river. A report of the Metropolitan Board of Works describes the situation in vivid terms: "[I]n hot weather an effluvium is given off from the putrefying organisms which . . . lie reeking in the sun as the tide continues to descend."[20]

Of course, as we have seen, filth and bad smells were not merely unpleasant, they also bore a range of threatening social meanings. The ravages of three cholera epidemics and the tireless campaigning of sanitary reformers were teaching the Victorian public to recognize a dirty environment and especially foul odors as sources of disease. Where there was smell, there was death. Because of this ready association, the metropolitan populace understandably trembled at the state of the Thames in 1858. The further association of dirt with social degeneracy surely compounded their fears. Again, as we have seen, within sanitary discourse a filthy environment was imagined to contribute not only to physical debilitation but also to moral degradation in all its forms —from profligacy to alcoholism, from adultery to prostitution. The causal link between filth and an immoral population, however, was frequently displaced by metaphor and metonymy. Thus, the people who lived in and suffered from an unsanitary environment—generally the poor—came to be identified with this environment: they did not merely live in waste, they were waste.

One very obvious instance of this conflation of moral and material conditions, of people and the filth they inhabit, occurs in *London Labour and the London Poor*. In the section titled "Of the Cleansing of the Sewers—Ventilation," Mayhew digresses from the technically specific topic announced in the subtitle to describe the immoral character of a particular quarter of the metropolis; but the apparent digression really leads to the heart of the subject, revealing as it does the difficulty of maintaining distinctions between "pollution" as excrement and "pollution" as criminality:

> Across Flint-street, Green-street, and other ways . . . hang, on a fair day, lines of washed clothes to dry. Yellow-looking chemises and petticoats are affixed alongside men's trowsers and waistcoats; coarse-featured and brazen-looking women, with necks and faces reddened, as if with brick-dust, from exposure to the weather, stand at their doors and beckon to the passers by. Perhaps in no part of the metropolis is there a more marked manifestation of

> moral obsceneness on the one hand, and physical obsceneness on
> the other. With the low prostitution of this locality is mixed the low
> and bold crime of the metropolis. . . . And all over this place of
> moral degradation extends the stench of offensive manufactures
> and ill-ventilated sewers. (2:423–24)

Mayhew substitutes a description of the neighborhood's sewer for a description
of something closely associated, if not interchangeable, with it: the residents
and their immoral behavior. Sexual promiscuity (marked by the indiscriminate
mixing of female undergarments with men's clothing on the line), prostitution, and other crime create an atmosphere that is the moral equivalent of a
poorly ventilated sewer. Within this imagined geography, Mayhew assigns the
degraded human population the role of refuse.

Representations of the Thames in the mid-nineteenth century similarly describe environmental degradation in social terms, frequently invoking a "waste
population" as a sign of the river's corruption. The river, defiled by the sewage
of London and marred by the presence of industrial activity, had become a
haven for petty criminals, paupers, vagrants, and other stigmatized peoples
who could linger unmolested on the shore. By day, scavengers sought out a
meager living from the river's dregs: "mudlarks" searched the mud near the
wharves for scraps of coal, iron, and wood; "dredgermen" surveyed the river
by boat, casting out their nets for bones, rope, coal, and—notoriously—dead
bodies. By night, the river provided a resting place for numbers of homeless
people who crowded under the arches of its bridges (fig. 2.1). The river also
provided a more permanent resting place for the suicides who leapt to their
deaths from Waterloo Bridge. The actual and imagined presence of this socially
and geographically marginalized population played a key role in inscribing
the river as a site of impurity and a source of danger.

We can gain a clearer understanding of the role the riverside population
played in the construction of Thames pollution by considering an illustration
of the river published in the *Builder* during the summer of 1858.[21] The image,
as well as the accompanying article, takes as its primary subject and target the
Thames mudflats (fig. 2.2). On the far left side of the drawing, the gaping mouth
of a sewer pours forth a quantity of sewage onto the muddy bank; the label
"poisonous accumulation" indicates that this process of expulsion and accre-
tion has been occurring for some time, to the detriment of the public health.

2.1. A marginalized population finds shelter on the Thames. Illustration by Gustave Doré, "Under the Arches," in *London: A Pilgrimage* by Doré and Blanchard Jerrold (London: Grant and Co., 1872), 185.

But the illustration does more than simply warn of the physical evils of the mudflats, their potential for generating miasmic vapors and attendant infections; for included in the iconography of the Thames along with sewer, mud bank, and polluted stream, is the human figure of the dredgerman, surveying the river from the shore. The appearance of the dredgerman highlights the social dimension of Thames pollution. The dredgerman's business of fishing for corpses established him as a figure of horror and mystery. In an article for *Household Words* describing waterside public houses and their customers, "Powder Dick and His Train" (1853), George Augustus Sala emphasizes the peculiar fascination and dread inspired by the dredgers, "surrounding whom there is a halo of deep and fearful interest."[22] By including the decidedly un-hallowed dredgerman in its depiction of the Thames, the *Builder* draws on this "fearful interest," the visceral unease, to make readers fear the river as a site of physical and moral corruption.

The idea that Thames pollution simultaneously posed an environmental and a social threat also emerges in descriptions of the river's youngest scavengers,

2.2. Constituent elements of the filthy shore—the sewer and the scavenger. Engraving titled "A Section of the Shore," from "The Condition of the Thames," *Builder,* 3 July 1858, 454.

the mudlarks. Representations of the mudlarks emphasize the intimate connection between these boys and girls and the filthy riverside environment where they work. Mayhew, for instance, describes the mudlarks he interviews as composites of filth: "[T]heir bodies are grimed with the foul soil of the river, and their torn garments stiffened up like boards with dirt of every possible description" (2:155). The distinction between mud and mudlark is effectively meaningless, for as Mayhew further reveals, the victims of pollution simultaneously serve as perpetrators. Observing the group of boy and girl larks he has assembled, Mayhew notes, "The muddy slush was dripping from their clothes and utensils, and forming a puddle in which they stood" (2:156). The mudlarks literally befoul every place they touch. But as in his account of ill-ventilated sewers, Mayhew moves swiftly and uncritically from the environmental to the social register. A description of the mudlarks' physical condition is displaced by judgments on their moral condition, which is also imagined to be contagious: "The majority of this class are ignorant, and without even the rudiments of education, and . . . many of them from time to time are committed to prison for petty thefts. . . . As for the females growing up under such circumstances, the worst may be anticipated of them; and in proof of this I have found, upon inquiry, that very many of the unfortunate creatures who swell the tide of prostitution in Ratcliff-highway, and other low neighbourhoods in the East of London, have originally been mud-larks" (2:156). The leap from filth to crime is a short one: the conditions of physical impurity on the Thames in which the mudlarks are immersed determine their social degeneracy, and vice versa. The social danger of the mudlarks, moreover, becomes particularly acute upon their departure from the riverbanks; for, as Mayhew insists, mudlarks grow up and contribute to another equally virulent form of pollution: they "swell the tide of prostitution in Ratcliff-highway." The real threat of pollution, then, is that it precipitates out; Mayhew's evocation of the prostitute, while seemingly tangential, precisely conveys the transgressive dangers of pollution. For as I discuss in the context of the sewer, the prostitute functioned as one of the most resonant symbols of pollution in the Victorian middle-class imagination. The physical danger posed by the prostitute lay in the risk of contracting venereal disease, but her infiltration of middle-class families through isolated but numerous sexual encounters also implicated her in a more broadly conceived moral corruption. As a figure of social transgression, the prostitute thus forged "the link between slum and suburb, dirt and cleanliness, ignorance and civilization, profligacy and morality," in Lynda Nead's assessment.[23] In other words, the danger of the prostitute lay in her mobility.

It is curious, in light of this perceived mobility, that so many nineteenth-century representations of fallen female sexuality fixate on the woman's demise, on her downward trajectory toward suffering and death. Nead argues that these representations helped defuse the perceived threat of prostitution by reinforcing "hegemonic notions of femininity and morality": female vice would not go undetected or unpunished.[24] Interestingly, the nadir of the prostitute's degradation, her ultimate moment of tragic suffering, is repeatedly represented as taking place on the Thames. When a sexually suspect woman makes her figurative fall, she comes to a halt quite literally on the banks of the river, the lowest point in London in both geophysical and social terms. The association of the prostitute with the river may seem at first an unlikely connection: her labor and identity, unlike that of dredger and mudlark, are not in any way confined to or dependent on the river. Yet the association played an important role in inscribing the Thames not only as a site of material and moral decay but also as a site where the dangers of pollution might be concentrated and effectively eradicated. Dickens provides a paradigmatic instance of this fall in *David Copperfield* (1849–50) when he describes David and Mr. Peggoty's meeting with the prostitute Martha down on the Thames at Millbank (fig. 2.3). As the male characters observing her quickly realize, Martha has gone to the river to commit, or contemplate, suicide. In a familiar move, Dickens uses the filth of the river to define the moral corruption of the miserable woman: he describes her as "stray[ing] down to the river's brink," "[a]s if she were a part of the refuse [the river] had cast out."[25] The metaphoric connection becomes even more explicit in Martha's own impassioned speech, in which she sympathetically identifies with the river: "I know it's like me! . . . I know that I belong to it. . . . It's the only thing in all the world that I am fit for, or that's fit for me. Oh, the dreadful river!"[26] Deploying the comprehensive conception of pollution that informs Victorian sanitary discourse, Dickens sets up an exact equation between Martha's tainted moral condition and the river's defiled physical condition. In the passage, the figures of the sexually suspect woman and the river are used reflexively to describe and define each other's degeneracy.

One of the earliest cultural representations of the death of the prostitute on the river Thames appeared in Thomas Hood's successful poem "The Bridge of Sighs" (1844). According to art historian Susan Casteras, as well as Nead, the poem was one of the most important sources for the myth of the prostitute as social outcast.[27] But the poem was also influential in establishing the Thames's reputation as a site of degradation and death. The short verse narrative, based loosely on the actual case of a woman named Mary Furley who attempted suicide, focuses on the plight of a sexually deviant woman who leaps from Waterloo Bridge into the Thames and to her death.[28] Because of the success of the poem, Waterloo Bridge and its suicides acquired mythic status. The poem's combined imagery of a fair, forsaken woman, the "dark arch" of Waterloo Bridge, and "the black flowing river" was incorporated into representations of prostitution throughout the century by visual artists influenced by the familiar work.[29] Thus, even as "The Bridge of Sighs" played an important role in writing the river into the cultural narrative of London prostitution, it also played a part in locating the prostitute within the cultural geography of the Thames.

The appearance of these degraded figures in representations of the Thames helped define the river as a site of impurity and, by extension, as a source of social disorder. At the same time, however, we can attribute the ubiquity and influence of these images to their implicit promise of social control. On the one hand, the use of the prostitute as an embodied referent for river pollution dramatized the danger that the Thames posed for the moral and medical health

2.3. The prostitute Martha sees in the polluted Thames an image of herself. Illustration by Hablot K. Browne (Phiz), "The River," in *David Copperfield* by Charles Dickens, vol. 1 5, *The Works of Charles Dickens* (New York: Scribner's, 1 9 o o), opposite 294.

of the urban body. On the other hand, the imaginative location of a waste population on the shore may have provided an anxious public with some degree of clarity and comfort: if pollution were embodied and localized, then it might be more easily contained. An article in the *Builder* from July 1 8 5 9 offers a version of this fantasy of containment and control when it implicitly links the eradication of the mudlarks to the aesthetic and sanitary renovation of the Thames. In its excoriation of the mudflats skirting the river, the *Builder* jests that at least the mudlarks are profiting from the filthy conditions, likening them to the "gold diggers of Australia."[30] But after marveling at the exploits of these marginal figures, the article concludes, "We hope . . . that the mudlarks will find better occupation, and that before long a splendid quay, lined with buildings pleasant to the eye will confine the river in such bounds . . . that in future no permanent stoppages will be made."[31] There is of course no explicit claim that removing the mudlarks will make the river clean, but the prospect of Thames purification and, in turn, urban renewal is nonetheless imaginatively tied to the fate of the lowly lark.

The Promise of Purity

Within this simplified narrative of accumulation, containment, and control, it is ultimately not the absence of a degraded population but the presence of the Thames Embankment—"a splendid quay"—that ensures the river's purification. Just as the mudlark, prostitute, or dredgerman served as a repository for negative judgments of the river, the Embankment served as a repository for a great city's aspirations and ambitions—an opportunity not just to cleanse the river but to aggrandize the capital. A prominent landmark in London still today, the Victoria Embankment (as it was named upon completion) stretches about a mile and a quarter along the north shore of the Thames from Westminster to Blackfriars bridges.[32] The structure reclaimed thirty-seven and a quarter acres of land, which was subsequently laid out to accommodate a road, a pedestrian promenade, and a public garden. As in the case of the Thames itself around the time of the Great Stink, an exaggerated rhetoric defined the Embankment in the cultural imagination. Dire proclamations on the state of the Thames were balanced against hyperbolic claims for the projected Embankment's purifying properties. For instance, although Augustus Granville dubs the Thames a "*cloaca maxima*" in 1865, he goes on to predict that once the Embankment is completed, the river "will exhibit to wondering Europeans a Castalian spring."[33] The *Times* similarly reflects and cultivates the great expectations attached to the Embankment: "Imagine a grand open quay all along the Thames," suggests an enthusiastic leader of 1860, "a river no longer polluted with filth and exhaling stench, but running in a deep and pleasant stream between strong embankments. Why it would be the finest walk in London; so that we should gain a place for the sewers, a new main road, a magnificent promenade, and a pure river all at one stroke!"[34] No matter that in its report to Parliament on the main drainage project, the Metropolitan Board of Works sought to temper expectations, insisting that "the Thames never could have been a 'silvery' stream"[35]; the vision of a pellucid river running past the Embankment retained a powerful hold on the urban imagination.

As the above litany of anticipated benefits suggests, the Embankment was imagined to fulfill a wide range of objectives: beautification of the capital, traffic relief, provision of recreational space, and sewage disposal. Yet the successful passage of the Thames Embankment Act in 1862 was most immediately tied to London's sanitary difficulties. Not coincidentally, it was in the wake of the Great Stink in August 1858 that Parliament finally approved plans for London's new main drainage system.[36] The Metropolitan Main Drainage, developed and executed under the auspices of the Metropolitan Board of Works, was designed to improve the sewerage of London and, related to that, the condition of the river. Three main intercepting sewers north of the Thames, running along an east-west axis, would serve to divert the city's sewage away from the river in central London and carry it to discharge points far downstream. Had it not been for the construction of these sewers, the Embankment may never have come to pass.[37] The idea of an Embankment for the Thames had a long history—appearing most notably in Christopher Wren's plans for rebuilding the City after the Great Fire of 1666—yet only in the context of the drainage project did the Embankment begin to seem practicable. First, the Metropolitan Board of Works promoted the Embankment in conjunction with main drainage as the only means to ensure Thames purification: by contracting the course of the river, the Embankment would remove the mudflats, which were as much of a problem as the sewage itself.[38] Second, the Metropolitan Board needed a viable route for the low-level interceptory sewer. Although the board had considered running the line underneath the Strand and Fleet Street, the disruption to traffic that would have attended construction there made the plan unworkable.[39] Running a new main sewer underneath a purpose-built Embankment, along ground that was essentially waste space, seemed like the ideal solution.

Clearly the construction of this sewer, as well as the removal of the mud banks, would play a key role in cleaning up the Thames in central London. But by bringing spatial and social order to a chaotic waste space, the Embankment also ensured the purification of the river in a broader sense, being designed to put all sorts of unsavory matter in its place. A sectional view of the Embankment published in 1867 in the *Illustrated London News* indicates the high degree of specialization and organization that the structure imposed on the river (fig. 2.4). The subterranean space is shown to support London's developing infrastructure: separate tunnels are provided for water and gas lines, the underground railway, and of course the low-level sewer. Aboveground, Charing Cross railway station looms over the scores of laborers and engineers applying their technical expertise to the taming of the river and mud. The fruit of their labor is the crystalline Thames, shown at right, contained within the gleaming Embankment wall. The spatial order of the Embankment, as envisioned in the *Illustrated London News* and elsewhere, reflected and sought to reproduce an ideal social order. Just as the city's wastes would be confined within proper bounds and transported out of the city, so too would the waste population necessarily be removed from the river by the erection of the Embankment in place of the spatially amorphous mudflats. The Embankment also reinforced a normative social order by providing an approved gathering place for less privileged social groups: the promenade and park were imagined to afford a socially acceptable form of recreation for the urban working class. The Metropolitan Board of Works expresses this hope in its promotion of the Embankment as a place for "quiet recreation of the people on Sundays and holidays."[40] And a letter published in the *Builder* in March 1870 reflects a similar hope, urging that "the Thames Embankment, properly carried out, should be for the poor women and children of Southwark and Lambeth, Seven Dials, [and] Holborn . . . what Hyde Park is for the upper classes . . . their Sunday promenade."[41] In his discussion of the spatial construction of social "outsiders," David Sibley identifies "pure" spaces as those "from which non-conforming groups or activities have been expelled or have been kept out through the maintenance of strong boundaries."[42] The Embankment's promenade and gardens, by excluding the river's waste population and encouraging socially acceptable forms of recreation for the "legitimate" working class, would ensure the river's continued social purity.

Although the Embankment was recognized foremost as a project of sanitary and, implicitly, social engineering, it was also seen as an opportunity to beautify the metropolis and enhance the city's public image. As Donald Olsen and James Winter have discussed, in mid-Victorian London, there was little public support for metropolitan improvements of a strictly aesthetic character.[43] "Grand gestures in the service of beauty," writes Olsen, "or visual expressions of municipal pride could be considered only if connected with projects remedying some undoubted evil or promoting obvious economic gain."[44] That the Embankment received the enthusiastic support that it did is attributable to its fundamental utility; but because of the rarity of improvement schemes of its magnitude, it quickly became the locus of the city's cultural aspirations. Promoting the Embankment in terms that became familiar

2.4. Imposing order on the chaotic waste space of the Thames shore. "Section of Thames Embankment," showing (1) water and gas lines, (2) low-level sewer, and (3) underground railway, in *Illustrated London News,* 22 June 1867, 632. Courtesy of Marion DuPont Scott Sporting Collection, Special Collections, University of Virginia Library, Charlottesville.

in the 1860s, the *Builder* claimed, "This stupendous undertaking . . . will confer a character of grandeur upon the whole metropolis."[45] Indeed, if the Embankment could be made the centerpiece of a comprehensive plan for the riverfront, then "we might eventually possess a metropolis which, architecturally considered, could not be matched by any in Europe."[46] A structure of such manifest engineering and architectural importance was imagined to bolster the reputation of London itself, to invest the metropolis with the kind of grandeur appropriate to its image as a world city.

Within the context of this vision of future glory, the squalid and irregular appearance of the condemned shore drew considerable comment and criticism. The industrial and commercial interests on the river—taking advantage of the vast, neglected spaces provided by the mud banks—had erected on the river's margin an array of unregulated structures, including wharves, temporary shelters and walkways, and precarious landing places. Old barges driven into the stinking mud regularly served as piers for steamships.[47] These chaotic conditions were repeatedly cited as evidence of the aesthetic degradation of the river, which, in turn, threatened to debase the image of the entire metropolis. The *Times,* for instance, charged in 1860 that at the riverside, "[a]ll is meanness and shabbiness and discomfort"[48] and repeated in 1863 that the river's banks had been "disfigured by every unsightly erection that trade and manufacture could devise for their convenience."[49] In one of its many articles devoted to the coming Embankment, the *Builder* included a series of sketches representing the unreformed shore (fig. 2.5). The illustration at the top of the page highlights the industrial character of the riverfront, with its coal wharves and brick manufactories. Apparent, too, is the lack of a "distinct margin," which has helped create the muddy expanse that serves as fertile territory for the mudlarks' excavations.[50] A trio of smaller images shows a near view of the narrow streets, shadowy corners, and decayed buildings abutting the river. Overall, the appearance of the riverfront is characterized as "shapeless," "dilapidated," and "unsightly," although with the Embankment on the horizon the hope remains that "in a few years our present illustrations will be looked at with wonder and doubt."[51]

As the text of the article goes on to suggest, these aesthetic judgments on the state of the Thames were connected to larger concerns about metropolitan identity. The squalid conditions of the shore needed to be remedied not simply for their own sake but because they prevailed on "the banks of the most populous, wealthy, and prosperous City in the world."[52] In other words, Thames pollution was understood to pose a threat not only to the public health but also to London's image of and reputation for prosperity on the national and world stage. This concern with London's threatened stature was repeatedly emphasized in arguments supporting the Embankment. Since the Thames is a "national river," according to a piece in the *Builder* in July 1859, its poor condition reflects upon and affects the entire nation.[53] In an article in the *Times* from March 1863, the stability of the empire itself is imagined to be contingent on the river's state, the "sordid appearance [of] which degrades our Imperial centre."[54] Londoners at midcentury saw, in David Owen's words, "a river front that was clearly unworthy of the growing magnificence of London."[55]

Developments across the channel in Paris added an urgency to the Embankment question. While London continued to suffer from the river's stench, Paris

Remains of the Savoy Palace.   A steep Road from the River to the Strand.   Thames Bank Architecture : a near View.

2.5. The *Builder* anticipates and promotes the Embankment by featuring scenes of squalor on the riverfront. "London on the Thames: The Desired Embankments," *Builder,* 25 January 1862, 61.

underwent massive urban surgery at the hands of Baron Haussmann and looked to surpass London as the premier European capital. As Olsen explains it, although Londoners rejected the kind of systematic urban renovation practiced in Paris, they nevertheless admired the monumental effect of the wide Parisian boulevards and hoped to infuse something of this spirit into their own metropolis.[56] The Embankment seemed uniquely capable of satisfying these aspirations toward a kind of urban splendor, toward the monumental. Located in a geographically and symbolically resonant place in the heart of London, the Embankment served as a visible manifestation of the city's prestige. Moreover, the Thames's status as an international waterway, the gateway to the empire, ensured that this prestige would circulate around the globe. Anticipating the completed Embankment in 1864, the *Times* praised it as "one of the most magnificent promenades of which Europe will be able to boast."[57] John O'Connor's 1873 rendering of the Embankment soon after its completion similarly conveys pride in a city that has built itself on commerce and industry, as indicated by the river traffic and smokestacks, but can afford time and space for enjoyment, as indicated by the gentlemen lounging on the balcony in the foreground (fig. 2.6). As a monument for London, the Embankment provided an unparalleled opportunity to consolidate the image of the metropolis as a site of material wealth, commercial preeminence, and imperial ambition.

The Urban Picturesque

Counterbalancing these prevailing ideas about the Thames, however, was the desire manifested in both cultural representations and urban practice to reject the rhetoric of reform in favor of a celebration of the river as a site of pleasure. While most commentators sought either to condemn or to control the river, a significant few sought to enjoy it. Although not all the celebrants of the river protested the Embankment explicitly, they rejoiced nonetheless in the very qualities of the river that the Embankment was designed to suppress. For a handful of writers, pollution was infinitely more fascinating than purity.

One example of this countercultural perspective appears in journalist Angus B. Reach's *London on the Thames; or, Life Above and Below Bridge* (1848), a genial tour guide that chronicles the activities and amusements transpiring on the modern river. Rather than re-create the beauties of the Thames in times

2.6. The Thames reclaimed—a monumental site where leisure and industry meet. Engraving by H. Adlard, from the painting *Thames Embankment from Somerset House* by John O'Connor, 1873. Reproduced by permission from the Guildhall Library, City of London.

past, Reach explicitly embraces the river of the present, asserting that "dearer to us than all such glimpses, antiquarian or poetic, is the glorious vision to be enjoyed from one of the bow-windows at Lovegrove's."[58] The view from the windows at Lovegrove's, one of the numerous riverside hotels at Greenwich, would have taken in nothing more glorious than merchant ships and steamers; yet Reach refers to this custom of dining at Greenwich as "one of the grand features of the Thames of our own day."[59] We might perhaps expect pollution to be conspicuously absent from an appreciation of the river in "its now-a-days' condition."[60] Reach, however, not only admits pollution into his representation but also dilates on the subject of filth with considerable enthusiasm. As the following descriptive catalogue reveals, the range of pollutants on the river enhances the enjoyment of the scene:

> Let the student, then, conceive an agglomerate mass made up as follows:—mud banks, dead cats, dead dogs, slimy hurdles, coal-barges, grimy wharfs, common sewers, police galleys, dishes of whitebait, coal-heavers, waterside public-houses, penny steam-boats, mudlarks, Jacks in the Water, tiers of colliers, ugly ballast boats, Dutch craft with Kennet eels, Boulogne steamers with railway

defaulters, yachts going as far as Erith on a voyage to the East In-
dies, gents conducting gentesses to the Red House at Battersea . .
. tiers of shipping, lines of old tumble-down houses, rigging, chimneys, wharfs, bridges, boats, and everywhere muddy water and restless currents—all moving—all commingling—and over all a
canopy of ever-rolling smoke.[61]

By means of such exhaustive listing (the single-sentence catalogue extends
over two pages), Reach re-creates the diverse pursuits and the restless motion
and noise characteristic of the Thames shore. Far from appearing as a source
of offense, the pollutants in the catalogue (including animal carcasses, sewage,
and mud banks) function as a source of visual interest and pleasure along with
the yachts, public houses, and whitebait. Although conventionally associated
with disease and death, in this instance uncontained filth becomes representative of "Life" on the river.

A similar exuberance inspired by the impurities of the Thames is expressed
by Edmund Yates, one of Dickens's protégés, in an article for *All the Year Round*
published in October 1863 at an early stage of the Embankment construction.[62] Entitled "Silent Highway-Men," the piece offers an energetic defense
of the Thames in the wake of the widespread negative publicity. While con-
ceding that the river is "thick, yellow, turbid, occasionally evil smelling," Yates
nevertheless proclaims his continued admiration for the maligned stream:
"The Thames is my mania, my love for it the absorbing passion of my life."[63]
The response to the river developed in the article differs radically from the
prevailing attitudes cultivated in the press. While the *Builder* and others de-
plore the filthy and irregular appearance of the Thames shore, the author of
"Silent Highway-Men" enthusiastically approves its notorious eccentricities:

> I know him [Father Thames] throughout; but I love him best in his
> own special territory, frowned upon by the great gaunt black ware-
> houses, the dreary river-side public-houses, the huge brewery
> palaces, the shot-towers, the dock-houses, the dim grey Tower of
> London, the congregationless City churches, the clanging factories,
> the quiet Temple, the plate-glass works, the export Scotch and Irish
> merchants, the cheese-factors' premises, the cement wharves, the
> sugar consignees' counting-houses, the slimy slippery landing-places,
> the atmosphere of which is here sticky with molasses, there dusty

with flour, and a little way further off choky with particles of floating wool.[64]

Instead of rejecting the unsightly riverside erections and the surprising combination of activities on the shore, Yates, in the style of Reach, embraces the
diversity and vitality of the scene. By juxtaposing the quiet of the Temple and
"clanging factories," for instance, he highlights the contrast of sounds and
shapes that the river provides. By crowding a multitude of occupations as diverse as warehousing, shipping, brewing, and manufacturing within a single
sentence, he suggests the wide variety of commercial pursuits transpiring
along the narrow shore. Furthermore, he uses an abundance of tactile imagery
("slimy," "sticky," "dusty") to re-create the sensory excitement of the work-a-
day river. Significantly, the very images that would have inspired horror in
the sanitary reformer, such as the "slimy slippery landing-places," become in
this passage a source of visual (and aural) pleasure.

As Yates imagines it, the Thames Embankment promised to put an end to
these pleasures. So while the Embankment, as we have seen, was widely recognized as the savior of the Thames, Yates portrays it in the "Silent Highway-
Men" as the cause of the river's social and aesthetic degradation. Following the
affectionately written inventory of the Thames shore quoted above is an un-
equivocal indictment of the structure being built in its midst: "Make your embankments, if you like; lay down your level road duly granited and palisaded off
from the river, and lined with buildings of equal height and of the same monotonous architecture; but, before you do that, you will have to clear away
hundreds of little poky dirty streets of a peculiar specialty nowhere else to be
met with."[65] From this perspective, the Embankment, because it promised to
regularize the appearance of the shore, threatened to annihilate the commercially and aesthetically vigorous environment imagined to epitomize Thames-
side London. For all its dilapidation, the riverfront offered visual interest and
diversity, while the Embankment in the course of squelching the heterogene-
ity of the shore promised visual stupefaction: "hundreds of little poky dirty
streets" were to be supplanted by "the same monotonous architecture." Of
significance here is the representation of Thames purification in terms of an
aesthetic controversy, a question of competing architectural styles. In this
context, the unreclaimed foreshore appears not as a degraded environment
but as an alternative visual model expressive of its own range of positive

meanings and values. Through an imaginative act, the "polluted" is refigured as the "picturesque."

The embanked river, as we have seen, provided London with an image of itself as a monumental city. At the same time, the prospect of the Embankment inspired—if only among a minority—the appreciation of the unreformed, degraded river reimagined as a site of the picturesque. While the monumental is essentially an urban image, expressing pride in the achievements of civilization, the picturesque provides an image of uncorrupted nature, pleasing because of its irregularity of form and its suggestion of aging and decay.[66] The pleasures of the picturesque were first cultivated on the aristocratic country estate in the eighteenth century, but in the nineteenth century the deceptive image of the unspoiled country was imported to the city in the form of the suburban villa. In his essay on the aesthetic characteristics of the Victorian built environment, Nicholas Taylor calls the picturesque "*par excellence* the image of the Victorian suburb."[67] The picturesque as bourgeois pastoral fantasy at first seems an unlikely image for the commercially active, urban Thames shore. Yet the celebratory descriptions of the Thames that we have considered consciously evoke the picturesque both thematically (by highlighting the variety and irregularity of the structural forms on the shore) and formally (by joining a host of fluvial images into surprising combination). This repeated evocation of the picturesque in representations of the urban Thames suggests a resistance not only to the monumental values of the Embankment but also to the modernization of the river and the capital more generally.

This complex form of resistance is expressed in *London: A Pilgrimage* (1872), a lavishly illustrated tour of the metropolis jointly produced by the journalist Blanchard Jerrold and the well-known artist Gustave Doré. Doré and Jerrold's artistic journey begins and ends on the Thames, and the river figures largely in both text and images throughout the volume. Doré provides multiple views of Thames shipping, of the docks, of riverside wharves, of bridges, and of boat races. Even the title page features a classically proportioned Father Thames surveying his domain from underneath the dark arch of a bridge, as if to advertise the river's graphic centrality (fig. 2.7). My focus, though, is on Jerrold's text because of its explicit commitment to the picturesque and to the Thames as an ideal vehicle for expressing this aesthetic.[68] Like the previous defenders of the Thames whom we have considered, Jerrold seems to value the river for

2.7. The Gothic Thames as an emblem of London life. Illustration by Gustave Doré, "Father Thames," in *London: A Pilgrimage* by Doré and Blanchard Jerrold (London: Grant and Co., 1872), half title.

the delightful confusion and even squalor that it presents. "The glimpses of dark lanes and ancient broken tenements; the corner public-houses delightfully straggling from the perpendicular; the crazy watermen's stairs": these are the characteristics of the river that the "artistic eye" especially appreciates.[69]

Throughout the volume, Jerrold challenges conventional standards of aesthetic worth by transforming "ugliness" and industry into art. His catalogue of riverside life, reminiscent of those from *London on the Thames* and *All the Year Round,* redefines the picturesque landscape in terms of the urban industrial experience:

> And in no part of London does Work wear more changing, more picturesque phases than in the narrow, tortuous, river-side street, that leads from the quiet of the Temple to the Tower—and so, on to the Docks. In this river-side thoroughfare there are more varieties of business activity than in any other I can call to mind. Glimpses of the Thames to the left, through tangles of chains, and shafts, and ropes, and cranes; and to the right crowded lanes, with bales and boxes swinging at every height in the air, and waggon-loads of merchandise waiting to be warehoused: and, in the thoroughfare itself immense vans and drays in hopeless confusion to the stranger's eye, yet each slowly tending to its destination:——a hurly-burly of clanking hoofs and grinding wheels, and clinking chains, and wheezing cranes, to a chorus of discordant human voices, broken by sharp railway whistles, and the faint thuds of paddles battling with the tide—this is Thames Street.[70]

Clearly this is not the picturesque of the aristocratic estate or of the Victorian suburb, with its highly individualized "rustic" cottages; rather, Jerrold has appropriated the term and applied it to an urban working neighborhood better supplied with filth than with shrubbery but displaying an individualism and architectural heterodoxy common to the suburbs as well. The urban picturesque offers not only surprising juxtapositions and diverse forms but also a profusion and variety of noise, activity, and people all crowded into the same overtaxed space. By re-creating the Thames shore in these terms, the text activates a range of meanings and values associated with typical images of the picturesque —individualism, diversity, and a connection to the past—values that in the modern urban context seemed increasingly endangered.

The image of the picturesque, then, functions partly as an expression of dissatisfaction with modern life. This dissatisfaction is made explicit when the Embankment is posed in antithetical relation to the river's affectionately remembered past. Jerrold indulges in a nostalgic appreciation of the Thames as it appeared centuries before, when "the dwellings of the great" lined its shores and when "the stream was crystal . . . and there were salmon in it."[71] But the reverie is achieved at the expense of the Embankment: "Standing by these Essex Stairs, amid the unsightly work of the Embankment; it is not difficult to conjure up the glorious days of the sweet-willed river."[72] Later in the same chapter, Jerrold acknowledges the utility of an embankment for the southern shore but still contrasts it unfavorably with the riverscape of the past: "[T]he beauty of the river scene has almost gone. The low southern bank is squalid and dirty: very busy at points—but unsightly everywhere. There is money-making behind: but the front, waiting the embankment, is a mud bank, garnished with barges. It was not to be helped perhaps—the river is in a transitional period. It was covered with picturesque life: it will be presently a stately water way, confined in granite walls and flanked by groves and gardens."[73] In what seems to be a reversion to a more conventional definition of the picturesque, Jerrold applies the term to the river's romanticized past, when watermen ferried people to and from the south bank theaters and royalty graced the waterway; the river of the present is dismissed as "unsightly." But despite the fact that a future embankment promises a remedy for this condition, it cannot compensate for the lost past. "Picturesque life" is succeeded by "a stately water way, confined in granite walls": in other words, as the use of the term "confined" suggests, vitality cedes to sterility, fluidity to fixity. As in Yates's piece for *All the Year Round,* the monumental Embankment is represented as formal and lifeless in comparison with the beloved riverscape it displaces.

The nostalgia of *London: A Pilgrimage,* however, in no way implies a rejection of urban life. Rather, as Griselda Pollock argues, the volume proffers "a particular kind of urbanism," made up of "a picturesque text with a romantic, Gothic visualization."[74] The Thames plays a key role in this project, in which modernity is not so much rejected as imaginatively transformed. For instance, included in the ambitious verbal description of the shore west of London Bridge are some of the more resonant markers of the modern city: "the heavy traffic . . . dragging over Southwark Bridge; trains glid[ing] across the railway arches into the prodigious Cannon Street shed."[75] The passage continues to pile up "factories, warehouses, mills, works; barges, wherries, skiffs, tugs, penny-boats" and other features both new and old on the river. But progress on the Thames need not cause its petrifaction, for there in the midst of the steam and bridges and railway sheds is "the heaving water churned from its bed and feverish in its ebb and flow."[76] By appropriating aspects of the contemporary Thames for the picturesque scene, Jerrold's text restores the vitality and eccentricity of the city, perceived to be at risk in a reforming age. In *London: A Pilgrimage,* the Thames serves as the quintessential image of "London life" in all its dizzying variety.

The image of the city as a site of the picturesque was necessarily challenged by the project of purification. The *Building News* certainly suggested as much. An article from 1870, critical of the immensity and emptiness of the Embankment promenade and roadway (which the author calls "dull, wide, cheerless, unoccupied"), laments the disappearance of the picturesque from the urban landscape: "[T]he whole of the picturesqueness about which there is so much talk in *old* towns is in the main due to the *narrowness* of the streets, and ways, and foot-pavements, and to the consequent thick grouping of the traffic through them. But we do not live in old or artistic days; the picturesque is confined to paper and art lecturings."[77] Condemning the dilapidated structures and irregularly disposed courts and alleys romanticized by some observers of the urban scene, sanitary reformers promoted wide thoroughfares and adequately sized, properly spaced structures. Ordering the environment in this way took precedence over sentimental attachments to urban squalor, refigured as delightful eccentricity. In a pamphlet on the improvement of the Thames published in 1856, Sir William Worsley speaks for the reforming interests when he insists that "the reminiscences of the past, must . . . yield to those improvements which the progress of Science, and the requirements of the metropolis, seem now gravely to demand."[78] But as Worsley suggests elsewhere and as Doré and Jerrold seem to have recognized, sanitary improvements and, more generally, "progress" invariably entailed a loss. As evocations of the picturesque in the urban context reveal, what is lost and often longed for in the modern city is not only a sense of vital connection to the past but also the vital connections among disparate individuals and experiences that seem most possible in an unplanned urban landscape. Proponents of the picturesque highlighted the diversity of human interests and activities and the surprising juxtapositions of people and structures as essential features of urban life. In the shadow of the construction of the monumental Embankment, they celebrated the round of daily life as it pursued its idiosyncratic course.

Life on the Embankment

As we have seen, the anticipated advantages of the Thames Embankment were multiple, ranging from the purification of the river to the relief of traffic congestion in the City. Moreover, it was imagined that the physical features of the project, including the retaining wall, sewer, roadway, and recreation ground, would redefine the spatial order of the Thames and in doing so reinforce the dominant social and moral order. The Thames became the stage for the aspirations of the metropolis and the nation. Whether we define the aims of the Embankment narrowly or in the broad social terms that the Victorians themselves adopted, we must conclude, nevertheless, that the project fell short of these expectations. As representations of the Embankment in the years following its construction reveal, much of the stigma attached to the Thames at midcentury was transferred to the structure that would purify it, suggesting a considerable gap between the lived experience of the river and the ideological imperatives of reform.

Purification, understood as a material and moral phenomenon, remained a problem on the river for the remainder of the nineteenth century, although the nature of the problem and the terms in which it was expressed changed in some crucial ways. For instance, after the completion of the Embankment, sewage was still discharged into the Thames as plans for the main drainage dictated. The perhaps predictable result was that the suburbs located downstream suffered from the pollution that had once afflicted the central part of the city. As early as 1868, the *Builder* recognized the detrimental effects of relocating the sewers' outfalls lower down the river: "The Metropolitan Board surely form a strange notion of their duties if they think that the purification of the Thames is effected by what they have done and what they are doing."[79] The befouled state of the river near the points of discharge came to public attention in dramatic fashion when the *Princess Alice* steamboat suffered an accident near Barking in 1878.[80] Many of the drowning victims reportedly choked to death on the untreated sewage, while several of the survivors later died from what was believed to be sewage poisoning. As this part of London's long history of waste-disposal problems suggests, the Embankment and main drainage had merely altered the patterns of environmental disorder on the river, rather than removing them altogether.

If regulating the physical environment of the river proved difficult, so too did efforts to rehabilitate the social life of the Thames. Even before its completion, the Embankment began to acquire a reputation as a haunt for the homeless and criminal populations of London, a reputation that—despite an active police presence—it kept throughout the century. Far from diffusing a moralizing influence among the "dangerous classes," the Embankment seemed to encourage what were interpreted as immoral or otherwise crude acts, partly because the area was often deserted. Ironically, although the magnificent Embankment roadway was designed to reroute traffic away from the busy Strand and to provide a new line of communication between the City and Westminster, the thoroughfare remained conspicuously untraveled. "While Fleet-street is gorged, crowded from end to end," commented the *Building News* in 1874, "a few foreigners or country people, or hansoms with uncommonly knowing drivers, have the Embankment almost entirely to themselves."[81] The inability of the Embankment to attract a steady flow of vehicular traffic not only was a disappointing result for a city increasingly plagued by traffic congestion, but also contributed to the discomfort and danger of the area for pedestrian use.

The lack of activity on the Embankment encouraged, according to an article in the *Builder* in 1882, a degree of "ruffianism" at odds with the civilizing impulse informing its construction.[82] Numerous letters appearing in both the *Builder* and *Building News* in the 1860s and 1870s complain of the unseemly and disruptive behavior regularly seen on the Embankment, including public urination, the defacement of railings and other public ornament, and the congregation of bands of rough children. One correspondent, writing in 1869, laments the degradation of an area intended for public enjoyment but appropriated by "the wild boys and tomboys of the streets"; noting "the unlimited license enjoyed by this wanton and uncultivated stratum of the town," he demands that "all riotous behaviour [be] put down with a strong arm."[83] Another correspondent writing in 1868 expresses in characteristically euphemistic terms his disgust over the excretions spoiling the Embankment: "[N]o reason exists why every nook and corner should be considered an improvised 'stop-ping-place.' The stains are painfully visible, and certainly are becoming detri-mental to the place."[84] Further commenting on these conditions in 1872, a metropolitan resident draws attention to the irony suggested by the signs posted in the area that read Decency Forbids: "The only present meaning they convey to my mind is that all decent-minded people are warned not to ven-ture on the Embankment."[85]

On the Embankment at night, minor annoyances reportedly gave way to more serious dangers, including robbery and physical violence. Reporting the occurrence of an attack there one night in March 1882, the *Times* confirms the Embankment's dubious reputation: "The extra police promised by the Home Secretary does not appear to have yet rendered the Embankment a safe promenade after dark."[86] In an editorial published a few days later, the *Builder* warns, "[N]ot a small section of the community has learned with dis-may that a thoroughfare brilliantly illuminated with the electric light has as much cause to be dreaded after certain hours at night as was ever Hounslow-heath or Crack-skull-common in the days of Tony Lumpkin."[87] Another reason the Embankment may have gained a reputation for being unsafe at night was that it attracted a considerable homeless population. Citing an informal survey conducted by the Salvation Army in the summer of 1890, General William Booth reports that on one evening, 270 people were asleep on the Embank-ment.[88] An engraving from the *Illustrated London News,* titled "How Some of the London Poor Spend the Night" (October 1887), captures the spirit of the statistics (fig. 2.8). A massed group of utterly destitute men, women, and children huddle together on one of the Embankment's benches in an attempt to sleep, or at least to remain through the night undisturbed. The scene be-came a familiar one in the cultural imagination.[89]

Despite the riverfront's continued association with poverty and crime, the Embankment was generally regarded with approbation. It was acknowledged as one of the most important sanitary improvements in nineteenth-century London, of benefit not only to the river's material condition but also to the health of the entire metropolis. It was also admired as an important architec-tural achievement, bringing an impressive visual coherence to what had been an irregular waste space. Without diminishing the success of the Embankment on these fronts, we can, nonetheless, clearly recognize that it did not meet the

2.8. The "waste population" continued to gather on the Thames shore, in spite of its embankment. Engraving from the series "How Some of the London Poor Spend the Night," *Illustrated London News,* 29 October 1887, 510.

expectations of either its supporters or its detractors. Referring explicitly to the Embankment, Olsen offers his thoughts on the often-unanticipated outcomes of urban planning: "The failure of the Embankment to relieve the congestion of the Strand and Fleet Street suggest[s] . . . that London has a mind of its own, pursuing inscrutable ends according to a logic that eludes the cleverest entrepreneurs and planners."[90] We can explain the failure Olsen speaks of in more specific terms by foregrounding the social dimensions of spatial change. Soja speaks to this issue in "The Spatiality of Social Life," where he describes the continual, fluid interaction between social life and spatial forms over time.[91] The processual nature of this relationship alerts us to the instability of space and, further, to the key role human activity plays in determining spatial outcomes. Purification thus must be seen as a transformative process that emerges from the interaction of social formations, spatial structures, and individual human behavior. For this reason, improvement schemes cannot always be expected to affect the social life of the city in a predictable pattern—a subject discussed at length in chapter 4. In the case of the Embankment, the site was used and perceived in ways that had not been intended. Although it succeeded in sending the sewage downstream and giving new definition to the river, it failed to exert a moralizing influence on the targeted population.

Happily, the Embankment also failed to drain the river of its imaginative energy, as had been feared. As envisioned in *London: A Pilgrimage,* the "turbulent stream of London life" continues to flourish on the Thames shore, while the "heaving water . . . feverish in its ebb and flow" continues to roll past the Embankment—its force undiminished.[92]

chapter 3

A More Expansive Reach

The Geography of the Thames in Our Mutual Friend

From Quilp's Wharf to Plashwater Weir Mill Lock, the river
belongs to Dickens by right of conquest or creation.

Algernon Charles Swinburne, "Charles Dickens,"
Quarterly Review (1902)

O ur Mutual Friend *is a novel surely best remembered for its filth. It opens*
on the river Thames in the heart of London, where dangerous-
looking scavengers trawl the river for human corpses and where
sewage washes up on the ill-defined shore. To the north loom the equally re-
pellent but economically valuable dustheaps, said to consist of "coal-dust,
vegetable-dust, bone-dust, crockery dust, rough dust and sifted dust,—all
manner of Dust,"[1] including perhaps the excremental dust of horses and humans. What is true of the novel is true of its critical history as well: filth has
been a defining concern. The dustheaps especially have received a thorough
critical sifting. In the middle decades of the twentieth century, Humphry
House, Edgar Johnson, and Earle Davis argued that Dickens uses the valuable
Harmon Mounds to highlight the moral bankruptcy of a grasping, Mammon-
worshipping society, of a society that in devoting itself to money immersed
itself in filth.[2] House's contention that the dustheaps consisted of excremental
matter gave a titillating twist to the argument, in addition to spawning a run-

ning debate about what exactly was in that dust.[3] Later literary critics, keeping the mounds front and center, have nonetheless modified the equation of waste with money.[4] Interpreting *Our Mutual Friend* in the context of roughly contemporary articles in Dickens's periodical *Household Words,* Nancy Metz has emphasized Dickens's appreciation of reclaimed waste as a source of real value.[5] The river has likewise been the subject of much critical scrutiny, understandably so: nearly one-third of the novel's sixty-seven chapters are set on the Thames, and experiences of drowning or near-drowning punctuate the action. Like the dustheaps, the river has been associated with both social corruption and moral regeneration. On the one hand, the befouled river is linked with the corruption of money because it is there that the dredgermen recover and rob drowned bodies. On the other hand, the river offers certain characters the possibility of transformation: after immersion in its waters, Eugene Wrayburn, for instance, is reborn a new (earnest) man.[6]

Given this keen critical interest in filth of both the wet and the dry variety, the fact that so few critics have explored the novel's immediate sanitary context is surprising.[7] At the time of the novel's publication in 1864–65, the riverscape was on the brink of a massive structural and cultural change. As discussed at length in chapter 2, perceptions of the river's pollution and its threat to public health had peaked in the late 1850s, and partly as a result of the outcry over environmental conditions, the Thames Embankment was developed and constructed in the 1860s. *Our Mutual Friend* began appearing in monthly serialization about the same time that construction of the Embankment was first becoming visible (fig. 3.1). The timing is significant, for it places the novel in a period of sustained public debate about the condition of the river, a period when the Thames had become the public stage for working out the problem of filth and the desire for purity in the urban context. This debate, as well as the anticipation of the river's renewal, may have provided the stimulus for the representation of the Thames in *Our Mutual Friend.*

But to suggest that the novel was a product of the rhetorical energies surging up from the river is not to discount its role as a participant in the debate. In fact, the novel joined fully in the contest to define the river's topographic contours and social meanings. The conception of the river developed in *Our Mutual Friend* ultimately challenges the view of the Thames that had gained cultural currency in the 1850s and 1860s. At a time when the river's limits were being literally contracted—narrowed and cemented over by the Embankment

3.1. The site of the Embankment works as it would have appeared during the writing and publication of *Our Mutual Friend*. "The Thames Embankment Works," *Illustrated London News*, 20 August 1864, 192.

—and when its meanings were likewise defined by an exclusionary rhetoric of purification, *Our Mutual Friend* expanded the river's topographic and imaginative reach, opening up the very questions that the Embankment was imagined finally and firmly to settle: what should the Thames look like, what are its possibilities for meaning, and how might it become a resource for metropolitan life?

"Now in the Town, Now in the Country"

Dickens, like most Londoners at the time, followed the activity on the river and eagerly anticipated its embankment. Two personal letters, in fact, reflect the civic pride that the prospect of the reclaimed river generally inspired. In November 1865, immediately upon completing *Our Mutual Friend,* Dickens wrote to his friend William de Cerjat in Paris, praising the Embankment as a work of great importance for the metropolis: "Meantime, if your honor were in London, you would see a great embankment rising high and dry out of the Thames on the Middlesex shore, from Westminster Bridge to Blackfriars. A really fine work, and really getting on. Moreover, a great system of drainage. Another really fine work, and likewise really getting on."[8] Several years later, in January 1869, he enumerates the many advantages of the Embankment to the same correspondent: "The Thames Embankment is (faults of ugliness in detail apart) the finest public work yet done. From Westminster Bridge to near Waterloo it is now lighted up at night, and has a fine effect. They have begun to plant it with trees, and the footway (not the road) is already open to the Temple. Besides its beauty, and its usefulness in relieving the crowded streets, it will greatly quicken and deepen what is learnedly called the 'scour' of the river."[9] The appreciation of a sanitary engineering project of such magnitude is just what we would expect from a committed advocate of sanitary reform, as Dickens was. The Embankment appealed to his public feelings; his expression of pride in a major metropolitan improvement was perhaps heightened in these letters because his correspondent was residing in Paris, the nineteenth-century exemplar of urban grandeur. But while Dickens's letters reflect the prevailing view of the river's transformation, approving the Embankment as a fitting guarantor of London's stature, his great novel of the period affords a different view of both the river and the possibilities of purification.[10]

An early clue to the imagined geography of the river in *Our Mutual Friend* appears in the novel's opening sentence: "In these times of ours, though concerning the exact year there is no need to be precise, a boat of dirty and disreputable appearance . . . floated on the Thames, between Southwark Bridge which is of iron, and London Bridge which is of stone" (43). Although Dickens feels no need "to be precise" about time, he apparently thinks it important to be precise about place, using familiar landmarks to specify the location of Gaffer Hexam's boat on the river. This topographic specificity is characteristic of the representation of the Thames in the novel: the river does not appear simply as an undifferentiated body of water; rather, each part of the river has its own distinct identity. At Greenwich, for instance, the river affords a scene of picturesque delight as sailboats and steamships from across the globe navigate the British waterway. At Limehouse, however, the river appears morbid and menacing, the watery grave of murdered men and the meeting place for low-life conspirators. Even as Dickens insists on the integrity of different sites along the river, he also emphasizes the river's range. Although the opening sentence of the novel stakes out clearly defined limits, these limits are continually surpassed. From the heart of the metropolis the river ebbs and flows, running downstream to Limehouse, then up to Millbank, running back out to Greenwich, then up to the locks; it even reaches the ironically pastoral factory town of Henley-on-Thames beyond the influence of the tides. The river redefines and extends the bounds of London by reaching out toward its upstream and downstream extremities.

Dickens invokes the river's range of motion, its notorious tidal flow, in describing the way the Harmon murder passes in and out of popular knowledge: "Thus, like the tides on which it had been borne to the knowledge of men, the Harmon Murder—as it came to be popularly called—went up and down, and ebbed and flowed, now in the town, now in the country, now among palaces, now among hovels, now among lords and ladies and gentlefolks, now among labourers and hammerers and ballast-heavers, until at last, after a long interval of slack water it got out to sea and drifted away" (74). The ostensible subject of the sentence is the Harmon murder and its topicality. Structurally, the river plays a subordinate role both as a figure suggesting the course a popular subject takes and as the medium, literally speaking, that bears and ultimately delivers up the Harmon corpse. But despite the grammatical agency afforded the murder, the evocation of the river's flux is what is most striking. The metaphor of the tides alerts us to the river's topographic scope, as well as to its local diversity: it appears alternately as a site of labor and recreation, as an image of beauty and squalor, in urban and rural guises. Rather than provide a single, unified vision of the Thames, then, the novel represents the river as an assemblage of local communities, each taking on a distinctive appearance and set of associations, yet still connected within the larger totality.

This reconception of the river's geography ultimately allows Dickens to work out the novel's sanitary ambitions. For as the imagery of the dustheaps and the filthy river make abundantly clear, a pervasive pollution threatens the world of the novel. In the context of the novel as in much of the sanitary literature, filthy material conditions reflect a perilous social condition. Here, urban pollution signals not only the moral degradation usually associated with poverty but also the decadence of a social order built upon material values. Of course, the hope is that material cleansing may also bring with it moral purification, the redemption of the individual and society. Part of Dickens's task as novelist, then, is to orchestrate at least a partial purification to achieve a narrative resolution in the form of a renewed social order: as Deirdre David explains it, this novel offers "a fable of regenerated bourgeois culture."[11] In *Our Mutual Friend,* this regeneration is a function of the reconceived geography of the Thames—of the topographically expansive, thoroughly localized river. Not only is the river large and diverse enough to accommodate sites of filth and purity, but because of its inherently fluid state it affords both an image and a means of mobility. Characters are seemingly free to move up and down the Thames according to their needs; while the river may be a source of pollution, it may also be a means to escape pollution. The fluidity of the river itself affords both characters and readers the refreshment that comes from a change of scene, as well as the promise of return.

This conception of the river and of urban purification differs significantly from the prevailing view of the Thames at the time of its embankment. Much of the outrage excited by the river's degraded condition in the 1850s seems to have derived from concerns about the city's public image. Just as appalling as the squalid appearance of the shore and the river's sewage-tainted waters was the fact that these conditions thrived in the symbolic center of the city, right outside the windows of the Houses of Parliament. By restructuring the ambiguous waste space that lay between Westminster and Blackfriars bridges, the Embankment promised not only to cleanse the Thames but also to transform the river into a monumental landscape, suggestive of London's national and imperial stature. In other words, the Embankment would transform a marginal space into a site of official power. In its representation of the Thames, *Our Mutual Friend* resists this monumental impulse. Whereas part of the function of the Embankment was to limit the meanings that could be applied to the riverfront and the uses to which it could be put, the novel emphasizes the river's range of motion and of imaginative associations. The imagined river offers in its course scenes of urban horror, pastoral beauty, and commercial energy; it appeals to sensations of fear and dread, pleasure and joy, serenity and peace. Moreover, the novel re-creates the river on a human scale to emphasize its significance for the individual, as much as for public life. This conceptual distinction is identified by Yi-Fu Tuan in his discussion of environmental perception: "At one extreme the city is a symbol or an image (captured in a postcard or a slogan) to which one can orient oneself; at the other it is the intimately experienced neighborhood."[12] By releasing the river from a narrow geographic range and a narrow range of meanings and by re-creating the river as a site of familiarity and intimacy, *Our Mutual Friend* restores the Thames as a resource for the emotional and imaginative life.

The remainder of this chapter charts the river as it passes through varied terrain, beginning—as does the novel—in the heart of London before turning to the downstream delights of Greenwich and, finally, to the pastoral landscape upstream. Investing in the river's local geography in this way enables us to recover the novel's sanitary strategy. For in *Our Mutual Friend,* filth and purity are functions of place.

The Attraction of Repulsion

The novel begins to challenge prevailing assumptions about the river, curiously, by seeming at first to reinscribe them. Set on the Thames and describing one of the most chilling occupations transpiring there—the act of "dredging," or searching the river for corpses—the first chapter plays into widespread fears about the material and moral degradation of the riverside. Dickens evokes the atmosphere of pollution through the language and imagery of filth: words such as "slime," "ooze," and "mud," coupled with images of "filthy water" and a "dirty and disreputable" boat, confirm the popular conception of the Thames as a sordid waste space (43–44). The ambiguity of the environment, which is neither liquid nor solid, finds an analogue in the dredgerman himself, Gaffer Hexam, who is described in equally ambiguous terms. Neither man nor beast, Hexam is likened to "a roused bird of prey"; he appears "half savage" with his matted hair and "wilderness of beard and whisker" (44–45). The dehumanized dredgerman is quite literally shaped by his primitive surroundings, since "such dress as he wore seem[ed] to be made out of the mud that begrimed his boat" (44). River, boat, and man merge by virtue of their shared element—filth. As we have seen so often, physical descriptions of filth inevitably become entangled with moral judgments: the filthy condition of Hexam's boat lends to it a "disreputable" appearance; the uses to which it is put further obscure the di-

viding line between matter and morals. The physical horror of the river's putrid ooze and the moral horror of Hexam's gruesome fishing expedition are
mutually constitutive. Only Lizzie Hexam, rowing her father's craft in quiet
dread, remains untouched by the river's taint.[13] Unlike her insensate father,
the girl shivers when she catches sight of a faded bloodstain in the boat. When
Hexam finds and hooks his corpse, she shrouds herself with her hood. As reluctant witness to her father's degrading acts, Lizzie provides a model for the
reader's own response: with her every shudder, the horror of the Thames is
magnified.

Despite the atmosphere of shrouded mystery, representations of the pestilential and sinister Thames would have been familiar to a British reading public
well acquainted with sanitary matters. Chapter 2 shows that lurid descriptions
of filth, exaggerated visions of the river's epidemic atmosphere, and shocking
representations of the "residual" riverside population were standard journalistic fare. The idea of the Thames as a site of disease and death was well established in the cultural imagination. One of the more striking visual evocations
of the death-producing influence of the river appears in the *Punch* cartoon
"The 'Silent Highway'-Man," published in the year of the Great Stink, 1858
(fig. 3.2). The cartoon depicts a shrouded skeleton—the Grim Reaper—rowing
on the filthy Thames amidst the corpses of small animals. In the middle distance
are the fetid mudflats, and in the background loom smoking chimneys and the
dome of St. Paul's Cathedral. The presence of the personified figure of Death
seems to have drained all the vitality from the river and likewise from the city
itself, transforming London into a virtual necropolis.

Visually reminiscent of "The 'Silent Highway'-Man" is Marcus Stone's first
illustration for *Our Mutual Friend,* "The Bird of Prey" (fig. 3.3). In this image,
showing father and daughter at work on the river, the mythic figure of the Grim
Reaper is replaced by Gaffer Hexam—no less a trader in decay and death.
Iconographically, the cartoon and the book illustration are similar: smokestacks, warehouses, and steeples define the background; the river occupies the
middle distance; and in the foreground floats a light skiff. More significantly,
both images represent pollution as an inversion of the natural and social order.
Rather than provide refreshment and fertility, the foul waters of the Thames
yield only human and animal corpses. In place of fishermen, we see the dehumanized "bird of prey" and the nonhuman figure of Death, who both sustain
their own lives by feeding on decay. Finally, in the cartoon's and in Dickens's

3.2. The familiar iconography of the Thames at the time of the Great Stink. "The 'Silent Highway'-Man," *Punch,* 10 July 1858, 15.

and Stone's representations of the Thames, the filth of the river is understood to precipitate out from the shore, involving the entire metropolis in an atmosphere of moral and physical corruption. *Punch's* inclusion of the dome of St. Paul's—a prominent London landmark—in its vision of the river clearly indicates the centrality of pollution to the urban experience. In *Our Mutual Friend,* the parallel drawn between the marginalized Hexam's pursuit of money and that of respectable Englishmen and women suggests the centrality of "dredging" to society at large.

These kinds of sensational representations of urban pollution could be an effective tool for reform. Sanitary reformers and social investigators frequently dramatized the dangers of filth and appealed to the fears and prejudices of the middle-class public in an effort to mobilize support for reforming efforts. But Dickens's representation of pollution in *Our Mutual Friend* functions very

3.3. Dickens's version of the London underworld. Illustration by Marcus Stone, "The Bird of Prey," in *Our Mutual Friend* by Charles Dickens, vol. 23, *The Works of Charles Dickens* (New York: Scribner's, 1900), frontispiece.

differently. For, as I have already suggested, in the novel Dickens expands the available meanings and associations of the Thames. Thus, while he invokes prevailing ideas about the degraded condition of the river, he also represents it as a powerful source of value. On the one hand, the first chapter of the novel introduces a sanitary and social challenge. Not only must the taint associated with Hexam be stayed, but more generally the vitality of river and city must be restored. On the other hand, while Dickens exploits the moral implications of pollution, he resists representing the degraded river in strictly moral terms or solely as a stage for social action. The river may be a source of danger and disease, but it is also a site of emotional and imaginative engagement. These meanings of the river emerge at the thematic level in the form of Dickens's aesthetic appreciation of filth. Throughout the novel, Dickens draws on the imaginative vitality of urban pollution for his own and his audience's pleasure. At the same time, the emotional richness of the filthy river emerges at the level of plot and character in Dickens's representation of Lizzie. For her, the forsaken river is her home—the source and site of domestic and filial affections. So while she may be horrified by the river, she is also deeply attached to it. Through Lizzie's story, we come to understand that a degraded waste space may have positive meanings for the individuals who reside there.

As far as Dickens's artistry is concerned, we know that the threatening, ugly aspects of city life held great significance for him. As Philip Collins and F. S. Schwarzbach have discussed, Dickens was fascinated by locations and events with dark, even criminal associations, so much so that he coined a phrase, "the attraction of repulsion," to describe his interest.[14] The phrase—appearing in John Forster's *Life of Charles Dickens* in connection with the rookeries of St. Giles and in Dickens's essay "The City of the Absent" in connection with a churchyard on a stormy night—aptly conveys Dickens's compulsion to witness and represent scenes of urban horror. We know from their recurrence in his novels and essays that certain grim scenes exercised considerable attraction: Newgate Prison, Covent Garden at night, the Paris morgue, decaying tenements. To this list we must surely add the river Thames in its murkiest, most menacing incarnations. For the river worked powerfully on Dickens's imagination, and its role as a site of drowning and death, as a source of fear and dread, haunts the fiction preceding *Our Mutual Friend*. In *Oliver Twist* (1837–38), Nancy, at that fateful meeting with Rose Maylie and Mr. Brownlow, wrongly predicts that she will die like many prostitutes in Thames water; in *David Copperfield* (1849–50), as we have seen, the suicidal Martha is found loitering by the river; and in *Little Dorrit* (1855–57), Dickens imagines the attraction the midnight river exerts on women just like Nancy and Martha—"a terrible fascination . . . for guilt and misery."[15]

In two articles for *Household Words*, "Down with the Tide" (1853) and "On Duty with Inspector Field" (1851), Dickens focuses on the darker, more disturbing associations of the river with obvious relish. In "Down with the Tide," the inspiration for which article was Dickens's nighttime excursion with the Thames Police, the narrator describes the criminal activity occurring on the Thames and lending the river its sinister atmosphere. Interspersed with a catalogue of the various "water thieves" working the area and an account of the appearance and manners of the many who commit suicide from Waterloo Bridge are the narrator's self-consciously morbid musings: he wonders aloud, "What a night for a dreadful leap from that parapet!" and reports hearing "uncomfortable rushes of water suggestive of gurgling and drowning."[16] In response to the officer asking him if he finds the river "so dismal," the narrator launches into an elaborate meditation before he is forcefully interrupted: "'So awful . . . at night. . . . [T]his river looks so broad and vast, so murky and silent, seems such an image of death in the midst of the great city's life, that—' That Peacoat [i.e., the officer] coughed again. He *could not* stand my holding forth."[17] Presumably Dickens could have continued to terrify himself and his readers with his description, but he uses the officer's forced cough to abort the monologue and, by so doing, draws attention to his terrible imaginings as a kind of self-indulgent pleasure.

In "On Duty with Inspector Field," Dickens continues to exploit the river's sinister associations. Wondering at Inspector Field's remarkable aplomb as he takes his rounds through the vilest rookeries and roughest neighborhoods, the narrator of "On Duty" compares his own fearful ideas about the Thames with those of the detective: "*He* does not trouble his head as I do, about the river at night. *He* does not care for its creeping, black and silent, on our right there, rushing through sluice-gates, lapping at piles and posts and iron rings, hiding strange things in its mud, running away with suicides and accidentally drowned bodies faster than midnight funeral should, and acquiring such various experience between its cradle and its grave. It has no mystery for *him*. Is there not the Thames Police?"[18] As the closing question makes clear, Dickens represents Inspector Field as a paragon of reason who trusts the Thames Police and the detective force to keep the river and streets clear of crime. At the same time, Dickens recognizes the woeful inadequacy of these efficient bodies to preserve the mind from its own dark imagination: for him, the river is a perpetual mystery.

A similar imaginative indulgence in the river's grim atmosphere recurs in *Our Mutual Friend* in the chapters "Tracking the Bird of Prey" and "The Bird of Prey Brought Down." After Rogue Riderhood wrongfully accuses Hexam of the Harmon murder, Riderhood and the police inspector, along with Mortimer Lightwood and Eugene Wrayburn, spend a long, dismal night on the Thames awaiting the dredgerman's return. As in Dickens's experience with the Thames Police recounted in "Down with the Tide," the silence and secrecy of the watch for Hexam set Mortimer's and Eugene's nerves on edge and activate their morbid imaginations. In the still night hours, the sounds of the river—iron chains, falling tide, plashing oars—are amplified. As night gives way to the ambiguous light of the predawn hours, the chill and silence of death prevail. The Thames is once again figured as a modern Styx, coursing through a city of the dead: "Very little life was to be seen on either bank . . . and the staring black and white letters upon wharves and warehouses 'looked,' said Eugene to Mortimer, 'like inscriptions over the graves of dead businesses'" (219). In light of Dickens's literary cultivation of "the attraction of repulsion," we can interpret Eugene's horrified response to the river as something like the horror of the aesthete, as opposed to the indignation of the reformer. The problem of the city's death by corruption remains, but under the influence of the menacing river, death is both feared and courted. The narrator, voicing the thoughts of Eugene and Mortimer, seems to delight in imagining the river as an agent of destruction: "Not a ship's hull, with its rusty iron links of cable run out of hawse-holes . . . but seemed to be there with a fell intention. Not a figure-head but had the menacing look of bursting forward to run them down. . . . Not a lumbering black barge . . . but seemed to suck at the river with a thirst for sucking them under" (219). The dark depths of the Thames tap into deep fears of death and dissolution—and therein lies the river's value. Because it has the power to fascinate the mind and to release the imagination, the morally and physically repulsive river provides a vital emotional and aesthetic resource.

This provocative tension between attraction and repulsion vis-à-vis the Thames is also critical to the development of the novel's plot. Through the stories of Lizzie Hexam and Bella Wilfer—the twin heroines of *Our Mutual Friend*—Dickens dramatizes both the threat of pollution and the imaginative value of the river at the individual level. By watching these young female characters navigate the dangers and resources associated with the river, we gain a better understanding of the complex geography of the Thames in the novel.

For Lizzie, whose story I take up first, the river is an intimately known place, and as such it provides the defining context for her emotional life. At the same time, she is appalled by the material and moral pollution that sustains her and her family. The novel introduces Lizzie's internal conflict in the first chapter when father and daughter reveal their feelings about the environment they know so well. Prompted by Lizzie's expression of revulsion against the river and what it yields, Hexam proudly, yet touchingly, reminds his daughter that the river's dregs have in fact supported her life: "How can you be so thank-less to your best friend, Lizzie? The very fire that warmed you when you were a babby, was picked out of the river alongside the coal barges. The very basket that you slept in, the tide washed ashore" (45–46). As Hexam insists, the river is their living, the source of the family's economic livelihood.[19] But his defense also suggests that for him the material meaning of the river is inseparable from its emotional yield: the polluted waters are the medium through which he expresses the abiding affection he feels for his daughter. Lizzie's response confirms that on some level she understands that the family's affective life is bound up with the river: she "took her right hand from the scull it held, and touched her lips with it, and for a moment held it out lovingly towards him" (46). For Lizzie, the river is physically repulsive and morally corrupting—the site of her father's shame—but it is also her home and, indeed, the only en-vironment in which she might sustain a relationship with her father.

Lizzie's ambivalent feelings about the river emerge in a conversation she has with her brother not long after their father's death. As brother and sister pace along the Thames shore at Millbank, Charley urges his sister to leave Jenny Wren's riverside home and to sever her connections to the sordid past, since the elder Hexam's death has made them free. Like other socially ambi-tious characters in the novel, Charley knows that one's geographic location is a determinant of social status. Lizzie's residence by the river in the company of a dwarfed daughter and alcoholic father troubles him because it seems to thwart his own social aspirations, to jeopardize his difficult rise into the middle classes. "It'll be a very hard thing, Liz," warns her brother, "if, when I am trying my best to get up in the world, you pull me back" (278). Although Lizzie knows too well the degradation of the river and for her own sake longs to es-cape it, she chooses to stay for the sake of her father and of the past. Gesturing toward the river, she struggles to explain her motives: "Any compensation—restitution—never mind the word, you know my meaning. Father's grave" (277). By remaining within the riverside world in which her father worked and living, moreover, with the granddaughter of one of her father's "finds," Lizzie hopes to redeem her father's past actions—to bring forth some bit of goodness from the river's muck.

To stay by the river, however, is to risk her own shame. Charley's concern about where and with whom Lizzie lives is strictly selfish, but in a certain respect he is right: Lizzie does risk her social and moral standing by remaining near the polluted urban river. The danger Lizzie faces is not so much actual filth as what Dickens refers to elsewhere in the novel as "moral sewage" (63). Dickens dramatizes the recognized danger of moral pollution—and the risk it poses for Lizzie specifically—in his representation of Miss Abbey Potterson and her strict management of the public house, the Six Jolly Fellowship Porters. Adopting the moralized language of filth, Miss Potterson explains to Lizzie that she has excluded Lizzie's father and Rogue Riderhood from the pub for the sake of its good reputation. Because of their link to the Harmon murder (Riderhood as accuser, Hexam as accused), both men, she insists, are "tarred with a dirty brush, and I can't have the Fellowships tarred with the same brush" (114). The taint that threatens to give Miss Potterson's establishment "a bad name" poses an equally serious threat to Lizzie herself (113). For by refusing Miss Potterson's offer of a refuge, Lizzie enters fully into her suspected father's degradation and alienation.

When applied to a woman of Lizzie's age and standing, however, the suggestion of moral degradation, or of a taint, acquires an implicitly sexual meaning: a "tainted woman" is one who has lost her sexual innocence. Dickens evokes the specter of fallen female sexuality and, specifically, of the prostitute when he describes Lizzie's lone wanderings in the "river-side wilderness" after she too has been cast out of the public house (114). The association of the Thames with prostitution—an association fully elaborated in chapter 2—would have been familiar to Dickens's readers through one of any number of literary and visual representations of the prostitute on the river. Lizzie's physical contact with the murky waters of the midnight Thames, with the "tidal swell of the river," thus signals the sexual nature of the danger to which she is exposed (114). Dickens revives these associations later in the novel in the scene at Millbank, for the site of Lizzie and Charley's meeting is the very place where Dickens had located the encounter between the prostitute Martha and the men trailing her in *David Copperfield*. As Dickens was well aware, this area along the river had been reconstructed in the years between the writing of *David Copperfield* and *Our Mutual Friend*: what was once all "broken ground and ditch" had become a "broad esplanade" formed by the new Millbank Road.[20] Martha's story nevertheless looms in the background of Lizzie's own story, casting a doubtful shadow over Lizzie's future. Dickens even uses similar language to describe the uncanny attraction the Thames holds for these two very differently fated characters. Martha, finding in the river's physically defiled condition an image of her personal degradation, muses, "I can't keep away from it. I can't forget it. It haunts me day and night."[21] Lizzie uses these words with only a slight variation to describe her connection to the river to her unsympathetic brother: "I can't get away from it, I think. . . . It's no purpose of mine that I live by it still" (278). When we recall that in the same chapter Lizzie receives a visit from the careless gentleman Eugene Wrayburn, we may appreciate just the kind of danger she faces.

The threat of urban pollution in the form of sexual sin ultimately impels Lizzie's flight from the city. What precipitates the crisis is Bradley Headstone's oddly menacing proposal of marriage, a proposal that simultaneously reveals the destructive potential of his disordered desire and forces Lizzie to see her sexuality as a threat to herself and those around her. Headstone, degraded in his own eyes by his sexual responsiveness, thrusts this degradation upon Lizzie, declaring, "Yes! you are the ruin—the ruin—the ruin—of me" (452). With his monomaniacal repetition of the name "Mr. Eugene Wrayburn" after Lizzie refuses him, Headstone sufficiently implies that just as Lizzie has been *his* ruin, Eugene will be *hers*. But in a corrupt social world, Lizzie's innocence is already compromised: while Headstone associates Lizzie's sexuality with the temptation of sin and the loss of reputation, Charley deploys it as a commodity to assist his social advancement. The environment in which these failed negotiations take place itself confirms the idea that purity cannot remain inviolate under the pressure of modern urban life: Headstone and Charley meet Lizzie in the City after working hours when "the closed warehouses and offices have a look of death about them" (450); moreover, their interview takes place around a church graveyard, "conveniently and healthfully elevated above the level of the living" (451). Decried by sanitary reformers and a favorite target of Dickens's satire, the inner-city burial ground with its half-buried corpses was a resonant sign and source of a uniquely urban danger.[22] In the city, the burial of the dead in densely packed churchyards in close proximity to the living was understood to pose a serious health risk. The very air seemingly bore the corruption of death. If, as Dickens suggests here, pollution is endemic to the urban environment, then Lizzie's best hope for purity lies in her escape.

"'Where Shall We Go, My Dear?' 'Greenwich!'"

Fortunately, the geography mapped by *Our Mutual Friend* is not without its resources. When the pressure of pollution builds, when life in the city becomes unbearable, characters and readers alike find a temporary release and a saving resource in the expansive topography of the river. For while the river is clearly a source of corruption in the novel, its flow also holds out the possibility of escape and even redemption. Whether they travel by steamboat or skiff, across the river's bridges, or along its marshy shores, characters chart their routes out of and back toward London by the Thames. Thus, Lizzie shifts her position from London's Millbank to a quiet stretch of the Thames upstream in an effort to evade the dangerous attentions of Headstone and Eugene. Similarly, the old pauper woman Betty Higden takes "the upward course of the river Thames as her general track," when she leaves London to try to win a meager living beyond the reach of the workhouse (566). Taking the opposite course, Bella and her father follow the river downstream to Greenwich to escape temporarily the responsibility of family and the cares of the city. In other words, the novel's solution to the problem of urban pollution is geographical: characters find purification, if they find it, in their strategic relocation on the river.

Before turning with Lizzie to the clear waters upstream, I consider Bella's flight from the city and the role the river plays in her "purification." For just as Lizzie suffers the threat of pollution troped as sexual danger, Bella is exposed to another urban pollutant in the form of money. Summing up the dangerous energies circulating around the two women, Adrian Poole notes in his introduction to the novel, "Both could easily go to the bad in familiar ways."[23] The taint that Bella faces is associated with the dustheaps rather than the river; for as the heiress to the Harmon fortune, her fate and her potential fall are tied to the staining "gold dust" that attracts "all manner of crawling, creeping, fluttering, and buzzing creatures" (257). This is a pollution to which Bella is particularly vulnerable, since, as she herself "confesses," "I am the most mercenary little wretch that ever lived in the world" (374). Bella's rehabilitation is effected in part by the dustman Boffin: by assuming a miserly persona, he lets Bella see for herself the spoiling influence of wealth. But Bella's purification, the cleansing away of dust to reveal her as "true golden gold at heart," is also achieved by water (843). Dickens orchestrates her escape down the river to Greenwich on two occasions. Bella and her father first travel there by steamship on holiday: they feast on whitebait fish and punch at one of the popular riverside hotels. Bella's second trip is more extended: after marrying John Harmon in Greenwich, she remains for a time outside the city in suburban Blackheath.

With the movement away from London, the river and the novel put on a holiday mood. For Bella and her much put-upon "Pa," unused to life's pleasures, "the little expedition down the river was delightful, and the little room overlooking the river into which they were shown for dinner was delightful. Everything was delightful. The park was delightful, the punch was delightful, the dishes of fish were delightful, the wine was delightful" (372). In a novel most often remembered for its somber mood and dark vision, the scenes at Greenwich provide a striking and welcome contrast, marked as they are by playful conversation, affectionate teasing, and innocent games of make-believe. When not ruffling her father's hair or hugging him round the neck, Bella charms her father with fanciful visions of her own future. Later, at the celebratory marriage feast, Bella, her father, and John Harmon playfully agree "that they would not reveal to mortal eyes any appearance whatever of being a wedding party" (735) (fig. 3.4). Bella's merriment sets the tone for the pair of chapters, a tone that seems to belong to a childhood tale of adventure and romance. Indeed, as Dickens describes it, the nuptial dinner reads like a fairy tale come to life: "What a dinner! Specimens of all the fishes that swim in the sea, surely had swum their way into it, and if samples of the fishes of divers colours that made a speech in the Arabian Nights . . . and then jumped out of the frying pan, were not to be recognized, it was only because they had all become of one hue by being cooked in batter among the whitebait" (735). In the scenes downstream, Dickens's transforming imagination is at its most lighthearted. The convivial atmosphere of the whitebait hotel and the bustling, commercially vibrant river provide the inspiration for a celebratory vision of both marriage and the city.

Although appearing in a very different guise from the menacing river in central London, the Thames at Greenwich similarly stirs the imagination. The barges and yachts, the ships and steamers "making their way to the sea" reflect the naval and mercantile preeminence of the British nation (373). But in Bella's

3.4. The Thames at Greenwich is bustling but lighter and brighter than it appears in the city. Illustration by Marcus Stone, "The Wedding Dinner at Greenwich," in *Our Mutual Friend* by Charles Dickens, vol. 24, *The Works of Charles Dickens* (New York: Scribner's, 1900), opposite 308.

eyes, the busy river traffic becomes the subject of stories and the inspiration for her dreams. As she and her father observe the activity on the river, Bella "imagine[s] all sorts of voyages for herself and Pa" (373). Pa takes the parts in quick succession of a rich coal merchant, an opium trader, and an imperialist adventurer, sailing "among the coral reefs and cocoa-nuts . . . to fetch a cargo of sweet-smelling woods, the most beautiful that ever were seen, and the most profitable that ever were heard of" (373–74). Bella imagines herself in the role of beloved and enriched wife first of a revivified John Harmon, then of a wealthy merchant, and finally of an "Indian Prince . . . who wore Cashmere shawls all over himself, and diamonds and emeralds blazing in his turban, and was beautifully coffee-coloured and excessively devoted, though a little too jealous" (374). Like the mythic adventurers she describes, Bella imaginatively plunders the empire, appropriating its wealth and cultivating its exoticism for her own girlish fantasies. Yet in these fantasies may lie Bella's salvation. As in those chapters that indulge in the river's morbid associations, the Thames here is not moralized, nor is it used as a vehicle for criticizing either the imperial project or the display of material wealth. Rather, the river serves as a site of imaginative engagement. The commercially vital river activates Bella's childlike fantasies of romance, adventure, and fabulous wealth—fantasies worthy of any fairy tale but also crucial to the restoration of Bella's moral health. For the imaginative life of the river allows Bella to indulge her potentially corrosive desire for money without risking her innocence. In other words, by using fantasy to express these dangerous desires, Bella is able to limit their power over her and, in a certain sense, to exorcise them.

But Bella's purification is complete only after her brief residence in a "modest little cottage" in suburban Blackheath (733). The middle-class suburb in close proximity to Greenwich provides a respite from the extremes of wealth and poverty in London and fosters instead a respect for modesty, order, and the domestic virtues. Here the newly wed Bella learns to live happily in moderation, finding joy in the regulation, rather than in the indulgence, of her desires. Demonstrating that she is quickly internalizing the middle-class ethic, Bella briskly declares to her mother and sister, "[W]e are economical and orderly, and do everything by clockwork, and we have a hundred and fifty pounds a year, and we have all we want, and more" (746). Bella embraces her new role as wife and efficient domestic manager, gladly exchanging the jeweled treasures of the Orient for the "treasures . . . of dry-saltery, groceries, jam and pickles"—the treasures of the pantry (733). Her early social ambitions are likewise replaced by domestic ones: she regularly consults the oracular volume "The Complete British Family Housewife" and dutifully studies the daily newspaper so she can join with her husband in intelligent conversation (749–50). Ultimately, the sojourn in Blackheath prepares Bella to return to the city and to accept her rightful position as heir with her husband to the Harmon fortune. Once Bella is cleansed of the taint of her mercenary desires, once she recognizes that money is after all another form of dust, then she is able to use her wealth wisely and well.

The turn to Greenwich in the novel holds significance not only for Bella's fate but also for the meaning of the river itself. For with the change of location, Dickens is able to provide an alternative perspective on the urban Thames. By representing the river as a recreational resource for Londoners, he recovers a deadened city's vitality and reminds his readers that the river is more than the sum of its pollutants. The wider implications of the excursions to Greenwich in the novel become clear when we recognize their debt to, and participation in, the popular cultural phenomenon of "dining down the river."

Taking a steamer from London down to Greenwich and dining on a meal of whitebait fish and champagne at one of the riverside hotels, the Old Ship or the Trafalgar, was a pleasure frequently indulged by Victorian Londoners— Dickens among them (fig. 3.5). As representations of the custom suggest, part of the appeal of Greenwich was the simultaneous feeling of escape from and enjoyment of the city that the excursion afforded. In his essay "Greenwich —Whitebait" (1844), William Thackeray, writing under the pseudonym Lancelot Wagstaff, relishes the experience of the whitebait dinner for the release from urban pressures it provides: "You rush after that little fish, and leave the cares of London behind you—the row and the struggle, the foggy darkness, the slippery pavement where every man jostles you, striding on his way, pre-occupied with care written on his brow. Look out of the window, the sky is tinted with a thousand glorious hues—the ships pass silent over the blue glittering waters—there is no object within sight that is not calm, and happy, and beautiful."[24] On the one hand, Thackeray posits a strict divide be-tween city and country, between London as site of struggle and fruitless labor and Greenwich as a scene of harmony and rest. On the other hand, as Thack-eray implicitly recognizes, the Greenwich dinner is an assuredly urban phe-nomenon: the "you" whom he addresses and sends to Greenwich is a besieged city-dweller. Other accounts emphasize Greenwich's ties to the city and its status as a place of amusement for Londoners almost exclusively. An "institu-tion . . . beloved by Londoners" is how Richard Doyle, noted *Punch* illustrator, describes the custom in the *Cornhill* magazine in 1862.[25] And in an article titled "The Business of Pleasure," published in *All the Year Round* in 1863, Edmund Yates includes the Greenwich hotels among London's premier pleasure indus-tries.[26] The key to their success lay in the fact that the trip to Greenwich al-lowed urban inhabitants to escape the city without ever really leaving it.

The Greenwich of *Our Mutual Friend* shares these urban motives and ener-gies. The characters who go there are all Londoners on holiday, and they ar-rive to find London in their midst. The river is crowded with ships engaged in the commercial pursuits of a great empire. The shore is populated with the urban dispossessed in the form of an old pensioner with two wooden legs and

3.5. Gustave Doré and Blanchard Jerrold feature "dining down the river" in their catalogue of Thames pleasures. Illustration by Doré, "Greenwich—In the Season," in *London:
A Pilgrimage* by Doré and Jerrold (London: Grant and Co., 1872), ii.

the boy mudlarks "bidding against each other to put their heads in the mud for six-pence" (737). But at Greenwich, urban pollution is refigured as the picturesque: the river is seen as a source of visual excitement, variety, and local color. What makes this celebratory vision of the Thames possible is the mediating effect of distance, distance not only between Greenwich and London but also between spectators and spectacle. The scenes emphatically coded as urban at Greenwich are invariably experienced as a *view,* from the vantage of balcony and window. Thackeray's romanticized vision depends on the mediating frame of the window ("Look out of the window," he advises), and so too does Bella and her father's view of the heavily trafficked Thames: they dine in a "little room *overlooking* the river" (372; emphasis added); and the amusing mudlarks are tellingly positioned "below the window" (374). This distance makes all the difference: whereas at ground level the individual may experience the city as a struggle against the crowd—a place, in Thackeray's words, "where every man jostles you"—once elevated above the fray, the protected observer can enjoy the city that in another context appears threatening.

In the scenes at Greenwich, Dickens offers his characters—and, by extension, his readers—the opportunity to appreciate the urban Thames at its best. His vision of the river is marked by an exciting profusion of forms and activities, by a range of imaginative associations, and by a playful energy. By taking a wider view of the river than that afforded by the vantage of the Embankment, Dickens is thus able to move beyond strict ideas of filth and purity. The Thames at Greenwich appears at once as a source of individual renewal, a site of commercial vigor, and—most important—a place of social pleasure.

A Sanitary Idyll

Like Greenwich, the quiet mill town upstream provides an escape and serves a restorative function for besieged Londoners. Identified by Robert Allbut's guide *Rambles in Dickens' Land* (1899) as Henley-on-Thames, the pastoral village lies some distance from London, in Oxfordshire. Yet, according to Allbut, . a day's outing from London to Henley affords "a delightful country excursion" and can easily be made by train (fig. 3.6).[27] When she leaves London seeking a refuge from urban danger, Lizzie relocates to this quiet stretch of the Thames

3.6. The pastoral Thames at Henley serves as the Edenic counterpart to the infernal Thames downstream. Painting by Helen M. James, "Henley-on-Thames," in *Rambles in Dickens' Land* by Robert Allbut (New York: Truslove, 1899), frontispiece.

beyond the influence of the tides. Here, in the novel's most salubrious environment, Dickens purifies his heroine of any potential or suspected taint. Moreover, in the sanitary denouement that transpires on the river, the novel's urban pollutants—materialized as violence, jealousy, and sexual predation—are finally either cleansed or destroyed. When he shifts the action upstream, Dickens creates a sanitary idyll, a powerful fantasy of moral and material existence restored to a state of perfect cleanliness.

The village and environs of Henley, dominated by the paper mill at which Lizzie works, exist in a state of almost mythic serenity. The river here appears very different from the grim urban Thames and different again from the recreational river at Greenwich. Closer to its source, the river is physically pristine and reflects an image of nature equally pure and fully beneficent: whereas human mirrors never "fail to reveal some scene of horror or distress," "the great serene mirror of the river seemed as if it might have reproduced all it had ever reflected between those placid banks, and brought to light nothing save what was peaceful, pastoral, and blooming" (585). To follow the Thames upstream is to return to a kind of golden age, an Edenic paradise, where there is "no immensity of space between mankind and Heaven" (757). The idealized natural order of Henley reflects and sustains an ideal social order. The mill community, as uncorrupted as the river that powers it, thrives on honest labor and innocent amusement. The daily exodus from the factory is marked by "the sound of laughter" and the appearance of "fluttering colours" (757). Even the village urchins tossing stones into the river are comprehended within "the ever-widening beauty of the landscape" (757).

The presence of the paper mill may seem incongruous amidst the gentle beauties of this pastoral scene. After all, as sites of industrial manufacture, paper mills were implicated in the problem of environmental pollution. Their effect on the health of rivers in particular was disastrous. According to Wohl, in the nineteenth century, "The paper mills along the Thames spewed forth carbonate of soda and lime, as well as the wash from old rags and bleaching powders."[28] But as Dickens imagines it, the mill at Henley is miraculously non-polluting: the river's waters are fresh and clear, and the neighboring village is emphatically "clean" (580). Moreover, under the benevolent management of a Jewish couple, the workforce of the mill is fairly treated and content. As Lizzie reports of her employers, "They most willingly and cheerfully do their duty to all of us who are employed here, and we try to do ours to them"

(579). In place of the dirty, oppressive atmosphere and the mental and bodily lassitude often associated with modern industry, Dickens represents an industrial landscape where people, land, and machines operate harmoniously.

In fact, when we consider the representation of the paper mill in *Our Mutual Friend* in the context of an earlier article Dickens had written for *Household Words,* we begin to recognize the centrality of the mill to the novel's vision of purification. Titled simply "A Paper-Mill" (1850), the article records Dickens's visit to and impressions of a paper mill in Kent. In the article, as in the novel, the mill is imagined to stand at the heart of a harmonious social and natural order. Not only does the river remain "sweet [and] clear," but the workers themselves are reported to be "thriving."[29] Although the argumentative frame of the article consists of a protest against the then extant tax on paper, the real energy and interest of the piece lie in Dickens's detailed description of how paper is made. The manufacturing process essentially entails the material conversion of old rags—a waste product—into new paper by means of shredding, boiling, bleaching, and cutting. Not surprisingly, the transformation delights Dickens, who was ever fascinated with the possibility of reclamation, of recycling. "Paper!" he rhapsodizes, "White, pure, spick and span new paper . . . can it ever come from rags like these?"[30] As the repetition throughout the article of the words "pure," "clean," and "white" suggests, Dickens represents the process of paper making explicitly as a process of purification, of cleansing. For instance, he uses the materially and morally inflected language of purity to describe the rags after they have been boiled in water: "Then, [the rags are] a dense, tight mass, cut out in pieces like so much clay—very clean—faint as to [their] colour—greatly purified—and gradually becoming quite ethereal."[31] Originally associated with clothing, the rag sheds its grosser origins to become the sanctified tool of artistic creation—writing paper.

As a literal vehicle of purification, the paper mill serves as an emblem of the novel's sanitary process. In the purer atmosphere upstream, certain characters —like rags in the mill—are cleansed of the taint acquired through urban experience, while others less worthy are discharged like so much moral effluent. The promise of moral cleansing is dramatized most fully in Lizzie's story, although Eugene Wrayburn and Betty Higden too find purification on the upcountry Thames. Indeed, Betty's experience provides the most extreme instance of the sanitation process applied to human life. Striving to maintain her independence but nearing death, she works her way up the river and takes her final rest within sight of the paper mill, in Lizzie's arms. The pastoral river, like its urban counterpart, is associated with death; but in the tranquil setting upriver, death appears peaceful and consolatory. Dickens adopts a contemplative tone in his representation of a river that provides an image of death not as a violent end but as a part of the natural life cycle: "In those pleasant little towns on Thames, you may hear the fall of the water over the weirs, or even, in still weather, the rustle of the rushes; and from the bridge you may see the young river, dimpled like a young child, playfully gliding away among the trees, unpolluted by the defilements that lie in wait for it on its course, and as yet out of hearing of the deep summons of the sea" (567). The vision of human life as a rushing river joins Wordsworthian imagery and sentiment with environmental literalism: just as the Thames runs from an up-country source through London and down to the sea, receiving the pollutants of the filthy capital on its way, so too is the innocence of youth jeopardized and sullied with the passage to adulthood. By traveling against the current toward the river's unpolluted source, Betty finds the purity imaginatively associated with both a pristine river and the moral innocence of childhood. Transcending the corruption of human experience, she finds the ultimate purification in death: "Lizzie Hexam very softly raised the weather-stained grey head, and lifted her as high as Heaven" (577).

Lizzie likewise finds her sanitary salvation on the river that had threatened to be her ruin. Working in the paper mill by the Thames, she is able to keep faith with her past without risking the corruption associated with the urban river. Inspired by the transformative power of the paper mill, Dickens offers a sanitary fantasy. He imagines the Thames-side village as a place where purity is inviolate and whatever is sullied is made clean again. Thus, even when the men whom Lizzie seeks to escape follow her upstream, she is protected; the clear river stands as the outward sign of her moral innocence. In what she hopes is a parting interview with Eugene on the river's banks, something of Lizzie's inner purity is revealed to her pursuer: "He held her, almost as if she were sanctified to him by death, and kissed her, once, almost as he might have kissed the dead" (764). Lizzie's "death" here is significant because it reflects her purity, understood as sexual innocence, and saves her from sexual victimization. Of course, the disturbing suggestion remains: the only way a woman can be truly pure is to be dead.

But while the river is a site of literal and figurative death in the novel, it is also the source of new life. The seeds of Hexam's dubious riverside exertions bear fruit in Lizzie's heroic action on the river upstream. Shortly after Eugene leaves her, he suffers a violent attack at the hands of Headstone; falling into the river, he is left for dead. Past deeds and future fate converge when Lizzie, responding to the noise, finds a boat and oars and rushes to Eugene's rescue. Inspired by "her old bold life and habit," Lizzie adapts the skills she gained in her father's service to the task of saving the drowning Eugene (767). Grateful for the chance to redeem her father's past by putting his legacy to good use in the present, Lizzie prays, "Now, merciful Heaven be thanked for that old time, and grant, O Blessed Lord, that through thy wonderful workings it may turn to good at last!" (768). By saving Eugene's life, Lizzie secures both his redemption and her own. Both are cleansed in the pristine waters of the rural Thames: Lizzie, having demonstrated her moral worth, is available as a bride to the socially superior Eugene; while Eugene, strengthened by her love, finds the vitality—the "mine of purpose and energy"—that he had previously lacked (825).

What cannot be salvaged or brought to good ends, however, must be discharged from the narrative flow. The gravitation of urban pollution upstream is a curious feature of the last quarter of the novel, given that the Thames in this region above Teddington lock is nontidal. But Eugene works his away against the current in his light skiff, Headstone follows him along the tow path, and the dastardly Rogue Riderhood gains a position as lock keeper at Plashwater Weir Mill Lock—an incongruity that Dickens emphasizes in his evocation of the tranquility of the river around the lock: "The voice of the falling water, like the voices of the sea and the wind, were as an outer memory to a contemplative listener; but not particularly so to Mr. Riderhood, who sat on one of the blunt wooden levers of his lock-gates, dozing" (695). Pamela Gilbert interprets the upstream migrations of the novel's most dangerous characters as evidence of the river's corruption all along its course, giving the lie to the "*apparent* purity" of the upstream Thames;[32] but seen another way, the purity of the rural river is more than equal to the novel's villains. Although the river is not a revivifying elixir to Headstone and Riderhood, as it is for Eugene, it cleanses the novel of their taint in another way—it kills them. They are found drowned, "lying under the ooze and scum" that has collected around the lock gate (874). Riderhood, we recall, was run over by a steam-boat and nearly drowned in the gritty London river; that he survives this ear-lier immersion in filth but not the immersion in purity is a testament to the cleansing power of the waters upstream.

Although this part of the Thames thus provides a stringent cure for urban pollution, it is manifestly never offered as an alternative to London. Indeed, the narrative's and the (still living) characters' movements out of the city are invariably followed by a return. Just as Bella and John Harmon ultimately leave the modest comforts of suburban Blackheath for their grander London residence, so too do the wedded Lizzie and Eugene Wrayburn leave the quiet beauty of Henley and return to London. But even as Dickens asserts the cen-trality of the city to his characters' fates, he also emphasizes the necessity of periodic escape for their moral and emotional health. For the characters of *Our Mutual Friend*, the extremities of the Thames function as a source of re-newal and purification; they provide an escape from the city that is, nonethe-less, a constituent part of urban experience.

In the context of the modernizing project of the Embankment, *Our Mutual Friend* provides a new perspective not only on the Thames but also on London itself. By emphasizing the topographic range and diversity of the river, Dick-ens creates an image of the metropolis as an aggregate of localities, each with its own identity and set of resources. While Greenwich promises lighthearted amusement, the Thames-side village inspires peaceful reverie. London, in other words, is conceived not as a static site of official power but as an organ-ism whose limits and meanings are constantly in flux. But as important as the difference and distance between places is the fact that they are all connected by the river. The secret of metropolitan life lies in this connection. For it is the possibility of movement from place to place that saves the urban inhabitant from collapsing under the weight of the city's refuse. It is the possibility of movement that ensures the city will remain vibrant, rich, and—ultimately— livable.

chapter 4

No Space for the Poor

Disillusionment with Reform in the 1880s

> In the general arrangements of London we have decidedly
> advanced during the last twenty years. We have added a grand
> system of drainage; but, as regards the houses of the poor,
> we believe that the flood of increased population has been too
> much for the little dykes reared by our organized philan-
> thropy and sanitary laws. . . . In many parts of London there
> are alleys where dirt defies the law, and where the sanitary
> officers are baffled by the circumstances of the case.
>
> Daily Telegraph (November 1874)

The movement for sanitary reform was from the start intimately concerned with the material, moral, and social condition of the working classes. Adherents readily understood that changes in the urban environment would improve people's lives, that a new sewer, for instance, had the potential to lift people out of poverty and ultimately stabilize the social order. We see this understanding in Dickens's endorsement of sanitary measures in the preface to the 1850 edition of *Oliver Twist:* "I have always been convinced that this Reform [sanitary] must precede all other Social Reforms . . . and that, without it, those classes of the people which increase the fastest, must become so desperate and be made so miserable, as to bear within themselves the certain seeds of ruin to the whole community."[1] Although the rhetoric seems rather to alarm readers about the danger of inaction than to tout the benefits of action, the message is nonetheless clear: sanitary reform will alleviate human misery and thereby preserve the "whole community." Growing disillusionment with reform, however, meant that in the 1880s this message was articulated with less confidence and was received more critically.

Typical of attitudes toward reform later in the century is this gloomy assessment of social progress from the journalist Arnold White's book *The Problems of a Great City* (1886): "Many a valiant soul fights gallantly to stem the tide of woe and want. But their efforts, if not fruitless, make no permanent and palpable impress on the mass of wrong to be cleared away."[2] The assessment may seem unusual for a book that itself offers a host of remedies for problems ranging from alcoholism to early marriages among the poor, but this sense of the enormity of the social problems facing reformers is repeatedly expressed in reformist texts of the period. Whereas reformers in the 1840s and 1850s expressed an implicit confidence in the power of material alterations to effect social change, those in the 1880s registered instead the sobering perception of the intransigence of poverty and the limitations of sanitary approaches to social problems. One reason for the perceptual shift was the recognized failure of housing reform policies of the 1860s and 1870s to alleviate the wretched living conditions of the London poor. We find another explanation in the changing conception of poverty, from the idea of poverty as a condition affecting the individual and subject to the immediate influence of sanitary and philanthropic intervention, to the idea of poverty as a sociobiological phenomenon bred into the population and over which reformers had little control. In this climate, sanitary reform came to seem less capable of meeting (at times even irrelevant to) the challenges of urban life. The East End Congregational minister George Sale Reaney speaks to this point in his article, titled "Outcast London," from 1886: "[T]he whole world is amazed at our magnificent sanitation, but stands aghast at the conditions of the life of our poor."[3] Here sanitary improvement and human improvement, which once had seemed almost synonymous, are imagined to have diverged. This chapter tells the story not only of this significant divergence but also of the increasing disillusion affecting social reformers.

The Irony of Improvement

We can better understand the disillusion with reform taking hold in the 1880s by tracing the history of a sanitary strategy that had long attracted controversy

—slum clearance. For many sanitary reformers, slum clearance was seen as an ideal means to improve both the public health and the moral condition of the poor. If the habitations of the working classes were exposed to the open air and to the beneficent influence of the prosperous classes, then they would be less likely to harbor either miasmic vapors or criminals—or so the argument went. The Royal Commission on the State of Large Towns and Populous Districts (1845), appointed in response to Chadwick's *Sanitary Report,* noted the tendency of "heaps of filth and ordure" to accumulate in areas isolated from the regular intercourse of traffic.[4] And in its report, the commission recommended driving thoroughfares through such areas not only to "ventilate" them but also to open them up to public scrutiny. Motivated by similar concerns about the health and especially the morals of the slum, the Reverend William Stone, speaking before the Select Committee on Metropolitan Improvements in 1838, pressed for the construction of a new street through his parish of Spitalfields; for, as he contended, the neighborhood was "the constant abode of fever and other infectious disorders," as well as home to "an exceedingly immoral population . . . [who] find in these obscure haunts concealment from the hands of justice."[5] Over thirty years later, the *Times,* in a piece urging the opening of a new street in St. James's parish, characterized the impenetrable haunts of the poor in terms that had hardly changed: "[T]hey are nurseries of disease, and they are nests of thieves."[6]

As is clear from the context of these remarks, sanitary reform and metropolitan improvement were often regarded as complementary processes. Strictly speaking, their aims differed: sanitary reformers typically advocated for the public health, and town planners promoted traffic relief. But they shared a conviction in the virtue of unimpeded circulation for the healthy urban body.[7] Thus, both groups urged the creation of wide-open thoroughfares in place of tortuous streets and narrow alleys, and both recommended slum clearances as a viable means to achieve this open urban landscape. In his essay examining the multiple motives of Victorian street improvements, H. J. Dyos explains that the several royal commissions and select committees appointed to consider metropolitan improvements before 1855 tended to prefer plans for new streets that would simultaneously serve sanitary ends.[8] For instance, the New Oxford Street scheme was recommended and ultimately carried out in the 1840s because the line of the new street would pass through the notorious slums of St. Giles and would thus, according to Richard Lambert Jones, "be the means of destroying a vast quantity of houses which are full of the very worst description of people."[9] Sanitary improvement may not have been the primary motive behind street construction, but to the Select Committee on Metropolitan Improvements, the sanitary benefits were nonetheless obvious and welcome; in concluding that "a good new street speedily effects the purification of the whole neighbourhood," the committee reinforced the conventional wisdom that clearances not only improved traffic flow, drainage, and ventilation but also improved morals.[10]

Although the conviction that clearance was a beneficial sanitary measure persisted throughout the nineteenth century and beyond, contemporary observers began noting the negative impact of slum clearance on the urban poor as early as the 1840s. Touching on the impact of street improvements, Dyos goes on to explain that outcomes rarely met planners' high expectations: "The naive expectation that, merely by redrawing the street map of London at key points, both the traffic and slum problems could be solved together had . . . a short life, while the problems themselves have had unwanted longevity."[11] The grim reality was that the demolition of slum property played a critical role in the perpetuation of slums and, more generally, in the housing shortage that plagued working London. Wohl describes this harrowing process in *The Eternal Slum,* a comprehensive study of the housing crisis in London: those tenants who were evicted in the name of improvement put pressure on the limited housing supply in adjacent areas, exacerbating already crowded conditions there and preparing the ground for new slums.[12] A prescient Chadwick had recognized the shape of the problem in 1842, when he asserted that in the case of slum clearance "existing evils are merely shifted, and, by being shifted, they are aggravated."[13]

But with the acceleration of slum clearance from the 1840s onward for the purposes of not only street improvement but also the creation of railways, docks, warehouses, and office blocks, the relation of clearance to the problem of overcrowding came into sharper focus. Demolition of housing was especially concentrated in the City of London, where throughout the century commercial interests were literally gaining more and more ground. Henry Jephson in *The Sanitary Evolution of London* (1907) emphasizes the impact that this transformation of the City had on working-class housing across the metropolis, calling it "one of the great, if not indeed the greatest of the economic forces at work which has unceasingly dominated the housing of the people not only in the 'City,' but in the metropolis outside and surrounding the 'City,' and in dominating their housing, powerfully affected also their sanitary and social condition."[14] Included among the economic forces working so powerfully in mid-nineteenth-century London was, of course, the railway, and its devastating effect on the built environment and on human lives alike stimulated much debate and concern. In 1861, the Reverend William Denton denounced the displacement of working people by railway schemes, noting that overcrowding was an inevitable consequence: "The poor are indeed displaced, but they are not removed. They are shoveled out of one side of a parish, only to render more over-crowded the stifling apartments in another part."[15] Whether the cause was a new street, a railway line, or a new commercial interest, the irony that so much devastation had been wrought by ostensible improvements was not lost on contemporary commentators. For one contributor to *All the Year Round* in 1866, improving interests of all sorts were no better than marauding "Attilas," laying waste the houses of the poor and causing "as much misery as a war."[16] In this context, the writer cannot help but mock those who applaud a new thoroughfare or new underground line: "Wonderful improvements going on everywhere, is the complacent cry."[17] A similar sensibility informs an 1879 article by politician and housing reformer William Torrens, titled "What Is to Be Done with the Slums?" Faced with the dislocation of poor tenants caused by wholesale clearances, Torrens denounces the "dilapidatory sweep of what are called metropolitan improvements."[18]

The key note of Torrens's piece is this recognition of the ironic link between improvement and slum. But what makes the irony particularly pointed for Torrens is that in 1875, with the passage of the Artisans' and Labourers' Dwellings Improvement Act (the Cross Act), slum clearance had become the centerpiece of the government's housing reform policy. Under the Cross Act, introduced by Home Secretary Richard Cross, the strategy of slum clearance was for the first time directed primarily at the problem of working-class living conditions.[19] The act directed that entire blocks of insanitary housing would be demolished and that the newly available sites would be used for rehousing as many working-class inhabitants as had been evicted. In London, the Metropolitan Board of Works was given responsibility for clearing the slums identified by local medical officers, compensating property owners, and then selling the cleared sites to one of the semiphilanthropic dwelling companies operating in the city. The Cross Act differed significantly from Torrens's earlier Artisans' and Labourers' Dwellings Act (1868) in its commitment to urban reconstruction on a large scale: rather than target the individual dwelling (as the Torrens Act had done), it targeted larger areas where not only the state of the houses themselves but also the structural arrangement of the houses and streets contributed to unhealthy living conditions. Of particular importance is the fact that it also promised to provide improved housing for those people displaced. Slum clearance, then, was conceived as the necessary first step in a comprehensive rehousing program; in fact, as J. A. Yelling explains in *Slums and Slum Clearance in Victorian London,* "[I]t was around the accordance of these two objectives that the logical structure of the Act was built."[20]

The Cross Act may have been logical, but in practice the twin strategies of clearance and rebuilding were hardly commensurate in their effects. The immediate impact of the demolitions, as in the case of so many London improvements, was increased overcrowding and higher rents. As many contemporary observers noted, the promised rebuilding was slow to materialize, and when model dwellings were erected, they very rarely rehoused the inhabitants who had been displaced, or even that same class of inhabitants. We can attribute the delays not so much to the unwillingness of the Metropolitan Board of Works to execute the Cross Act, as to the financial difficulties that the act entailed. Compensating owners of condemned property proved time-consuming and expensive, but more troublesome still, the cleared sites that the board made available for sale were not immediately attractive to the philanthropic housing organizations.[21] Many of these sites, located as they were in the densest parts of central London, were exceedingly valuable from a commercial standpoint, and the board was reluctant to sell or lease them at a reduced price for purposes of rehousing. As a result, many sites lay cleared and empty for long periods of time: for instance, Yelling shows that in Whitechapel one of the sites to receive the board's earliest attention was ready for construction in July 1878 but did not find a buyer until June of the following year (and at terms to the board's disadvantage).[22] In *Outcast London,* Gareth Stedman Jones explains that although those suffering from chronic poverty were the usual victims of slum clearance, they were also the least likely to benefit from the construction of new housing.[23] The Royal Commission on the Housing of the

Working Classes reached this conclusion in 1885, noting that the rents of the model dwellings were too high and the regulations often too stringent to "reach the class whose need is the greatest."[24]

The disastrous results of the policy were, indeed, quickly recognized. Throughout the 1880s, pamphlets and periodicals, Parliament and the press —having seized on overcrowding as the most urgent social problem of the day—criticized the mass evictions and clearances prosecuted under the Cross Act. "Space after space has been cleared under the provisions of this Act," charges the popular writer George Sims in his exposé *How the Poor Live* (1883); "[T]housands upon thousands of families have been rendered homeless by the demolition of whole acres of the slums where they hid their heads, and in scores of instances the work of improvement has stopped with the pulling down."[25] Cross himself reported in 1882 that 20,335 people had been evicted under the requirements of the Cross Act; although he also anticipated that housing for 23,000 residents would be available within another year, this was scarcely consolation for those evicted, nor did it distract social commentators from the plight of those displaced.[26] In his immensely popular tract *The Bitter Cry of Outcast London* (1883), Andrew Mearns laments that the abject poor are quite literally "cast out" of their dwellings by the act and ultimately "driven to crowd more closely together in the few stifling places left to them."[27] We find similar rhetoric, emphasizing the passivity and helplessness of the poor in the face of the act, in a leader from the *Daily Chronicle* in 1879: "The working classes have been hunted from their houses and driven far from the market-place of their labour."[28] In the years immediately following the passage of the Cross Act, many would have agreed with the *Saturday Review*'s assessment in 1879: "[T]he sole effect which the Act of 1875 has at present had is to make things worse than it found them."[29]

For a brief period in August 1878, the problem of the mass evictions authorized by the Board of Works crystallized around a single case: the death of an infant whose family had only recently been evicted because of an impending clearance scheme. The family of six (including the child's mother, Elizabeth Mason) moved into a single-room dwelling in Half Moon Court off of Gray's Inn Road after being forced to leave their lodgings in Red Lion Square. As the grandmother explained, "We were turned out of our last place, as the houses were coming down."[30] The thirteen-week-old child was presumed to have died by suffocation in the "stifling atmosphere" of a room and a house that were both overcrowded; the verdict at the inquest was "death from want of fresh air."[31] For the coroner, Dr. Hardwicke, the inquest served as an opportunity to strike out against the Metropolitan Board of Works for carrying out improvement schemes so detrimental to the welfare of the poor. In his testimony, in fact, he comes close to laying the death at the Board of Works' door: "It is all very well for that energetic body to obtain their Acts of Parliament and make metropolitan improvements, but crowding the poor more and more, and forcing them to live in such dreadful dens as they do is cruel in the extreme."[32] In reporting the case, the daily press for the most part sympathized with the victims of improvement, although we do find some reluctance to condemn improvement schemes outright. The *Daily News,* for instance, seemed fully aware of the ambiguous effects of improvements such as the creation of new streets, which, on the one hand, "sometimes have a lamentable result" and, on the other hand, offer "an immense convenience to all of us, poor and rich."[33] Providing a less accommodating response was the *Daily Telegraph;* its sensationalist account of the Mason case played up the cruel irony of improvement: "And yet it would appear that there is another manner in which poor people can be got rid of when they obstruct the 'march of improvement.' They can, it seems, be choked and asphyxiated until the feeble flicker of life in their sickly bodies goes out in darkness amidst the foul and putrid air that quenches its last faint spark."[34] The accounts of the Mason child's death indicate, first, how unpopular the Metropolitan Board of Works had become in its role as executor of the Cross Act and, second, how skeptical the public had become about urban improvement in its bearing on working-class life.

To say that the Cross Act caused this disillusion would be an overstatement, but it did help bring the limitations of sanitary reform into focus. Cross had deliberately defined the housing crisis as a sanitary problem because doing so allowed him to argue for and justify state intervention. Subsidizing or providing improved housing for a particular group of citizens was, he reasoned, beyond the scope of the law; but destroying and rebuilding unhealthy areas —"plague spots"—where the death rate was demonstrably higher than in other places benefited the entire community.[35] "No one will doubt the propriety and right of the State to interfere in matters relating to sanitary laws," he argued.[36] After the 1880s, however, the sanitary approach to the housing crisis lost ground. The publication of Mearns's *Bitter Cry* in 1883, with its explicit attacks on "overcrowding and its moral hazards," helped reshape the debate by shifting the emphasis away from sanitation and toward overcrowding as the primary concern in working-class housing reform.[37] A key sign of this shift was Lord Salisbury's speech before the House of Lords in 1884, in which he detailed the limits of the sanitary solution and concluded that "as long as you confine your attention to purely sanitary legislation, and do not bear in mind this difficulty of overcrowding . . . your sanitary legislation will be in vain."[38] Salisbury and others recognized that slum housing, with its attendant ills of overcrowding and demoralization, was a complex problem that would not be solved by a new street or a new sewer. This recognition was hastened by the devastating consequences of the Cross Act, which—as we have seen—relied on a sanitary approach to the slums and in doing so made those conditions worse. Under pressure of these events, the ideals associated with sanitary reform had to be modified: no longer could sanitary improvement be seen as the essential vehicle for human improvement.

This sense of the limitation of sanitary reform in the period is expressed by the pioneering social reformer Lord Shaftesbury. In 1884, at the end of a successful career as champion of the poor, Shaftesbury appeared before the Royal Commission on the Housing of the Working Classes. His testimony, which sounds at times like a retrospect of the sanitary movement, alternately reflects pride in reforms that have palpably improved the sanitary condition of the metropolis and doubts that the very poor can be helped by material reforms at all. Looking back on a half-century of improvements, Shaftesbury cannot resist a feeling of satisfaction: "Many of the worst places have been swept away."[39] At the same time, he recognizes the toll that large-scale clearances have taken on the poor: "The opening of the Embankment and of the streets going down to it has aided wonderfully . . . and in many parts of London all these clearances have produced the most beneficial effect upon the health and upon the decency of the people, but they have been the cause of great suffering to those who are driven away."[40] Although the suffering of the dispossessed poor does not escape Shaftesbury's notice, he is unwilling to condemn alterations that have supported the "health" and "decency" of the larger portion of the population. But perhaps more significant is his inability to imagine the kinds of reforms that might ultimately aid the minority of the population—"those who are driven away." When he begins to consider this class, Shaftesbury's assurance wanes; to the commission he confesses, "The very lowest class are the migratory class; and I have never been able to see any one mode, except by a complete alteration of the state of society, in which we could benefit them. . . . I have not a notion what to do with them, and I have never been able to come to a conclusion about them."[41] The apparent intractability of the "very lowest class[es]" baffles Shaftesbury, leading him to utter merely a series of negatives: "I have never," "I have not," and again "I have never." He wants to believe in the efficacy of reform, but the very existence of the "migratory class," of a class that cannot be helped, challenges this belief. Shaftesbury's testimony, in vividly suggesting the limitations of improvement, raised disquieting possibilities: perhaps the improved city was not necessarily a more humane city; more troubling still, perhaps the abject poor were beyond the reach of improvement.

Unfit for Reform

In the literature treating the housing question, the poor are very often represented as unwitting victims of processes beyond their control. They are "shoveled out," "hunted from their houses," and "driven to crowd more closely together." But the idea of the poor as victims tends to shade into the seemingly contradictory idea of the poor as sanitary perpetrators, willingly embracing conditions of filth and degradation and thus responsible to some degree for the failure of reforming efforts. In the case of the death of the Mason child from "overcrowding" in 1878, we recall the coroner's angry rebuke of the Metropolitan Board of Works for treating evicted tenants so callously; however, a very different response to the same case appeared in the *Globe* under the revealing title "Objectionable Lodgers." The newspaper uses the case as an opportunity both to defend the board and to blame the poor for choosing to live in overcrowded, insanitary dwellings: "[T]here are thousands of persons within the metropolitan district who appear to have a deeply rooted aversion to decent living, and who, turned out of one foul nook, hurry with their families to another, not because more wholesome habitations are not to be obtained, but in deference to a sort of burrowing instinct which leads them to seek out the dark holes and corners."[42] According to this line of argument, the poor, like rats, prefer to wallow in filth, and this preference is both instinctual and "deeply rooted." From this perspective, sanitary solutions to the housing crisis appear limited and naïve. George Sims makes this very point in *Horrible London* (1889) when reflecting on the difficulty of improving the living conditions of people who are thought to be naturally inclined to dirt: "Take them from their dirt to-morrow, and put them in clean rooms amid wholesome surroundings, and what would be the result?—the dirty people would not be improved, but the clean rooms would be dirtied."[43] Here, disillusion with reform seems to be linked not to the efforts of reformers but to the deficiencies of the poor themselves.

As both Peter Keating and Gareth Stedman Jones have shown, a pessimistic response to urban poverty dominated the social reportage of the 1880s. Many reformers were beginning to accept that a certain portion of the population was permanently sunk in poverty.[44] Related to this response was the belief, stated more firmly by some than by others, that existing social institutions and reforming methods were wholly inadequate to solve social problems or uplift the poor.[45] We can trace the changing conceptions of poverty in the period to specific economic and political conditions, as well as to the increasingly influential social-scientific discourse of degeneration. Jones has identified several factors that contributed to intensified middle-class anxiety about the poor in the 1880s: the economic depression in the middle of the decade, which helped create conditions of chronic unemployment; the working-class housing shortage, which as we have seen drove up rents and exacerbated overcrowding; and the emergence of socialist movements, which threatened to give a powerful and disruptive voice to those suffering from the aforementioned conditions.[46]

In this context, degeneration theory had a powerful hold. Drawing on the Darwinian theory of natural selection, degeneration theory posited a pathology of urban life to explain the paradoxical existence of an unfit population, the residuum of society.[47] Hostile environmental conditions were sustaining this population, but they were also contributing to its physical and moral deterioration. More alarming still was the belief that the acquired defects of the poor could be passed down through the generations—a process referred to as "hereditary urban degeneration"—creating a diseased and dangerous new "race" of the London poor.[48] White, in his analysis of urban conditions in *The Problems of a Great City,* is especially alarmed by the propagation of a new race of the unfit and describes the process in language that quite typically blends biology and morality: "Tainted constitutions, brains charged with subtle mischief, and languishing or extinct morality, transmit a terrible inheritance of evil to the next generation."[49]

The proper role of reform in relation to the residuum was subject to debate. Some social Darwinists believed that sanitary reform had already done too much to prolong the lives of weak individuals, who—for the sake of the nation—were better off dead.[50] Many more reformers, however, believed that solving the problem of the residuum required the kind of aggressive measures that only government intervention could supply. So, for instance, the liberal economist Alfred Marshall recommends sending the "descendents of the dissolute" to industrial colonies outside London so that the poor of abler bodies and sounder minds might have space to live.[51] But even this approach, which entailed a limited socialism, did not aim so much at rehabilitating the dissolute poor as removing them for the sake of the "legitimate" working classes. Marshall is explicit about the goal: to "rid London of its superfluous population."[52] Degenerationist ideas, then, played a key role in suggesting the limitations of reform, even when they spurred new, more interventionist measures.[53] These tensions are apparent in Harold Boulton's article on the housing question in 1888, in which he urges that local authorities have a responsibility to provide housing for the working classes but dismisses a whole swath of the population from his consideration. He states matter-of-factly, "There must always be a residuum of unhelpables [*sic*]."[54]

The residuum may have represented only a small portion of London's working-class population, but the idea and imagery associated with this lowest social stratum dominated the literature of housing reform. We see again and again images of the poor as animals and as waste in addition to references to the superfluity and intransigence of the poor. In *The Bitter Cry of Outcast London,* for instance, Mearns uses the metaphor of waste trickling into a cesspool to describe the concentration of a poor and immoral population in certain areas of the city: "The low parts of London are the sink into which the filthy and abominable from all parts of the country seem to flow."[55] Sims, in *How the Poor Live* (1883), similarly likens the low lodging houses and homes of the

poor to "receptacles" for the "crime, disease, and filth . . . which has already
been bred elsewhere, and which is deposited gratis, to swell the collection."[56]
The association of the poor with waste is a familiar trope in the literature of
the sanitary movement, but in representations from the 1880s on, the image
of waste is deployed in a way that emphasizes its stagnancy and its mass, rather
than its ability to travel as so much miasmic vapor. The poor are shown massed
together in a figurative cesspool, from which it is not easy to emerge. This use
of waste imagery converges with the image of the abyss, which, as Keating explains, was used frequently around the turn of the century to express both the
perceived intransigence of poverty and heightened class fears.[57] The "people
of the abyss," to borrow the title of Jack London's 1902 book, seemed to live
outside the pale of productive society: "There is no place for them, in the social fabric, while all the forces of society drive them downward till they per-
ish. At the bottom of the Abyss they are feeble, besotted, and imbecile."[58] The
downward course into the abyss is imagined to be inevitable and irreversible,
which is precisely the point: the image of the abyss implies a condition of
degradation from which there is no recovery. The recurrence of these related
images—the abyss, the sinkhole, the filthy mass—reflects the growing sense
of crisis among reformers in the period. Moreover, descriptions of this sort
reinforced doubts both about the capacity of the poor for improvement and
about the efficacy of reform.

The emphasis on the superfluity of the poor served a similar function. Not
just the size of the population but also its rate of reproduction alarmed many
social investigators and reformers. In discussions of the housing question,
children are frequently represented in dehumanizing terms, like so much
waste product, thereby suggesting the intractability of the mass. For housing
reformers such as the philanthropist Octavia Hill, children exacerbated one
of the great problems facing working-class Londoners—the problem of limited space. Lamenting this shortage in *Homes of the London Poor* (1883), Hill re-
counts her attempt to navigate an overpopulated court: "[T]he children are
crawling or sitting on the hard hot stones till every corner of the place looks
alive, and it seems as if I must step on them, do what I would, if I am to walk
up the court at all."[59] The imagery in Hill's account becomes more explicitly
animalistic in London's description of a group of children outside a house in
Spitalfields: "A spawn of children cluttered the slimy pavement, for all the

world like tadpoles just turned into frogs on the bottom of a dry pond."[60] Representing the children of the poor as frogs reflects the influence of degeneration theory: implicit here are fears that the race of the urban poor is devolving. Implicit also are concerns that this rising generation, with its apparently large numbers, might threaten the security of a less prodigal middle-class population. In *From the Abyss* (1902), the settlement worker and, later, politician Charles Masterman focuses a great deal of nervous attention on the overwhelming number of poor inhabitants, a "number continually increasing, multiplying without pause."[61] The specter of the excess population may have posed a threat, but it also served to magnify the difficulties that reformers faced. Helping the poor out of overcrowded housing and out of poverty itself comes to seem less and less feasible if the poor are represented as a vast fecal mass.

As I have been suggesting, representations of the residuum produced a distortion, which in turn placed limits on what reformers could imagine and do. These imaginative limits are especially apparent in discussions of slum clearances, evictions, and suburban relocation—all measures connected with the relief of overcrowding. For a wide variety of reasons, some of which we have seen, these approaches did not relieve overcrowding and did not meet the needs of the most destitute urban inhabitants. Yet many reformers persisted in attributing these failures to the deficiencies of the poor, even when they acknowledged alternative explanations. For instance, in the minutes of evidence from the Royal Commission on the Housing of the Working Classes, the commissioners repeatedly grapple with the question of why the poor remain in overcrowded neighborhoods rather than moving to less-populous suburban districts. Referring to the residents of Clerkenwell, Lord William Compton provides one answer to the question: "I suppose they are accustomed to live there. . . . [T]hey have lived in the district probably ever since they were born."[62] The commission follows this explanation with a suggestion of its own, revealing firmly held assumptions about the indolent habits of the poor: "And it is too much of an enterprise for them to leave the neighbourhood?" To which Compton replies, "I think so. They do not like change."[63]

A very similar exchange appears in the testimony of the Reverend Benjamin Oswald Sharp. Again referring to the crowding in Clerkenwell, Sharp explains, "In one case where I had to clear a house myself, everybody went within one hundred yards of it."[64] And the commission again responds with the query, "I suppose there was something in the want of initiative and enterprise?"[65] Sharp agrees with the assessment but also clarifies: "Partly, and also that they are clannish and kind to one another. . . . They are very good people socially in that matter; they keep to their surroundings; they do not want to be driven away."[66] The testimony offers two ways of interpreting the behavior of people living in overcrowded conditions. We see, on the one hand, people with strong allegiances to their communities and friends; we may even sympathize with their efforts to stick together despite the evictions, clearances, and rent goug-ing that had become characteristic of life in central London neighborhoods. On the other hand, we see people too insular and indolent to leave the places they know, despite the obvious benefits of doing so. The latter assumption, driving the questioning and shaping the answers as it does, emerges as the dominant view: the poor themselves pose the greatest obstacle to reform.

One of the more dramatic versions of the recalcitrance of the poor in the face of improvement appears in accounts of evictions—or, rather, accounts of evicted tenants who fail to leave their condemned residences. The *Daily News* reported this problem in 1879 in connection with clearances near Drury Lane authorized under the Cross Act. Although "a clean sweep" of the area is to be made, "further embarrassment is threatened by the inclination of some of the inhabitants to remain in their wretched rooms and cellars until actually ex-pelled."[67] In his essay "Evicted London," Sims provides a closer look at the slum dwellers who ignore eviction notices and stay on, clinging to the bit of house property left to them with a siege mentality (fig. 4.1). The essay, appear-ing in *Living London* in 1902, describes the challenge of the residuum in terms that had changed little in twenty years. Sims still wonders how to reconcile the "public good" accomplished by slum clearance with the hardship experi-enced by those beyond the reach of improvement: "What is to become of the people who are unfit (by reason of their ways or their families) for the new buildings? What will happen to the areas in which the 'undesirables' (*i.e.* the criminal and vicious) scatter themselves?"[68] The dilemma informs the repre-sentation of evicted residents at the moment of crisis, when the actual work of demolition forces them to take to the streets. Such is the case of one woman whom Sims describes as the last remaining inhabitant in a block of condemned property: "The roof, the doors, and the windows were removed while she . . . still remained crouching in a corner of the miserable room. . . . When bricks and plaster began to fall in showers about her, and the point of the pickaxe came through the wall against which she was leaning, then at last she scrambled for her belongings and went out into the streets."[69] Sims addresses the difficulties associated with eviction, including (of course) the scarcity of replacement housing, but expressions of sympathy are followed by reproofs: although the people have many weeks to look for new accommodation, "it is the nature of the slum dwellers to live only for to-day and to trust to luck for to-morrow."[70]

Suggestions such as this of the inherent deficiencies of the poor appear frequently in discussions of the housing question. This perception, when combined with the recognition of environmental deficiencies, created a sense of disillusionment with current approaches to reform. Although images of stagnation and superfluity may have been intended to cordon off the most destitute of the urban population, to mark and exclude them from social life, the strategy had the opposite effect. It gave to the idea of the residuum an imaginative life that far outstripped reality and that ultimately challenged belief in the transformative power of sanitary improvement.

The Residuum Rising

One of the greatest fears associated with the residuum was that it would corrupt not just future generations but also working-class inhabitants slightly higher up the social scale. Of the many detrimental effects imagined to come from overcrowding, one of the most serious was the tendency for the "honest" poor to live in greater intimacy with the "dishonest," or criminal, poor. The articulation of the problem in the *Contemporary Review* (December 1883) is typical: "The honest and worthy poor . . . are mingled with those given to evil."[71] Fears of the moral decline of "outcast London" inevitably merged with fears of a social or political disturbance. So, for instance, an article for the forum Common Sense and the Dwellings of the Poor in the *Nineteenth Century* (December 1883) warns that "there exists at the present moment, in the heart of the wealthiest city in the world . . . a mass of men and women . . . committed to an existence of crime and disorder . . . which, terrible in itself, constitutes a grave danger to the community."[72] Sims's imagination of the dan-

4.1. The house she lives in is scheduled for demolition, but the old woman—a "besieged resident"—remains. "Lot 1," photograph, in "Evicted London" by George R. Sims, vol. 1, *Living London: Its Work and Its Play, Its Humour and Its Pathos, Its Sights and Its Scenes,* ed. Sims (London: Cassell, 1903), 206.

ger of the mass in *How the Poor Live* (1883), though in a similar vein, takes a decidedly more thrilling turn: "This mighty mob of famished, diseased, and filthy helots is getting dangerous, physically, morally, politically dangerous. . . . [A]nd it may do the State a mischief if it be not looked to in time. Its fevers and its filth may spread to the homes of the wealthy; its lawless armies may sally forth and give us a taste of the lesson the mob has tried to teach now and again in Paris."[73] Sims evokes the terrifying memory of the Paris Commune of 1871, when revolutionaries seized control of the city from the French government. As Matthew Beaumont explains, in the 1880s when domestic anxieties were already high in England, the Parisian example of a decade before gripped the middle-class imagination.[74] In 1883, the quiescence of the English "mob" would seem hardly to have warranted the alarm, but events in the capital in 1886 and 1887 made Sims's vision of insurrection seem eerily prescient.

In those years, marked by rioting in the West End and frequent demonstrations in and around Trafalgar Square, the phantasmic forms of the suffering and neglected poor seemed to rise up and to take possession of the city in unprecedented ways.

In the 1880s, Trafalgar Square had become a popular site for demonstrations and gatherings of all kinds, but one event in particular gained for the square a new notoriety. On February 8, 1886, a massive march and demonstration on the part of the unemployed was planned by the antisocialist Fair Trade movement, while the socialist Social Democratic Federation planned a counterdemonstration in response.[75] According to the report in the *Times* the following day, fifteen to twenty thousand people attended, constituting a remarkable but not extraordinary gathering: "The whole of the square where the fountains are was densely packed with people, the roadways on each side were filled, the steps of St. Martin's Church were thronged, and down to Pall-mall, as far as could be seen, were onlookers."[76] The police and the Home Office were not unduly concerned by the event, arranging to have only five hundred reserve officers in the vicinity. What authorities did not observe at the time of the demonstration and what turned out to be the signal event of the day, however, was the breaking off of a large group of demonstrators from the mass gathered in the square and the subsequent riotous march of these demonstrators through the West End. This group—variously estimated at one to two thousand and three to five thousand strong[77]—was led out of the square into Pall Mall Street by the Social Democrats, who intended to reconvene and then disperse in Hyde Park; but once roused, the group proved difficult to control. For nearly two hours, the crowd rampaged through the West End unmolested, smashing windows, looting shops, and stopping carriages to oust their occupants. The representation of the riot in the *Graphic,* titled "Here They Come!—The Mob in St. James's Street," conveys the anger and resolve of the crowd as it passes quickly through the street (fig. 4.2). At the center of the image is a bearded man, identifiable as the socialist leader John Burns: this figure holds aloft a red flag that served as a potent rallying point on February 8 and quickly became associated with the call to socialism.[78] Surrounding Burns and filling the frame are countless bodies in a swirl of activity: men's mouths are open as if in midshout, and their arms are upraised, ready to launch bricks and stones. The English mob here seems to have shaken off its apathy and to be channeling the spirit of the Parisian revolutionaries.

4.2. No longer confined to East End tenements, "outcast London" imposes its force on West End streets. "'Here They Come!'—The Mob in St. James's Street," *Graphic,* 13 February 1886, 177.

Representations of the riot in the succeeding days and weeks reveal the public's alarm at the freedom of action allowed the mob and the destruction that occurred. Much of the criticism was directed toward police mismanagement of the situation, especially the failure of anyone in authority in Trafalgar Square to notice the sizeable crowd heading west into Pall Mall; this and other lapses became the focus of a Parliamentary inquiry. Of more immediate concern was the fear of further outbreaks of rioting occurring on an even vaster scale and over large areas of London. In *Outcast London,* Jones describes the two days after the riots as a period of heightened anxiety, as rumors circulated throughout South London and the West End that thousands of men were on the march and bent on destruction: at one point, it was widely believed that a force of ten thousand men was marching on central London from points south.[79] A telegram sent to the office of the *Times* and reprinted in the paper on February 11 suggests the degree of panic that had been reached: "Fearful state all round here in South London. Thirty thousand men at Spa-road moving to Trafalgar-square. Roughs in thousands trooping to the West."[80] For Jones, the real significance of the riot lay less in the event itself than in the wild rumors of an imminent uprising that the riot generated: he sees this as the moment when middle-class fears of the residuum reached a climax.[81] But a more fundamental point is that the riot revealed the London poor in a new guise: in this one moment, at least, they were not suffering victims, contained in crowded rooms; they were in the open air and on the move, claiming the space they were ordinarily denied.

Of course, that the riot took place in the West End made all the difference. In the evidence delivered before the Parliamentary committee inquiring into the riot and the police response, the novelty of a crowd of demonstrators moving westward is repeatedly emphasized. When questioned about the failure of police to follow the demonstrators who marched up Pall Mall, Commissioner of Police Edmund Henderson responded, "[W]e never follow them; we are only too glad when the mob goes away, and are only too ready to facilitate their going."[82] On February 8, however, the expectation that the poor would just go away was subverted, as the demonstrators made the bold move of heading west. In his testimony, Henderson insists that those attending meetings in Trafalgar Square in the past have "never gone westwards."[83] And this statement is confirmed by Assistant Commissioner of Police Richard Pearson: "My experience is that they [demonstrators] generally go back to the place from whence they come; that is, if they come from the east they go back to the east."[84] The riot thus appears in the light of a foreign invasion, one that, moreover, seems to have permanently breached that imaginary dividing line between west and east.

For after the events of February 1886, Trafalgar Square and other West End public spaces continued to attract an outcast population. In fact, as Jones explains, the depression in trade through 1887 coupled with mild temperatures in the summer and fall encouraged more open-air sleeping, especially in Trafalgar Square, in St. James's Park, and—as shown in chapter 2—on the Thames Embankment (see fig. 2.8).[85] The *Times* reported in October of that year that when police decided to disperse the occupants of the square on one particular evening, "between 300 and 400 homeless wanderers of both sexes" were on the scene.[86] The *Graphic* also reported the phenomenon in the fall of 1887, noting the way in which use of public space shifted according to the time of day: "During the past summer months a large army of poverty-stricken wretches have taken up their quarters by night in Trafalgar Square, where

4.3. An invasion of a different sort—the homeless poor lay claim to urban space. "Our Homeless London Poor—St. James's Park at Mid-Day," *Graphic*, 17 September 1887, 301.

they sleep on newspapers or pieces of matting and sacking, and by day in St. James's Park, where they sun themselves in an enclosure known as the 'Bull Ring.'"[87] The accompanying illustration, "Our Homeless London Poor—St. James's Park at Mid-Day," makes an interesting companion to the image of the rioting mob published in the *Graphic* a year and a half earlier (fig. 4.3). On the surface, the two images seem quite different: the fierce energy of the mob in St. James's Street contrasts sharply with the almost corpselike forms of the sleepers in St. James's Park. Yet there is a spirit of defiance common to both illustrations—explicit in one, implicit in the other. The sleepers may be passive, but they have completely taken possession of the aristocratic park. The male figure at the very center of the image stares ahead with an easy assurance, as if daring the viewer to displace him. The text even refers to the people as "a large army," further suggesting the perceived aggression behind the act of public encampment.[88]

The presence of these assembled crowds of clearly disaffected individuals attracted the attention of socialist organizers, religious preachers, and charity workers alike. Throughout October and the first part of November 1887, socialist groups worked to mobilize the crowds, staging meetings in and marches from the square almost daily, much to the consternation of area property owners and police, who looked on these activities as, at best, a nuisance and, at worst, a prelude to the revolution. The "struggle for Trafalgar Square," as Donald Richter dubs it, describes the conflict that ensued between socialist-led demonstrators, who wanted to continue to use the square as a rallying place, and government authorities, who wanted to suppress such activity.[89] The struggle came to a crisis on November 8, 1887, when Police Commissioner Charles Warren (who had succeeded the disgraced Commissioner Henderson) banned public meetings in the square. The ban served as the impetus for a massive demonstration planned for November 13, in which socialists were joined by other radical organizations and Irish nationalists to support the right of free speech and of public meetings. The numerous contingent groups that planned to converge on Trafalgar Square that day were ultimately blocked by police and military forces in a series of sometimes-violent encounters that earned for the occasion the title of "Bloody Sunday." According to Richter, some two hundred people ended up in the hospital in connection with the skirmishes, although published sympathy for the demonstrators seems to have been limited to the *Pall Mall Gazette*. Even after this defeat for the socialists, the attempt to win the square for public meetings and the police repulse of such attempts continued through 1887 and 1888, becoming something of a routine; but a demonstration of the scale seen on Bloody Sunday was not repeated.

The true political import of the events in and around Trafalgar Square in 1886 and 1887 was subject to competing interpretations. On the one hand, we see the impulse to minimize the significance of the disturbances by attributing them to the residuum, cast as a troublesome but numerically insignificant segment of the London poor. For instance, in discussing the riots of February 1886, the *Saturday Review* claimed confidently that "the unemployed workmen had no share in them."[90] The *Review* was echoing the prevailing view, articulated by the *Times* (among others), that a clear distinction could and should be made between actual working men, who were "honestly assembled" in the square to hear what might be done in the way of employment, and "ruffians," who were bent solely on violence and destruction.[91] Similar distinctions were employed in discussing the meetings of the following year. The *Times* again was eager to dissociate the problem of unemployment from the protests against unemployment: "The distress of London is one thing, the meetings in Trafalgar-square another thing totally distinct."[92] In contrast, Reaney's article, titled "Outcast London" and appearing in December 1886, sees the politicization of the suffering poor as a very real, and worrisome, possibility. Reaney first characterizes the condition of the poor in terms that should be familiar: "[D]ull, awfully passive, and infinitely patient."[93] But he continues, "Things are undergoing a marvelous change. Socialism, physical-force Socialism, is amongst us. The red cap of Continental revolutionary thought is passing along like a spectre of scenes not a century old."[94] Although he greets the transformation with dread, Reaney nonetheless registers a change from passivity to mobilization in the attitude and behavior of the urban poor. Henry Hyndman, founder of the Social Democratic Federation, presents a similar diagnosis of the state of society in the *Contemporary Review* (July 1887), though with very different emotions. He too imagines the passivity of the poor as a defining characteristic—"the endless patience in terrible misery, the calm bearing up under almost unendurable suffering"; and he likewise locates this characteristic in the past.[95] In the present, he identifies a "new spirit . . . abroad among the workers" and seems to warn readers against ignoring such a potent new force: "Peaceful and law-abiding as they [the workers] are . . . they will not be patient for ever."[96]

Clearly it suited Hyndman's political purposes to insist on the awakening of a political consciousness among the working classes. That such a politicization was occurring at the end of the nineteenth century seems, however, doubtful. The Fabian socialists certainly did not believe that the recent agitation portended revolution. Commenting on the irrelevance of politics to most of the London poor, the Fabian Hubert Bland quipped, "The revolt of the empty stomach ends at the baker's shop."[97] And Bernard Shaw in an essay on the subject acknowledged regretfully that the proposed "militant organization of the working-class and general insurrection . . . proved impracticable."[98] Jones's work has largely confirmed Fabian opinion: he argues convincingly that the casual laborers of London were both too fragmented in their interests and too absorbed by immediate concerns to become deeply involved in any kind of organized political program. He concludes that "the most striking characteristic of the casual poor was neither their adherence to the left, nor yet their adherence to the right, but rather their rootless volatility."[99]

Yet the absence or presence of a political consciousness among the demonstrators did not ultimately affect the impact they made: for every good reason or for no good reason, the city's dispossessed were staking a claim on urban space. For some reformers and observers, this fact mattered more than either the motives or the affiliations or the moral character of the assembled crowds. Looking back on the riots of 1886 at the end of 1888, the Reverend Samuel Barnett, founder of the settlement house Toynbee Hall, writes in the *Nineteenth Century,* "Three years ago London was startled by the evidence of its great 'fluid population.' The unemployed, by crowds and riots, forced themselves into notice."[100] Salvation Army founder William Booth similarly highlights the role played by events of 1887 in making the London poor starkly visible: "The existence of these unfortunates was somewhat rudely forced upon the attention of Society in 1887, when Trafalgar Square became the camping ground of the Homeless Outcasts of London."[101] As both excerpts make clear, crowds of poverty-stricken individuals on the march, or simply out in the open, may be rude or startling, but they cannot be ignored. Whether sleeping in the park, listening to a speech in Trafalgar Square, casting a brick, or casting a vote, the London poor were making their presence felt as active sharers in public space and public life.

The incursion of the poor into West End space was, of course, alarming for all the reasons I have discussed, but the point I want to make here is that it also seemed to forecast a shift in the condition of the masses that could be interpreted positively. One did not have to be a socialist to feel that some sort of self-assertion—however feeble—on the part of outcast London seemed to point a way out of the stultifying narrative of failed social progress. We may be surprised to find this view expressed in Masterman's account of the London poor, *From the Abyss.* In many ways, Masterman's text reinscribes the poor as a degenerate race of inarticulate and dangerous creatures. Recalling the celebrations on Mafeking Night in 1900, when working-class crowds flooded the streets to celebrate the relief of an English garrison in the Boer War, Masterman paints a nightmarish picture of the residuum rioting in the West End: "Our streets have suddenly become congested with a weird and uncanny people. They have poured in as dense black masses from the eastern railways. . . . [T]hey have been hurried up in incredible number through tubes sunk in the bowels of the earth, emerging like rats from a drain, blinking in the sunshine.

They have surged through our streets, turbulent, cheerful, indifferent to our assumed proprietorship."[102] As in 1886 and 1887, the poor are once again seen as staking a claim on middle-class urban space, coming en masse from the East End into "our streets." The dehumanizing imagery is also familiar from earlier evocations of the residuum in representations of the housing crisis, although Masterman's suggestion of the anarchic energy and sheer magnitude of the crowd makes his representation that much more chilling.

But elsewhere Masterman displays a small degree of optimism about the future of these inhabitants of the abyss. In the midst of apparent stagnancy, he detects signs of motion and life: "A pool that looks stagnant and motionless is, in reality, subject to a continuous heavy and slow circulation."[103] The "circulation" referred to is literally the tendency of the poor to change residences frequently, to move from one tenement to the next, but this rather unremarkable fact becomes for Masterman a sign of some importance. In fact, he calls it "the most welcome feature of Abysmal life" because of what he believes it represents: "It exhibits, at least, a refusal placidly to acquiesce: a reaching out of the human spirit towards a life larger and less confined: a protest, however vague and uncontrolled, against a purely material satisfaction: a movement resistant to that stagnation which is the precursor of inevitable death."[104] The language—"protest," "refusal," "movement"—indicates that what Masterman discerns is an inchoate resistance on the part of the poor to the subhuman living conditions that have too long been their lot. The possibility opened up by this idea is the very liberating one that the poor might uplift themselves. Although only rarely imagined, this was certainly one way out of the impasse that late-century reformers had created for themselves and those they sought to help.

chapter 5

Intransigence and Limited Mobility

Competing Geographies in The Nether World

Look at a map of greater London, a map on which the town
proper shows as a dark, irregularly rounded patch against the
whiteness of suburban districts, and just on the northern
limit of the vast network of streets you will distinguish the
name of Crouch End.

And if life ever seemed a little too hard, if the image of the
past grew too mournfully persistent, she knew where to go
for consolation. Let us follow her, one Saturday afternoon
early in the year.

George Gissing, *The Nether World* (1889)

*B*y the 1880s, the recognition of the link between urban poverty and reform
had become inescapable. No longer could reformers and others ignore
the negative impact that urban improvements often had on the disempowered populace. As chapter 4 shows, this recognition and the growing
sense of disillusionment that accompanied it coalesced around the housing
reform movement of the 1870s and 1880s. The demolitions carried out for
the purpose of housing reform and the dispossession and overcrowding that
resulted highlighted the divergence between urban improvement and human
improvement—a divergence so great that even committed reformers began
to lose confidence and to look for new approaches. George Gissing's novel
The Nether World dramatizes this perception of the failure of reform. Informing

the novel at every level is the conviction that reforms of all kinds—from street building to charitable soup kitchens—routinely fail to improve the lives of the poor; indeed, both the aims and the achievements of reform are seen as debilitating and dehumanizing. But the novel is also significant for its precise representation of urban space and spatial processes, as well as its recognition of the way in which space is used by its inhabitants. By examining the spatial dimension of the novel, we can better understand its vision of reform.

On the one hand, the novel follows the critique of many contemporary reformers by implicating urban improvements—that is, large-scale spatial processes—in the suffering of the poor. On the other hand, the novel affords a very different way of looking at the relation between poverty and urban form through its representation of characters' idiosyncratic movements through the city streets. One of the notable characteristics of the novel is in fact its scrupulous attention to the precise routes that characters take when they move from one location to another. From this perspective, characters seem less like victims of a hostile and unyielding environment than autonomous subjects with unique ways of negotiating an often-challenging landscape. We can sum up the differences between the two ways of representing urban experience with the help of two phrases from the novel: "Look at a map of greater London" and "Let us follow her."[1] The geography of *The Nether World* is multivalent; it shows us the city both from above ("Look at a map") and at ground level ("Let us follow"). In doing so, the novel provides not only an objective critique that reproduces the prevailing disillusionment with reform but also an experiential view that suggests there may be limits to the critique. It shows us the suffering mass in the grip of powerful social and spatial forces, but it also shows us the individual racing home, running an errand, or plying a trade.

Realism, Reform, and the Novel

In a scene toward the end of *The Nether World,* Clem Peckover and Bob Hewett meet on the Thames Embankment, where Clem urges her former suitor to murder her husband. The location of the encounter at the river's edge reinforces the state of extremity to which both characters have been driven: Bob, as the head of a counterfeiting ring, is weakened and maddened by his entrapment in a life of criminality and the consciousness of his degradation; Clem,

who marries for a fortune that fails to materialize, is enraged by an unquench-
able lust for wealth and supremacy. Although the Embankment forms a natural viewing station, these characters quite literally have no prospect: the two
"kept . . . apart, looking sullenly at the ground" (331). Even the river, which
might be expected to provide some image of change or release, appears static,
impenetrable: "They both stared down at the water; it was full tide, and the
muddy surface looked almost solid" (331). Gissing may have felt a kind of
grim satisfaction when deciding to set this scene on the Embankment, for
what could be more appropriate than locating two murderous characters in
a public space that had become notorious as a haven for criminals and outcasts? But the choice of setting is also ironic when we consider that one of the
desired ends of the Embankment was the revitalization of an area recognized
for its social degradation. In the case of the Embankment, the expectations associated with improvement were subverted. Gissing understood this and
forcefully reminds us of the failure by using the site as the meeting place for
two of the novel's most cruel and forsaken characters. This scene and those
immediately following it thus serve as a succinct introduction to Gissing's famously pessimistic views about the value of improvement in relation to the
wasted lives of the urban poor.

Throughout the novel, Gissing represents the city as a place hostile to
human life. Urban experience in the netherworld might best be summed up
by the image of the baffled crowd, moving to and from work, struggling to
navigate the mud-soaked streets. What is significant about the novel's negative
vision, however, is that it places human suffering within the larger context of
urban projects—such as the Embankment, model industrial dwellings, and the
new Clerkenwell Road—that were explicitly designated metropolitan improvements. Far from alleviating the pressures of urban industrial life felt most
acutely by the poor, improvements, Gissing suggests, only intensify these pressures. In *The Nether World,* this insight is developed into a sustained critique of
spatial and social reform. The novel not only marks the futility of urban alterations to solve the real problems of the poor but also implicates these alterations
in the dehumanization of the city and its populace.

The implicit connection between a failed reform effort and human degradation comes into focus when we follow Bob's course after he leaves the
Embankment. Parting from Clem in tacit acceptance of her criminal propo-

sition, Bob begins a long and frantic, but ultimately circuitous, flight through the streets of central and northern London. In a state of desperation, with the guilt of both his past and his future crimes upon him, he seeks and finds a kind of oblivion in walking. He roams the City for hours until striking homeward to Merlin Place, stopping there briefly to beat his pathetic wife, Pennyloaf. From there, Bob heads north to Pentonville, King's Cross, Holloway, and finally Hornsey, some five miles away, before turning back to Islington and his own neighborhood, where he is shocked to overhear himself given up to the police by a fellow counterfeiter. The journey is remarkable not so much for the distance traveled, which is considerable, but for the lack of distance gained: Bob can escape neither his crime, nor his guilt, nor his place of origin. He is "goaded . . . along, faster, faster" (334), until he finally makes his way back into a Clerkenwell slum.

In describing a movement that ultimately goes nowhere in spatial terms, Gissing also describes a movement that is a decidedly downward one in social and biological terms. As the man rushes on, he seems to be devolving, to be sinking down the scale of human life. When describing Bob's fleeting abuse of Pennyloaf, Gissing notes that as he delivers the blows, he "utter[s] a strange sound, such as might come from some infuriate animal" (334). Bob's degradation is inscribed even more forcefully in the streets: he moves through them like a "stricken animal," until in his frenzy to escape the notice of the police, he rushes blindly into traffic and is struck down by a London cab (335). Suffering from this blow, wanted by the police, pelted by rain, Bob is reduced to seeking refuge with Pennyloaf's alcoholic mother in a squalid room in Shooter's Gardens, the most wretched slum in Clerkenwell. Having "let himself sink there," he rises no more: Bob is dead before the police can take him into custody (339). In relating Bob Hewett's history, Gissing draws on degenerationist ideas and imagery, particularly the image of the human residuum, that segment of the London poor that was considered unfit and beyond reclamation. At various points in the novel, Gissing challenges the idea of social progress by evoking the image of residuum, often in the context of some metropolitan improvement. We see this juxtaposition specifically in Gissing's representation of Bob Hewett's last day alive: the narrative of Hewett's decline, his journey into the abyss, is prefaced by the cultural narrative of failed reform embodied in the Embankment.

Gissing's cynical representation of the failure of reform has long troubled readers and critics. Many are understandably frustrated by the competing tendencies of his novels of working-class life, which on the one hand evoke appalling social conditions and on the other hand assert the absolute futility of reform. Whereas organized philanthropy is the particular target of *The Nether World*'s satire, seemingly every type of systematic reform is considered and found wanting in the novels—from socialism in *Demos* to popular education in *Thyrza*. Gissing seems to hold in equal disdain aid "from above" (middle-class intervention) and collective activity on the part of the working classes themselves. And often accompanying this refusal of reform is the question of whether the most degraded individuals even have the capacity to be reformed. The biological determinism that seems to underlie the representation of many of his characters obviously limits the possibility of individual change. In this context, David Grylls's definition of Gissing's novels as "anti-reformist" may sound like an understatement.[2]

Complicating this view are Gissing's own comments about his role as novelist just prior to writing *The Nether World,* as well as the responses of some contemporary reviewers. We know that Gissing wrote *The Nether World* quickly, from March to July 1888. This period of inspired production followed closely on the heels of a personal event, both distressing and liberating—the death of his estranged wife, Marianne Helen (Nell) Gissing. Gissing's relationship with Nell is a well-known part of the artist's biography.[3] The two met in Manchester, where Gissing was a student and Nell was a prostitute. In an idealistic attempt to save her from that life, Gissing (who was poor himself) gave her all his money and began stealing from his college classmates. Upon the discovery of this crime, Gissing was expelled, his promising future as a scholar was destroyed, and he moved temporarily to America. When Gissing returned to England, he and Nell reunited and eventually married, although their life together was very unhappy and tumultuous, largely because of Nell's chronic alcoholism. They ultimately separated, so that when Nell died in February 1888, it had been many years since Gissing had seen her. After years of contending with his wife's self-destructive and erratic behavior, Gissing must have felt a sense of relief upon her death. But he was also depressed by seeing the remnants of her sad and sordid life and, as he tells it, inspired by his memory of her to recommit to his work as a socially engaged writer. To his brother, a fellow novelist with whom he often discussed his craft, he wrote four days after Nell's death: "For me there is yet work to do, & this memory of wretchedness will be an impulse such as few men possess."[4] The resolution is elaborated in a diary entry made on March 1: "[A]s I stood beside that bed, I felt that my life henceforth had a firmer purpose. Henceforth I never cease to bear testimony against the accursed social order that brings about things of this kind."[5] Key here is Gissing's conviction that his writing has a social purpose and, moreover, that his art could serve as an effective medium for social protest. As we will see, this is not a view of his art that Gissing subscribed to with any consistency. Still, such statements articulated just weeks before Gissing began *The Nether World* should caution us against defining Gissing's relation to reform too monolithically.

Interestingly, some of the readers of the novel seem to have divined Gissing's privately expressed purpose. Chief among these was Frederick W. Farrar, archdeacon of Westminster, whose unconventional review of *The Nether World* in the *Contemporary Review* appeared in September 1889. In the piece, Farrar deliberately disregards the book's literary qualities and instead focuses entirely on its social significance, claiming somewhat paradoxically, "[T]his realism gives to it a far deeper significance than at all belongs to it as a novel."[6] He recommends the novel on the grounds of its realism, by which he means that it provides a "true," documentary picture of the degradation and horrors of poverty. Reading about such things can provide an important moral education, for they may stimulate sensitive middle-class readers to take up the cause of reform, to right society's great wrongs. A book like Gissing's, despite the fact that it "has little or nothing to impress upon us as to the nature of the remedy," can nevertheless "bring the careless, the indolent, the selfish, the luxurious face to face with problems which it will be impossible for Government or Society much longer to ignore."[7] Other reviewers, although not clerics, similarly stressed the novel's importance as an educational tool and, thus, as a vehicle for reform. The anonymous reviewer for the *Court Journal* recommends the book as one "to be read and read again," since it teaches about how life is really lived in the "terrible underworld of London."[8] The *Whitehall Review* praises it for the same reason: "Such books as this one do an infinitude of good."[9] And in the introduction to the Colonial Edition (1890) of *The Nether World,* the writer insists on the "deep significance" of the work "for all classes of Philanthropists."[10] Whether this particular recommendation was made in ignorance of the novel's extremely unflattering depictions of philanthropists or whether it was made in an effort to conciliate this group of potential readers is unclear. What is clear is that among at least some of its influential readers, *The Nether World* was received and recognized as "a novel 'with a purpose.'"[11]

Gissing, however, was understandably uncomfortable with the equation of his art with a sociological inquiry. In an article on Gissing published in the German periodical *Deutsche Presse* just a few months after the above reviews appeared (November 1889), Eduard Bertz addresses this very issue, insisting, "Gissing does not write to a thesis. . . . [H]e is, first and foremost an artist."[12] As a close friend and regular correspondent of Gissing's, Bertz was very much aware of the novelist's views of his art and in sympathy with his aims and achievements. Presumably Gissing was pleased to have Bertz emphasize his artistic integrity and, more specifically, to counter Archdeacon Farrar's interpretation of *The Nether World* as an important social, rather than literary, document. Referring explicitly to Farrar's review, Bertz states, "Gissing does not write with this purpose in mind; any effect his books may have in the direction of reform can be ascribed to his artistic realism."[13] The emphasis on "artistic" realism is important, suggesting as it does the difficulties involved in understanding realism, and even in using the term, in the last decades of the nineteenth century. One of the problems with the term was that it tended to imply an objectivity that obviated the need for artistry, as Aaron Matz has explained in his work on Gissing's vexed relation with realism: "Realism" to writers such as Gustave Flaubert and Thomas Hardy "implied something unimaginative and indeed insipid, the mere duplication of everyday life."[14] Hence, Bertz attempts to correct any such misperception by defining Gissing's realism as "artistic." In Gissing's own thoughts on the subject in "The Place of Realism in Fiction" (published in 1895 as part of a forum on the subject in the *Humanitarian*), he does not reject what he sees as the true aim of realism ("artistic sincerity in the portrayal of contemporary life"), but he does recognize the potential danger for the realist writer not just in being mistaken for a sociologist but in actually becoming one: "[N]ovels nowadays are not always written for the novel's sake, and fiction cries aloud as the mouthpiece of social reform."[15]

But for all Gissing's and Bertz's careful distinctions between art and social reform, the boundary refuses to remain definite. Later in the same article in which Bertz makes the case for Gissing's "artistic objectivity," he remarks on what can only be described as Gissing's strong social conscience—his hatred of injustice and his sense that "the rich and the powerful are to blame . . . for the degenerate condition of the poverty-stricken masses."[16] Bertz concludes the discussion of Gissing's social principles by returning to Farrar's point about Gissing's reformist fiction—this time with a difference: "Gissing lets the facts speak for themselves, and the facts speak eloquently. Farrar is quite right: this is the way to provoke conscience."[17] Gissing lets "the facts speak," but then his novels also "provoke conscience." The two phrases nicely capture the paradox at the heart of the discussion of Gissing's relation to reform. On the one hand, Gissing's novels are artistically pure, not written with a distinct social purpose or agenda; on the other hand, because they represent the sufferings of the poor with honesty and indignation, they can be highly effective at inspiring sympathy or even social action. The very title of Bertz's article suggests that he was aware of the paradox and sought to preserve it: "George Gissing: Ein Real-Idealist." Matz concludes that the term *idealistic realism* is probably the most satisfactory way to describe Gissing's work, encompassing as it does the competing ideas of artistic neutrality and a moral awareness that, nevertheless, refused allegiance "to a specific program or politics."[18]

Many of Gissing's critics, however, have been less willing to accept such an expansive definition, tending to label his work as either reformist (in the case of the contemporary reviewers we have considered) or bereft of social purpose —whether for good or for ill. This latter assumption has played a significant role in twentieth-century criticism. In his review essay "George Gissing" (1948), George Orwell contends that Gissing "had no very strong moral purpose. He had, of course, a deep loathing of the ugliness, emptiness, and cruelty of the society he lived in, but he was concerned to describe it rather than to change it."[19] For Orwell, the amoral quality of Gissing is surprisingly "a point in his favour," apparently because it allows him the objectivity and freedom of the artist.[20] Here again we see the association of a scientific realism with an art divorced from politics. Turning to the tradition of Marxist criticism, however, this perception of Gissing's disinterest in—or worse, refusal of—social change is regarded as a serious shortcoming. According to Stephen Arata, Georg Lukács's negative assessment of the late-Victorian novel in general is especially applicable to Gissing.[21] Whereas in Lukács's formulation, the classic realist novel performs the crucial social function of "criticiz[ing] life" and thereby paving the way for meaningful political change, the naturalist novel reifies the existing social order in its staunch adherence to empiricism.[22] The reification that Lukács attributes to the naturalist novel, Frederic Jameson associates with all realistic representation, including that of Gissing, since it has a narrative and aesthetic "stake in the status quo."[23] In his discussion of *The Nether World*, Jameson suggests that Gissing's introduction of the philanthropic plot (Snowden's plan to make the feeble Jane the dispenser of aid among the poor) has the potential to destabilize the narrative for the very reason that it calls into question the inevitability and inevitable rightness of the status quo. But the utopian possibilities of *The Nether World* are ultimately ridiculed and neutralized, so that in the end we are left with the politically conservative "indicative mode."[24] In their studies of Gissing, both John Goode and Adrian Poole point to the limitations of Gissing's representations of the class structure and working-class experience, respectively, representations that again tend to reify the existing social order.[25] Clearly we have a strand of Gissing criticism that, whatever else it argues, emphasizes the refusal of his work to take seriously the possibility of social change.[26]

When taking up this issue, however, we need to pay close attention to the discourse of reform as it was articulated in the 1880s. The fact that several of *The Nether World*'s reviewers interpreted the novel as a reformist text seems significant. Whatever we may think of this assessment, it indicates how closely aligned Gissing's work appeared to be with what reformers and journalists were saying about urban poverty at the time, particularly in the context of the housing crisis. Both the novelist and reformers shared an understanding of the limitations of environmental alterations when applied to social problems; both understood that reform could and often did fail the poor. We see evidence for this shared perception when we compare the geography of Clerkenwell as it was represented and produced by reformers in the 1870s and 1880s, and as it is imagined in Gissing's novel.

The Geography of Poverty

It is fitting that a novel interested in the relation between poverty and reform should be set in Clerkenwell in the early 1880s. For this area experienced a dramatic shift in its spatial and social topography during the second half of the nineteenth century, largely as a result of urban development schemes vigorously pursued in both the City of London and Clerkenwell itself. As more and more working-class housing was razed to make way for warehouses and office blocks, railways, and street improvements, the evicted residents migrated into neighboring areas such as Clerkenwell so that they could still live near their workplaces. John Hollingshead, describing the character of Clerkenwell in *Ragged London in 1861,* estimated that two-thirds of the population worked in the City; the district was "filled with labourers, artizans, needlewomen, and girls employed in many fancy trades, and the capital and enterprise of the city of London are largely responsible for them all."[27] The influx of population brought about changes in the use of existing space and in the class structure of the neighborhood. Houses that had previously been occupied by independent middle-class families were carved out into tenements that often housed as many families as there were rooms. The vicar of St. Peter's Clerkenwell witnessed the transformation during his tenure in the neighborhood and described it before the Royal Commission on the Housing of the Working Classes: "I know that not in one case, but in a hundred cases where a family had, when I first came to the parish, four, six, or eight rooms, they now reside in the suburbs . . . and meanwhile every room in the house is occupied by tenants."[28] The Reverend William Dawson confirmed the trend in his 1885 history of the parish of St. John's Clerkenwell, noting that most of the tradesmen, lawyers, and wealthy watchmakers and jewelers had given way to a new class of residents—dockworkers, bricklayers, charwomen, costermongers, and artificial-flower makers.[29] Once an area of middle-class respectability, Clerkenwell had been reduced by 1861 to one of those "neighborhoods that have 'seen better days.'"[30]

A closer look at a representation of Clerkenwell from the *Builder* reveals, in fact, a long-standing pattern—a geography defined by continued improvements and persistent overcrowding, seemingly bound in a reflexive relationship. In 1853, the *Builder* ran a feature on the homes of the London poor north of the City and skirting the valley of the Fleet River.[31] Directing attention first to the "dense masses of buildings thickly populated" east of Farringdon Road, the article leads the reader into the midst of this warren of courts and alleys by way of Frying Pan Alley.[32] The entrance to this alley measures, we are told, two feet and six inches wide, and the alley runs for twenty feet before turning off into other courts and alleys. Conveying equally the cramped

nature of the surroundings and their fatal influence on inhabitants is the resonant remark that "there would not be room to get a full-sized coffin out of this
court without turning it on its edge."[33] The rest of the article and its accompanying illustration, titled "A Clerkenwell Interior," turn to the living quarters
of the local population (fig. 5.1). Although we are told that "these dilapidated
buildings were inhabited . . . by human beings," the scene as it is depicted
does little to humanize these inhabitants: the room is dark and bare of furni-
ture, the women and children are "dirty and ill-clad," and vials of holy water
hang from the ceiling, suggesting the lodgers' Irish Catholic affiliation.[34] While
on the left side of the frame a woman sorts her findings of "bones, pieces of
iron, [and] cinders" and on the right a small group huddles around an empty
grate, toward the middle of the frame an unattended infant sprawls across
the floor, a fit symbol of the ruin and neglect into which the housing of the
poor has fallen.[35] Of particular importance here is the context of this representation. Before describing the overcrowding in Clerkenwell, the article
refers to an earlier improvement scheme—the northern extension of Farringdon Street in the 1840s, which destroyed much of the slum housing of the
notorious Saffron Hill neighborhood. According to the *Times,* sixteen hundred
houses were taken down to build this street, and an estimated population of
sixteen thousand was subsequently displaced.[36] The *Builder* links this event to
conditions in Clerkenwell in the 1850s: "The buildings have been swept away,
and those who inhabited them have been *driven to equally unfit lodgings in other
districts.*"[37] Thus, the article ties the unfit lodgings of the Irish women in Clerkenwell to clearances executed ten years earlier in the name of improvement.

Awareness of the cost to the local population did not slow the march of improvement through Clerkenwell. Charting the dramatic changes to his parish
occurring within recent memory, the Reverend Dawson notes, in addition
to the extension of Farringdon Street in the 1840s, the opening of Farringdon
Station and the Metropolitan Railway in 1863, which "swept away more
houses . . . forming in this parish a vast deep trench, from whose murky recesses, the screaming whistle and the rolling thunder of the train, seem, as the
shrieks and groans of the lost souls in the lowest circle of Dante's Inferno."[38]
An alteration he regarded more positively was the construction of Clerkenwell Road, a project executed by the Metropolitan Board of Works under the
authority of the 1872 Metropolitan Street Improvements Act. The line of the

5.1. The unsanitary living conditions depicted are linked to urban improvement—the extension of Farringdon Street in the 1840s. "A Clerkenwell Interior," *Builder,* 12 March 1853, 161.

new street ran through Clerkenwell along an east-west axis and, together with the widened Theobald's Road, linked Old Street in the east with Oxford Street in the west. For Dawson, the street provided a welcome breath of fresh air (quite literally): "[T]he great new street opens up all the Parish to the bracing blast of dry east wind, and to the fresh breezes of the west, pregnant with cleansing rain-storms."[39] The language of purification here tells us everything we need to know about the kind of property taken out by the new street: like so many other Victorian improvements, this one destroyed its share of working-class housing. In this instance, among the targeted areas was the one that the *Builder* had singled out in 1853—the closely built courts and alleys located off of Turnmill Street, including Frying Pan Alley (fig. 5.2). Looking at the plan for the Clerkenwell Road, we see that the line of the new street passes right through the densely built space bounded by Turnmill Street and Red Lion Street: here are Lamb Court, Bit Alley, Frying Pan Alley, and Rose Alley. In *Ragged London,* Hollingshead had called Frying Pan Alley "a rampant court" and put forth his view that the reform of such a court was "beyond the reach of anything, except an earthquake or a new railway, and even then

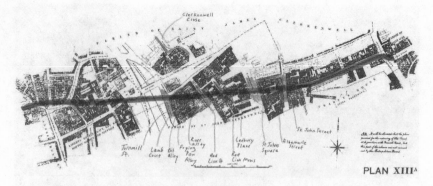

PLAN XIII^A

5.2. The line of the new Clerkenwell Road was designed to break up the slums of Clerkenwell, especially those courts and alleys east of Turnmill Street. It also passed through and "disfigured" St. John's Square. "Metropolitan Street Improvements—Old Street towards New Oxford Street," in *History of London Street Improvements, 1855–1897* by Percy J. Edwards (London: London County Council, 1898), plan 13a, labels added by author.

the inhabitants would only be pushed somewhere else."[40] Hollingshead was right on both counts: an act of destruction did ultimately "reform" the habitations of Frying Pan Alley, and the residents displaced by the new street did have but one choice—to crowd into equally unfit lodgings nearby.

Whereas the courts off of Turnmill Street were incidental casualties of improvement, the site of Pear Tree Court just to the north was specifically targeted for destruction under the Cross Act around the same time. Following the procedure established under the act, Clerkenwell's Medical Officer of Health John Griffith made a representation to the Metropolitan Board of Works at the end of 1876, requesting that a group of buildings "unfit for habitation" be removed.[41] The site to be cleared comprised all of Pear Tree Court, Yates's Rents, and Cromwell Place, along with some of the houses of Waterloo Place and Clerkenwell Close (fig. 5.3). In the Parliamentary inquiry preparatory to approving the scheme, the area's unfitness is established by virtue of the medical and moral risks it posed. According to Griffith, partly because of the "depressing" environment and partly because they are "free from the public eye," the inhabitants of the court "take their drops."[42] More seriously, the area posed a risk to the neighborhood at large because it was a "plague spot" where the death rate was "nearly double that which prevails over the whole Parish."[43]

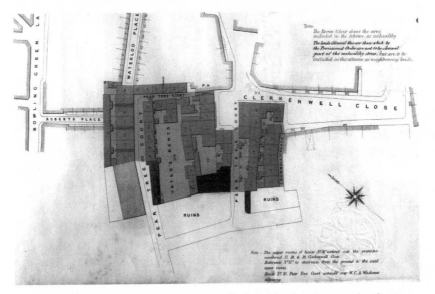

5.3. Houses deemed unfit for habitation and scheduled for demolition under the Cross Act. Pear Tree Court Improvement Scheme, 1877, papers of the Metropolitan Board of Works, shelf mark 1847, London Metropolitan Archives. Reproduced by permission from City of London, London Metropolitan Archives.

Asked to comment on the health of the inhabitants, the district relieving officer Henry James Stranack offered this medically vague but emotionally resonant assessment: "Many of them you cannot tell their appearance because they are so filthy dirty. You cannot tell whether they are healthy or not."[44] In keeping with the mandate of the Cross Act, the cleared Pear Tree Court site was to be used for rehousing working people displaced by improvements. The Board of Works finally sold it and the adjacent Coppice Row site to the Peabody Trust in 1879, after the usual difficulty of finding a buyer willing to build working-class housing, and a block of Peabody Buildings, still remaining on the site, was completed in 1883.[45] But six years had passed since Pear Tree Court had been destroyed, and its four-hundred-plus residents had already been sent someplace else.[46]

We should not be surprised, then, that Clerkenwell received its share of critical scrutiny when overcrowding became an issue of national importance in the 1880s. In fact, when the Royal Commission on the Housing of the

Working Classes was convened, the commissioners selected Clerkenwell and its environs (the area between, roughly, Euston Road and Holborn) for a more focused investigation. Their report traces the problem of overcrowding in the area to demolition, mentioning specifically the Gray's Inn Road improvement (in progress at the time) and the Pear Tree Court scheme: "In St. Luke's the district has never yet recovered [from] the pressure which was caused by the pulling down for the building of what is known locally as Peabody Town."[47] Elsewhere within the record of evidence taken by the commission, one examiner posits that overcrowding in Clerkenwell has "increased concurrently with the destruction of . . . Frying Pan Alley, Turnmill Street, Ledbury Lane, Pear Tree Court, and others."[48] The pattern of the "shifting slum" is unmistakable. In 1853, the courts behind Turnmill Street had been denounced as uninhabitable; thirty years later, their destruction was linked to the deplorable overcrowding in the streets and courts above Wilmington Square, an area identified by the Reverend Alfred Fryer of St. Philip's Clerkenwell as the worst part of the parish.[49]

Gissing locates *The Nether World* in the midst of this overtaxed space. The geography of the novel is marked not only by appalling slums and overcrowded tenement housing but also by new streets, model dwellings, railway lines, and other signs of vigorous improvement. It is the same geography that had been defined by Hollingshead, by the Royal Commission on the Housing of the Working Classes, and in the *Builder*. And although the novel does not posit a causal relationship between improvement and overcrowding, it does evoke a world where urban alterations and material and spiritual destitution seem inevitably to coexist.

A surprising number of recent metropolitan improvements in and around Clerkenwell appear in the novel: the Thames Embankment, the Holborn Viaduct, Clerkenwell Road, and the Farringdon Road Buildings. These latter two sites seem to represent for Gissing everything that is wrong with the current economic, social, and aesthetic conditions. He maligns the new Clerkenwell Road in the context of a fond reverie on the ancient precinct of St. John's Priory. The road, in addition to taking out the squalid courts behind Turnmill Street, cut through and disfigured St. John's Square; however, St. John's Gate was left standing, "a survival from a buried world" (51) (fig. 5.4). For Gissing, the medieval gate conjures the image of a community bound together by its

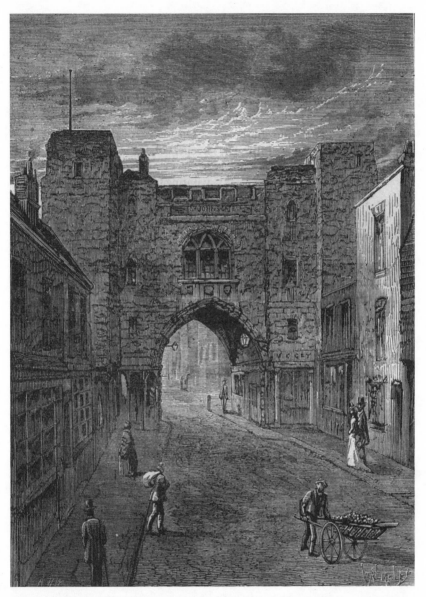

5.4. Clerkenwell Road broke up St. John's Square, but the medieval gate was allowed to remain. Engraving by John Walmsley, "St. John's Gate, Clerkenwell," in *Old and New London* by Walter Thornbury, 6 vols. (London: Cassell, Petter, and Galpin, [1872–78]), 2:318.

spiritual ideals, while the new road and the modern buildings around it reflect the triumph of commercial values over those ideals. As the narrator imagines it, the gate looks "depressed, ashamed, tainted" in its new context, "packed in among buildings which suggest nothing but the sordid struggle for existence" (51). The presence of the gate at all seems a strange anomaly and only throws into relief the banality of contemporary life: "The wonder is that it has not been swept away, in obedience to the great law of traffic and the spirit of the time" (51).

The Farringdon Buildings similarly horrify Gissing because of their stark utilitarian character. Erected by the Metropolitan Association for Improving the Dwellings of the Industrious Classes in 1874, this model dwelling was typical of those provided by semiphilanthropic housing societies of the period: a multistoried housing block divided into flats of two or three rooms.[50] This arrangement—housing people in flats, as opposed to detached or semidetached dwellings—derived chiefly from economic concerns: the dwelling companies certainly wanted to provide accommodation for as many people as possible, but they also recognized that by maximizing the number of tenants at a given site, they had a better chance of receiving a return on their investment. Economic pressures also influenced the dull, monotonous character of the architecture. The model housing blocks were widely felt to have an impersonal, institutional appearance, more suggestive of a workhouse or barrack than of a home, and Gissing assails the Farringdon Buildings on precisely these grounds: "What terrible barracks, those Farringdon Road Buildings!" (274). He goes on to describe the "vast, sheer walls, unbroken by even an attempt at ornament" and the "row upon row of windows in the mud-coloured surface" (274). To some degree, we hear in these criticisms the voice of Gissing the aesthete, whose sensibilities are assaulted by the ugliness of the modern industrial world.[51] Yet, as the narrator of *The Nether World* insists, everyone's life—not just the life of the privileged observer—is made worse by improvements conducted in accordance with "the great law of traffic and the spirit of the time." The real horror of the Farringdon Buildings lies in their distorting effect on the people who live in them. The unrelieved expanse of brick and countless rows of identical windows literally depress the individual and "crush . . . the spirit" (274). Clara Hewett is even tempted to commit suicide by throwing herself out the window and down the central stairwell, an act that, as Gissing suggests, would not have been extraordinary: "Had not this place tempted other people before now?" (275). Gissing's criticism is significant because it traces urban improvement back to economic imperatives and commercial values prevailing in the capital; moreover, it implicates improvement schemes in the mental and bodily suffering of the poor.

This latter implication emerges more clearly in the representation of the overcrowded dwellings of the netherworld, specifically the Peckovers' tenement house in Clerkenwell Close and the slum property called Shooter's Gardens. The novel opens at the tenement house in Clerkenwell Close, where we find several key groups of characters living together—Mrs. Peckover and her daughter (Clem), the Hewett family, and the unlikely heroine Jane Snowden. The tenement is representative of houses in the area: once a single-family home, it has become the lodging for at least thirteen people from several families. The Hewett family alone is made up of eight members occupying only three rooms: Mr. and Mrs. Hewett sleep with the baby in one room, three children and the eldest daughter (Clara) sleep in another, and the eldest son (Bob) shares a separate room with an unrelated inmate. Using even this small area of house space, however, was considered unusual, according to Gissing: "This was great extravagance, obviously; other people would have made two rooms sufficient for all, and many such families would have put up with one" (21). The decrease in available house space was, as we have seen, characteristic of the changes occurring in Clerkenwell after the 1850s and was usually linked to nearby improvements. Gissing's choice of Clerkenwell Close, in particular, for the setting of his fictional tenement could not have been more appropriate, since this street directly abutted Pear Tree Court and Coppice Row, sites cleared by the Board of Works in the 1870s. We know that these clearances put additional pressure on the population and housing of the Close.

Even more crowded are the tenement houses located on the slum property Shooter's Gardens (the exact location of which Gissing leaves unspecified). Whereas the Hewetts cling desperately to three rooms, the families of the Gardens accept one as a matter of course. Gissing describes the living arrangements of the house in which the Candy family lives, portraying it as typical of the houses in the slum: "It contained in all seven rooms, and each room was the home of a family; under the roof slept twenty-five persons, men, women, and children; the lowest rent paid by one of these domestic groups was four-and-sixpence" (249). The restrained, reportorial style of the description, as well as its substance, recalls accounts of overcrowding in Clerkenwell gathered by the Royal Commission on the Housing of the Working Classes. The physical layout of the slum also corresponds to the definition of the slum adopted in housing reform legislation. Shooter's Gardens is a closely built area, penetrated by a low archway and winding alley, and thus cut off from public intercourse. Because of its inaccessibility, it serves as a harbor for filth and noxious air, as well as for immoral and criminal activity. Slums such as Shooter's Gardens were seen as perfect candidates for demolition and clearance because of their structural deficiencies, so it is perhaps not surprising that Gissing projects just such a future for his fictional slum. In what must surely be an implicit indictment of current housing reform policy, Gissing explains that Shooter's Gardens has been targeted for improvement: "This winter was the last the Shooter's Gardens was destined to know. . . . [I]n the spring there would come a wholesale demolition, and model-lodgings would thereafter occupy the site" (248). What Gissing describes here is the process of clearance and rebuilding authorized by the Cross Act. But he must have advanced this promise of renewal with a full sense of its irony, for the problems associated with demolition, and with the Cross Act in particular, were too well understood for them to have escaped either Gissing's or his audience's notice. Slums such as Shooter's Gardens might be destroyed, but what of their inhabitants? Unsuited for residence in the anticipated model lodgings by virtue of their occupations (including rag picking) and habits (including drinking and brawling), they would have been left to crowd into neighboring tenements that would, in turn, become new slums. Gissing also suggests the difficulty, if not impossibility, of trying to control human behavior by means of environmental intervention: most of the slum-dwellers, Gissing explains, preferred a home in the Gardens "to that offered them in a block of model lodgings . . . [for] here was independence, that is to say, the liberty to be as vile as they pleased" (74). The possible benefits of reform seem even more doubtful when we recall Gissing's disparaging representation of the Farringdon Buildings. The dreary model dwellings appear every bit as demoralizing—and dehumanizing—as the slums. For if we could see behind the forbidding walls of the new building, we would find there a "weltering mass of human weariness, of bestiality, of unmerited dolour, of hopeless hope, of crushed surrender" (274). Like the slums that it replaces, this "improved" housing contributes to the human degradation that so thoroughly defines the netherworld.

Of course, Gissing is less interested in tracing the causes of overcrowding than in dramatizing its effects on the impoverished inhabitants. The demonstration is far from consolatory: in *The Nether World*, the severe limitation of resources endemic to a life of poverty makes human life seem superfluous. Housing in Clerkenwell is in short supply, as are employment and its fruits of food, fuel, and clothing. Coupled with these shortages, however, is the ceaseless fecundity of human life: work may be scarce, but there is always another mouth to feed. The idea of human superfluity was part of the larger discourse of urban degeneration, as I discuss in earlier chapters. That stratum of the poor labeled the residuum was deemed superfluous by virtue of its threatening abundance and its apparent physical and moral worthlessness. In *The Nether World,* Gissing takes the idea of human superfluity or excess to its familiar, but deeply disturbing, end: the equation of people with excrement.

The problem of superfluity is embodied in the Hewetts, whom Gissing explicitly designates "A Superfluous Family" in the chapter introducing their domestic life. The family's superfluity is determined, on the one hand, by John Hewett's inability to find work in London's flooded casual labor market: the aging Hewett's skill and sinew are superfluous when, in his words, "there's twice too many of us for the work that's to be done" (26). On the other hand, the family's superfluity is determined by its unchecked fertility: in addition to two adult children, Hewett and his wife are responsible for three young children and an infant. Although Hewett is able to respond to his young children with some degree of affection, he remains indifferent to the baby, who must seem to him a cruel redundancy: "[H]e stepped to the bed and looked at his latest born. The baby was moaning feebly; he spoke no word to it" (20). Hewett's eldest son, Bob Hewett, expresses a more callous view of his own paternity, but one that is nonetheless representative of attitudes in the netherworld: "The infants were a nuisance; no one desired their coming, and the older they grew the more expensive they were" (212). The sheer number of children crowded in wretched rooms and spilling out into the streets of Clerkenwell conveys the sense of a horrifying superfluity. But, as Gissing suggests, just as troubling as the excessive procreation of the inhabitants is the idea of a diseased fertility, of unhealthy human beings producing ever-weaker offspring.[52] Instead of robust, healthy babies, the miserable people of the netherworld produce distortions of humankind: "[B]ald, red-eyed, doughy-limbed abortions in every stage of babyhood, hapless spawn of diseased humanity" (130). The description is dehumanizing in the extreme: like "swarm," which Gissing frequently associates with children in the novel, "spawn" suggests the animalistic character of the population; and the phrase "doughy-limbed abortions" indicates quite literally that these beings have not and never will achieve full humanity.

Reinforcing this dehumanization, Gissing invokes images of actual refuse to describe both the netherworld and its inhabitants. Indeed, the novel's epigraph encourages us to equate its subject matter with waste matter: Gissing implicitly likens his literary representation to "La peinture d'un fumier," the painting of a dung heap.[53] While the dung heap serves to define the squalid physical environment of the netherworld, it serves also to define the population that lives there: as sanitary discourse insisted, it is rarely possible to live amidst filth and receive no taint. The convergence of human beings and habitat in a shared atmosphere of filth finds its fullest expression in those scenes describing Shooter's Gardens. The very name of the slum suggests the site's original function as a dust or manure yard, a place where refuse was "shot." In its present incarnation, the slum harbors a kind of human detritus, seemingly closer to the condition of decaying vegetable matter than to that of fully individuated human beings. Almost indistinguishable from their surroundings, where "the walls st[and] in a perpetual black sweat," are the "beings" who live in the Gardens and appear "soaked with grimy moisture, puffed into distortions, hung about with rotting garments" (248).

Here we have the answer to the question of what makes the tone and vision of *The Nether World* so bleak: it is these images of a waste population combined with Gissing's evocation of an urban structure that is responsive to the laws of traffic and commerce but not to human suffering and deprivation. Together these aspects convey the idea of stagnation, of stasis, that is thematically central to the novel and that is so vividly expressed in the novel's metaphor of the netherworld as Dante-esque hell—an equation made explicit by the minor character Mad Jack when he addresses the tenants of Shooter's Gardens: "This life you are now leading is that of the damned; this place to which you are confined is Hell! There is no escape for you" (345). We find a more sophisticated —and for our purposes more significant—articulation of the conditions defining life in the netherworld in a passage describing the view of the city from the vantage of the Farringdon Buildings. Through the eyes of Clara Hewett, Gissing directs the reader's gaze southward across Clerkenwell and the City and down into the streets below. We see first St. Paul's at a distance, then Newgate, Smithfield, and Bartholomew's Hospital. Nearer still is the "tract of modern deformity, cleft by a gulf of railway, which spreads between Clerkenwell Road and Charterhouse Street" (280). But just below Clara's window is a sight more distressing still: "[H]uman beings, reduced to their due paltriness seem[ing] to toil in exasperation along the strips of pavement, bound on errands, which were a mockery, driven automaton-like by forces they neither understood nor could resist" (280). Here are human beings in all their insignificance buffeted about by implacable and incomprehensible forces that, in the final phrase of the novel, Gissing terms "those brute forces of society which fill with wreck the abysses of the nether world" (392). Rarely are the characters themselves afforded such an expansive, generalized perspective on urban life, but the perspective is one that Gissing reproduces several times in the novel, always as a vehicle for withering social critique.

The passage thus allows us to sum up some of the key features of the novel's geographic imagination. First, by locating the image of human toil and suffering within the carefully defined urban landscape, Gissing makes the point that oppressive social forces exert themselves spatially. It is no accident that our view of the dehumanized individual encompasses also the church, prison, market, hospital, and railway—architectural embodiments of institutional power. The built environment oppresses the inhabitants of the netherworld in a very real way because the interests of the powerful are expressed and reproduced through the environment, through physical space. The second point is that this vision of London—of the human swarm caught in the grip of a mechanistic urban order—is the vision we are most likely to associate with *The Nether World*. Gissing comes back again and again in the novel to the view of the downtrodden from "above," that is, from a vantage that is both physically elevated and intellectually or morally superior. Like Clara looking out from the Farringdon Buildings, Michael Snowdon and his granddaughter Jane, for instance, look down on the "desolate tracts" of the East End from the window of a train. The train, that preeminent symbol of modernity, travels "across miles of a city of the damned" and "*above* streets swarming with a nameless populace" (164; emphasis added). John Goode has considered this distanced, objectifying vision of the city as characteristic of Gissing's representation of London: it is the city as "biological phenomenon," as "fate."[54] Interestingly, Goode draws a connection between Gissing's perspective on the city and that of Charles Booth, who conducted the most significant study of poverty and its spatial distribution in the 1880s. Relying on a team of investigators and using data provided by the London School Board, Booth produced a topographic survey of the metropolis that displayed street by street the economic conditions of the inhabitants.[55] According to Goode, the "extreme empiricism" of Booth's approach tended to produce a vision of the city and its inhabitants similar to Gissing's, that is, a city of stasis, locked into an unyielding and apparently natural spatial and social structure.[56] The revealing connection between Booth and Gissing leads to a third point, a point made clear in the preceding pages: Gissing's representation of Clerkenwell evokes the geography of poverty as it was being defined—and in some cases created—by social reformers in the 1880s. In this respect, *The Nether World* appears less marginal to, or in ironic relation to, the late-century discourse of reform than very much in tune with this discourse.

The City Humanized

Nevertheless, while we must recognize the determinist strain in Gissing's representation of city life, we must also guard against defining Gissing's vision solely in these terms. For Gissing provides another, very different perspective on life in the netherworld, one that both complements the first and contributes to the complexity of the novel's geographic imagination. In the novel, Gissing also represents the city on a human scale, as it is experienced by the characters who inhabit and move through it. In other words, Gissing affords a view of the lived city, defined by what Yi-Fu Tuan calls "the daily patterns of work and play."[57] Tuan's theory of urban development and perception is useful for understanding Gissing's representation of the city; for while Tuan explains that cities are shaped predominantly by large-scale, organized interventions, he also recognizes the very limited but significant role that the mundane activities of ordinary citizens play in shaping the life of the city.

We can begin to appreciate Gissing's multivalent conception of the geography of poverty by looking at the way in which individual characters use and respond to urban space. The first general feature to note is Gissing's emphasis on the characters' movements through the city: as we have already seen, Gissing often takes great pains to specify the precise route a character takes. That characters in *The Nether World* move about from place to place is an obvious point but one worth reflecting on, given the emphasis on human stasis in much of the contemporary literature of urban exploration and in the novel itself. In journalistic exposés and Parliamentary reports, it is the intrepid investigator who is most likely to move through the streets of poverty, while the poor are imagined to be crowded together in some bare room or back court. Recall the illustration of "A Clerkenwell Interior" in the *Builder,* in which the inhabitants are huddled together in small groups like primitive cave-dwellers. Gissing likewise shows us poverty-stricken people prostrate in their desolate rooms, hunched over empty grates, and sprawled on staircases, but he also shows us characters in motion as they run errands, go to work, or meet friends. In this way, the novel recognizes the poor as actors in the urban environment. Characters may not be altogether exempt from the pressures of urbanization, but they do have some room to maneuver. David Trotter also has sought to highlight this middle ground between freedom and imprisonment in which Gissing's characters seem to operate, arguing, "There is no way out of the nether world. But there are ways out within it."[58] For Trotter, this qualified "way out" has to do with several of the characters' successful attempts to gain independence and self-respect within the confines of a working-class identity and working-class city. The "way out" that I identify has to do with the imaginative possibilities of the city, as well as the possibilities it affords for human connection and mutual support.

As an illustration of the former point, urban space in the netherworld is often invested with deeply personal meanings. How a character perceives or interacts with the environment may have more to do with the thoughts and feelings of that individual in the moment than with any of the prescribed uses and meanings of a given space. For instance, what brings Michael Snowdon to Clerkenwell Close at the novel's opening is the search for his granddaughter

Jane; however, his hesitating gait reveals that his mind is divided between his search in the present and memories of his past: he "walked slowly across Clerkenwell Green, and by the graveyard of St. James's Church stood for a moment looking about him" (2). Snowdon's explicit purpose is to inquire in the neighborhood for Jane, and he does just that; but he also pauses by the graveyard and pauses again by the prison, absorbed in bitter thoughts of past sufferings and continued injustices. No other character could walk through the heart of Clerkenwell with these same thoughts and in this same way.

We see this very personal response to space in the scenes that show Sidney Kirkwood meditating on St. John's Gate. We recall that the narrator comments on the anomaly of the gate's presence, given the fact that so much of Clerkenwell's medieval fabric has been destroyed in the name of modernization. But the narrator goes on to explain that "St. John's Arch had a place in Sidney Kirkwood's earliest memories," associated as it is with the stories his father told him when a boy about the history of Clerkenwell (51). As an adult, Sidney has the arch often before him because he can see it from the window of the jewelry workshop where he is employed, and its "grey battlements" inevitably take him back to his boyhood, when his father not only told him stories but also encouraged his artistic talents. Gissing does not provide too many details about the father and son's life together, but he tells us enough to suggest that the father nourished interests and aspirations in his son beyond the merely material. The arch quite naturally connects Sidney to this aspect of his past because it, too, represents a world imagined to be very different from the nineteenth-century world of industry and commerce, labor and capital, speed and efficiency. The arch, just by the fact of its existence, has the power to take the adult Sidney momentarily out of the present world. On a morning at work that is like many others, for instance, he sees it and is transported: "The glimpse before him . . . aided the revival of old impressions; his hand ceased from its mechanical activity, and he was absorbed in a waking dream" (90). The suspension of "mechanical activity," though fleeting, is significant; although it is only for a moment, Sidney is able to escape his monotonous labor through reverie. As in the case of Snowdon, Sidney's relationship with St. John's Gate is deeply personal; the associations could be his alone. And in both situations the interaction between cityscape and urban inhabitant results not in feelings of entrapment but in a qualified transcendence.

Gissing's city affords other possibilities for relief—specifically, the relief that can come from human connection and sympathy. Many times throughout the novel we see characters wending their way through the city streets not to escape some new indignity or a malevolent pursuer but to reach another human being who can provide words of encouragement and comfort. This is true of Jane Snowdon's errand to call Sidney from his workshop and bring him back to the tenement house in Clerkenwell Close. At this early point in the novel, Jane is still a downtrodden servant running errands and doing chores for her relentless mistresses the Peckovers. On such errands, "it was her custom . . . to run till she could run no longer, then to hasten along panting until breath and strength were recovered" (11). She runs so fast, we are told, in a usually fruitless effort to avoid the Peckovers' criticism and abuse. There is, however, "another reason why she sped eagerly on her present mission" (12). The reason is her sheer eagerness to reach Sidney, who "was one of the very few persons who had ever treated her with human kindness" (12). Sidney's sympathy and the kind words he invariably offers Jane afford her a respite from an emotionally and physically hostile environment. Indeed, in this particular instance, the relief that Sidney's words provide is tangible and bodily: although it is a bitterly cold and rainy evening, his "old tone of kindness . . . entered into [Jane's] blood and warmed it!" (13). The scene is pathetic, but for all Jane's weakness she gets what she so desperately wants. She is able to use the city to her advantage and to fulfill her desire for sympathy, to a small degree, by walking.

The city can appear as a hostile force, intent on humiliating its weakest victims, or it can provide the possibility of blessed relief. This ambiguity is even more dramatically realized in the case of Pennyloaf Candy, who develops a close attachment to Jane over the course of the novel. On what turns out to be her darkest day, Pennyloaf takes her sick child to the hospital. The weather always makes travel more arduous for the inhabitants of the netherworld, and when Pennyloaf sets out, it is windy and raining heavily. Pennyloaf suffers quietly, as the small miseries and indignities of her situation continue to multiply: "She had to stand for a long time at a street-corner before an omnibus came; the water soaked into her leaky shoes, but that didn't matter; it was the child on whose account she was anxious. Having reached her destination, she sat for a long time waiting her turn among the numerous out-patients" (267).

Before she can even see a doctor, however, the child dies. At this point, the nearly defeated Pennyloaf seeks relief in a meeting with Jane, who has always had the ability to soothe and comfort her, and she makes her way to Hanover Street north of the City Road in a dazed state. Despite Pennyloaf's longing to see her friend, her wretchedness and a deeply ingrained sense of worthlessness almost prevent her from knocking on the door of Jane's lodgings. When the two women do meet, however, the relief is immediate: "Ah! that was the voice that did good. How it comforted and blessed, after the hospital, and the miserable room in which the dead child was left lying, and the rainy street!" (268). For characters such as Pennyloaf, the city is usually experienced as a kind of battlefield, but some resource remains: while one street leads to the hospital and the misery of her dead child, another street leads to the "blessing" of Jane.

It is certainly not always true that wandering brings relief for characters in *The Nether World*. We need only think back to the scene with which I opened this chapter—Bob Hewett's desperate flight to escape the authorities, in which he races blindly through the London streets without any real hope or possibility of escape. As if to reinforce the inevitability of Bob's doom and the active, antagonistic role the city plays in it, Gissing arranges for Bob to be mortally wounded by the shaft of a cart when he rushes into the street. Clara Hewett, too, although she does not suffer a violent death, seems less in control of her actions than driven by feelings of desperation. Gissing describes her as "a creature beset by unrelenting forces" (86) at the moment when she decides to live as Scawthorne's mistress. And her physical actions, her movement through the streets during this period of transition, reflect the idea of her as as a being buffeted by fate. In the following passage, we see Clara as she suddenly changes lodgings so neither her family nor friends can find her: "[S]he left the house and walked with a quick step towards a region of North London with which she had no acquaintance. In an hour's time she had found another lodging, which she took by the day only. Then back again to Islington. She told her landlady that a sudden necessity compelled her to leave; she would have a cab and remove her box at once" (95). Clara's movements are deliberate, but Gissing makes clear that they are also reckless and ultimately self-destructive: "Now she had cut the last bond that fretted her, and the hours rushed on like a storm-wind driving her whither they would" (95). She, like her brother Bob, moves quickly but goes nowhere: rather than achieve her ambition to become an actress and to leave the netherworld behind, she ends up scarred (literally), married to the man she has known from her childhood, and living in the significantly named suburb of Crouch End.

Both Clara's and Bob's experiences would seem to support the idea that characters in *The Nether World* are victims of a hostile urban environment. The metaphor is literalized in Bob's case: he is killed by traffic. Still, we should not let this aspect of the novel define our vision of it. Although Gissing represents urban space as oppressive and dehumanizing, he also represents it as a repository of human feeling and a potential resource for distressed inhabitants. The novel ends with Jane's journey to her grandfather's grave, a pilgrimage she makes annually: "She left the work-room in the dinner-hour, and did not return. But instead of going to Hanover Street, she walked past Islington Green, all along Essex Road, northward thence to Stoke Newington, and so came to Abney Park Cemetery; a long way, but it did not weary her" (391). On this occasion, as on every occasion, she meets a fellow mourner in Sidney Kirkwood. This final passage evokes ideas of loss—loss not just of Snowdon himself but of Sidney's and Jane's earlier aspirations—yet it demonstrates once again the opportunities for connection and remembrance that are possible in the city. To represent the city in this way is to restore some measure of integrity to the dispossessed people of the netherworld. At the same time, it challenges the idea that urban space, even planned space, exerts a unilateral influence on inhabitants: characters in *The Nether World,* like human beings everywhere, use and interact with space in ways that can be unpredictable and sometimes even liberating.

Afterword

They find their own dreams; but I look after the drainage.

George Bernard Shaw, *Major Barbara* (1907)

*I*n *George Bernard Shaw's play* Major Barbara, *the title character Barbara* abandons her post in the Salvation Army when she is confronted with its susceptibility to economic forces. Her father, the wealthy munitions manufacturer Andrew Undershaft, plays a critical role in Barbara's disillusionment when his tainted money is gladly accepted by the Salvation Army in furtherance of its mission to feed the poor and save souls. The older, more pragmatic Salvation Army worker, Mrs. Baines, accepts the contributions of Undershaft and Bodger (the whisky maker) with thanks and praise; stage directions have her "taking the cheque" as she muses, "Who would have thought that any good could have come out of war and drink? And yet their profits are brought today to the feet of salvation to do its blessed work."[1] Barbara, however, is shattered upon suddenly seeing herself as "her father's accomplice," in the words of Shaw's preface to the play (27). Recognizing that the Salvation Army is financed by "war and drink," by the very entities responsible for the suffering it strives to combat, Barbara turns away from the sullied business of saving souls.

Of course, the play does not end here with the events of act 2. As Stanton Garner points out in his article "Shaw's Comedy of Disillusionment," the Shavian character's loss of faith is succeeded by a "deepening sense of reality," as well as feelings of invigoration, as limiting frameworks are stripped away.[2] In Barbara's case, the reality she comes to know is expressed by Undershaft's (and Shaw's) maxim that poverty is a crime. As Undershaft explains to Barbara, "Poverty blights whole cities; spreads horrible pestilences; strikes dead the very souls of all who come within sight, sound, or smell of it" (142). For Undershaft (and again, Shaw), the only true social reform begins and ends with ensuring that every person has enough money to live and that he or she works to earn it—an aim that Undershaft is able to accomplish, at least within the confines of his factory town, Perivale St. Andrews. The play closes with Barbara's declaration of faith in this gospel of St. Andrew Undershaft and her determination to save the souls not of the starving East Enders but of the well-fed munitions makers. "I have got rid of the bribe of bread," exults the reborn Barbara (152).

Shaw's play provides a useful coda to this study of reform and resistance in the nineteenth century because it allows us to reflect briefly on the changing landscape of social reform at the turn of the twentieth century. Through Barbara's experience, Shaw exposes the limitations of the Salvation Army, both in its conflation of economics and spirituality and in its complicity with a socioeconomic system that requires people to be poor. This latter point emerges in an exchange between Undershaft and Mrs. Baines, in which Mrs. Baines remarks approvingly that Christianity alleviates the bitterness of the poor against the rich. Fully aware of the irony in the Salvation Army's position as a friend at once to the poor man and to the capitalist, Undershaft responds, "It is certainly most convenient and gratifying to all large employers of labor" (105). But Shaw's criticism extends beyond the Salvation Army to the entire tradition of Victorian social reform, with its soup kitchens and model dwellings, its female rent collectors and university-educated settlement workers. In the preface, Shaw addresses the failure of nineteenth-century reforming liberalism, which spoke eloquently but accomplished nothing:

> The nineteenth century saw the same lesson repeated in England.
> It had its Utilitarians, its Christian Socialists, its Fabians (still extant): it had Bentham, Mill, Dickens, Ruskin, Carlyle, Butler, Henry George, and Morris. And the end of all their efforts is the

Chicago described by Mr. Upton Sinclair and the London in which
the people who pay to be amused by my dramatic representation of
Peter Shirley turned out to starve at forty because there are younger
slaves to be had for his wages, do not take, and have not the slight-
est intention of taking, any effective step to organize society in such
a way as to make that everyday infamy impossible. (28–29)

Shaw's immediate point is that art and politics without the threat of force
come to naught: "[H]ard words . . . break no bones" (28). In a more general
sense, this invocation of some of the most important social reformers of the
past century only to emphasize their futility is in tune with other expressions
of disillusionment we have seen. The machinery of reform rumbles on, and
unemployment, starvation, and slums remain.

Yet *Major Barbara* also points to a change in the idea and practice of reform.
The play projects a utopian vision of a new society, ushering in the revolutionary force that Gissing, for one, may dream about but refuses to provide. In
The Nether World, Gissing suggests in bitter seriousness the necessity of revolution, rather than reform, if the condition of the poor is to be improved:
"Destroy, sweep away, prepare the ground; then shall music the holy, music
the civilizer, breathe over the renewed earth, and with Orphean magic raise
in perfected beauty the towers of the City of Man."[3] In *Major Barbara,* Shaw
brings together all these energizing forces in his creation of an Undershaftian
"City of Man": he does what Gissing dreams. The Salvation Army band provides the music in the East End, with Adolphus Cusins on drum and Undershaft on trombone; and the presence of the explosives shed at Undershaft's
armory provides the always-imminent means of destruction. In this charged
atmosphere, the audience is invited, with the characters, to marvel over the
"horribly, frightfully, immorally, unanswerably perfect" factory town that
Undershaft has built for his workers (130). Perivale St. Andrews is paradoxically a model socialist community with schools, libraries, magnificent civic
buildings, gardens, and even a "William Morris Labor Church" (133). In fact,
the abundance of the town leads the conventional Stephen to worry about
the moral characters of its residents: "I cannot help thinking that all this provision for every want of your workmen may sap their independence and weaken
their sense of responsibility" (131). To this essentially Victorian argument
in support of self-help, Undershaft replies jauntily that if society is to be or-

ganized at all, it may as well be organized so as to eliminate all "trouble and anxiety" (131).

Major Barbara thus places Barbara's individual journey from disillusionment to renewed faith in the context of a shift from old modes of reform—the Salvation Army and other paternalistic schemes—to new ones, embodied in the model socialist village. These parallel developments are significant because they point outward to a reinvigorated culture of reform in turn-of-the-century London.[4] While the limitations of reform were becoming clear in the 1880s, new conceptions of and approaches to reform were just on the horizon. Characterizing the period between the 1880s and 1920s, Stuart Hall explains that "old laissez-faire conceptions began to be challenged, new philosophies of state action took shape, the scale of state activity enlarged and the state did begin to pioneer new modes of action of a more interventionist kind."[5] For instance, in the debates about working-class housing, many came to recognize that the problems would not be solved by private enterprise alone. John Tarn notes that one of the significant outcomes of the Royal Commission on the Housing of the Working Classes in 1885 was "the grudging acceptance of the role that the state must take in the future financial solution of the housing problem."[6] Also influential in encouraging more ambitious environmental reforms were fears of urban degeneration, of the enfeebling effect of town life on inhabitants. Anthony Sutcliffe links the growing interest in comprehensive urban planning schemes to recruitment drives in 1900 and 1901 for the Boer War, when the physical unfitness of the male urban population became a subject of national concern.[7] Around this time, the garden city movement was founded, with the aim of creating self-contained communities that combined the best features of the city and the country.[8] Distinct from the garden city, but sharing in many of its aims, were the planned suburban communities and suburban housing estates that were also developed in the first decades of the new century.[9] At the same time, socialist organizations (such as the Social Democratic Federation and the Fabian Society) were becoming influential in municipal politics and used this influence to bring health, housing, and poverty to the forefront of the urban agenda.

In London, one of the most significant developments of the last decades of the century was the creation of the London County Council in 1889, the first representative government to treat London as a single entity. Municipal reform was arguably essential to combat housing problems effectively and to rationalize city services, such as gas, water, and sewerage. Such administrative reform, labeled "centralization" by detractors, had been fundamental to Chadwick's vision of the sanitary city in the 1840s; not until a year before his death did such reform come to pass. The immediate context for the formation of the London County Council was the abolition of the Metropolitan Board of Works, which was beset by charges of corruption and malpractice.[10] With the board discredited and disbanded, the council took up its duties, becoming responsible for main drainage, street improvements, working-class housing, and Thames works, among other areas.[11] Although it followed the course set out by the Board of Works, continuing to pursue slum clearances and street improvements, the council approached the housing difficulty much more aggressively. After the passage of the Housing of the Working Classes Act in 1890, the council undertook the work of building working-class housing, in addition to simply clearing and selling sites on which others might build (as the Metropolitan Board of Works) had done.[12] By 1915, over thirty thousand new rooms had been constructed under the auspices of the council,[13] although the problem of housing the most destitute urban inhabitants was still not broached directly.[14] But as Tarn has discussed, perhaps more significant than any single initiative was the London County Council's attitude, its commitment to making the metropolis a better and healthier place for all its citizens: "The public spirited way in which the L.C.C. pursued its role as the sanitary guardian and spatial arbiter of the metropolis made it clear that a new kind of local government organisation, more positive and willing to act for the public good, had sprung into existence."[15]

The energy and optimism associated with the creation of the London County Council finds full expression in a *Punch* cartoon by John Tenniel titled "New London" (fig. A.1). Published in December 1888 in *Punch's Almanack for 1889,* the double-page illustration celebrates the passage of the Local Government Act, which established the London County Council. Filling the frame is a host of allegorical figures representing the political, social, and material life of the metropolis. To the left are the bad old figures of corruption, represented by a seedy-looking Father Thames, an indignant beadle, and a rotund Lord Mayor of London. The group holds aloft signs advertising its affiliation with jerry-building, usury, slum lodging, sweated labor, and of course the disgraced Metropolitan Board of Works. Symbols associated with the City of

A.1. The forces of purity and progress, under the banner of municipal reform, drive off the forces of corruption and obstructionism. Illustration by John Tenniel, "New London," *Punch's Almanack for 1889,* 6 December 1888.

London are prominent, among them the giants Gog and Magog and the heraldic griffin, slinking off with his tail between his legs. The City Corporation did not in fact lose its autonomy under the new act; nonetheless, the illustration suggests that a blow has been delivered to the luxurious habits and parochialism of public bodies such as the City and the vestries. Administering this blow are the regenerative forces of progress and public-spiritedness. Led by a triumphant Britannia are the graceful female figures personifying Light, Clean Water, Fresh Air, and Charity—the latter tenderly escorting two ragged children. Behind the forward sanitary guard are three male figures representing Science, Art, and Literature. The appearance alone of these figures of progress contrasts sharply with that of the moribund figures of corruption. The former appear graceful, erect, and of solid Anglo-Saxon stock; some of the latter appear fat and coarse, and others are given Jewish or Asian features as if to suggest that the racial integrity of the city is also at stake in this battle between old and new governments.[16] "New London," under the banner of municipal reform, promises to be a city of purity—physical, moral, and racial.

Clearly the ideals and aspirations associated with the sanitary reform movement retained—and still retain—their powerful hold on the urban imagination. Indeed, as Jon Peterson has argued, sanitary reform laid the foundation for the city planning movement of the twentieth century by promoting the idea of an urban environment shaped according to public needs and for the public good.[17] But, ironically, as a more comprehensive and progressive approach to environmental planning took hold in cities, the role of sanitation itself began to change, becoming at once more technical and more limited in scope. Martin Melosi in his ambitious study of American sanitary history links the change to the rise of bacteriology, which gave to environmental sanitation "a narrower context within a broadening field."[18] That is, sanitation was only one component, albeit a crucial one, of the healthy city. Its promotion and implementation, moreover, were no longer within the purview of writers, philanthropists, and politicians. Instead, sanitation became the specialized work of laboratory scientists, seeking ways to keep water safe from biological pollutants, and municipal engineers, focused on the technology of waste and water carriage; responsibility for individual and public hygiene shifted to the medical community.[19] Thus, Victorian sanitary reform both did and did not outlive its era. Sanitation came to mean managing one specific part of the urban environment—its refuse. Gone was the idea of sanitary reform as a broad movement promising material cleansing and moral uplift and demanding the support of every well-to-do citizen. These impulses persisted, but they were absorbed by the new field of city planning.

And what of resistance? Did opposition and ambivalence toward reform also survive into the new century? A brief look at one of the London County Council's most important improvement projects reveals that while the ideals associated with sanitary reform persisted, so too did expressions of regret at the passing of the familiar, if tattered, urban fabric. The idea for a major north-south thoroughfare connecting Holborn to the Strand just west of Lincoln's Inn Fields had been discussed as early as the 1830s.[20] Not until the London County Council took the project up in the 1890s, however, did it finally come to fruition, as the new Kingsway-Aldwych improvement. The project was of the type pursued by the preceding Metropolitan Board of Works, but it was more ambitious, taking a greater amount of private property so that rebuilding could proceed according to a more uniform plan. According to Dirk Schubert and Anthony Sutcliffe, Kingsway-Aldwych was "the most extensive and expensive new street project which had ever been submitted to Parliament."[21] In the more subjective assessment of Hermione Hobhouse, the project "was responsible for the devastation of a larger area than any other previous event but the Great Fire."[22] But if the scale had changed, many of the objectives were familiar. The new road, one hundred feet wide and extending in a straight line from Holborn to a crescent road that connects it to the Strand, would improve the traffic flow in the central corridor between the City and Westminster. It would also clear long-standing slums, notably around Clare Market, and destroy the disreputable Holywell Street, a narrow offshoot of the Strand known equally for its Elizabethan buildings and its shops selling obscene books and prints.[23] In its report of 1895, the council's Housing of the Working Classes Committee pressed for the demolition and reconstruction of the Clare Market area, stating, "This is the largest and worst of those crowded collections of the courts and alleys to disgrace central London."[24] Promoting the Holborn-Strand improvement as a whole, George Shaw Lefevre of the council's Improvement Committee argued that the clearances would have a positive impact on the area's working-class inhabitants: "The labouring people will also be greatly benefited by the clearing away of the unsanitary slums through which the new street will pass, and by the erection of new houses for them on the best sanitary principles at no great distance."[25] More than three thousand residents were displaced, and although the council took responsibility for their rehousing, it is hard to imagine that this fully compensated for the loss of community, the disruption of daily habits, and the economic hardship associated with eviction and relocation. Indeed, according to Jonathan Schneer, there was some opposition to the project from Radical members of the council who believed that street improvements were not in the real interest of the London poor, despite efforts to cast them as humanitarian endeavors.[26]

Kingsway and the Aldwych, as the street and crescent were named, opened in 1905, and in the succeeding years, stately buildings projecting an imperial image were erected along the roadway.[27] But the dingy alleys, the out-of-the-way houses and shops existing paradoxically in conditions of obscurity in the heart of central London—those were missed. As I have shown throughout this study, urban improvements often inspired nostalgia for the sites and sensations that were swept away, even, and perhaps especially, when the sites were filthy and the sensations veered toward repulsion. Such is the case for Wilfred Whitten, author of a deeply nostalgic evocation of the city, *A Londoner's London* (1912). Whitten's theme is the ceaselessly changing metropolis and the experience of dislocation that it produces. In the chapter titled "The Veils of

Yesterday," he reflects, "While we grow older the London we knew disappears, and at double speed we are separated from streets where we remember to have stood in leisure."[28] The Kingsway-Aldwych scheme is invoked in this context, but Whitten recurs to it throughout the book, making of it an exemplar of the regrettable march of progress. Of Holywell Street, destroyed in the course of the project, he says, "Good old, hospitable, not quite reputable street . . . whose beckoning glow is lost in municipal day-shine, I doubt if we had a right to pull you down. You should be there still—in the arms of the Aldwych."[29] Clare Market, characterized by its "populous dirt and colour," is similarly lamented as a casualty of metropolitan improvement.[30] Its destruction sparks a more general elegy for the passing of an uncontrolled, and thus authentic, cityscape: "All the traditions of piecemeal change, casualness, and compromise which have made London picturesque were flouted in the Kingsway and Aldwych scheme."[31] Once again, squalor is reinterpreted as the picturesque and fondly embraced when it is perceived to be a target of improvement.

It is difficult to judge the impact of expressions of this sort, those voices of ambivalence and resistance that I have been concerned to trace. Certain kinds of criticism, such as the criticism of slum clearances carried out independently of a rehousing plan, did play a part in changing approaches and attitudes to reform. The London County Council, for instance, was much more sensitive to the housing needs of the working classes and the pressures put on them by improvements than the Metropolitan Board of Works had been. Other kinds of opposition to reform, however, such as that based on an appreciation of picturesque London, may have had no appreciable impact on the practice of reform or the shape of the urban environment at all. Still, these voices matter not because they changed reform but because they change the way in which we understand reform. They remind us that the sanitary modernization of the Victorian city was not a seamless, uncontested process, but an anxious and disorienting, if sometimes exhilarating, experience. They remind us of the contradictory impulses of human beings when it comes to progress, on the one hand, and the emotional pull of the familiar, on the other. They remind us that purity, in its way, can be just as challenging as filth.

notes

Introduction

1. Nancy Aycock Metz, "Discovering a World of Suffering: Fiction and the Rhetoric of Sanitary Reform, 1840–1860," *Nineteenth-Century Contexts* 15 (1991): 68–69.

2. Charles Girdlestone, "Rich and Poor," in *Meliora, or Better Times to Come,* ed. Viscount Ingestre, 1st ser. (1853; repr., London: Cass, 1971), 23.

3. Anthony S. Wohl, *Endangered Lives: Public Health in Victorian Britain* (London: Methuen, 1983), 329.

4. "Some London Clearings: Eastcheap," *All the Year Round,* n.s., 35 (8 November 1884): 103–9. Further references to this article (abbreviated as "Eastcheap") are cited in the text.

5. "Some London Clearings: Clerkenwell," *All the Year Round,* n.s., 34 (7 June 1884): 126. Further references to this article (abbreviated as "Clerkenwell") are cited in the text.

6. "Some London Clearings," *All the Year Round,* n.s., 33 (26 January 1884): 231.

7. "Some London Clearings: Soho," *All the Year Round,* n.s., 36 (13 June 1885): 312. Further references to this article (abbreviated as "Soho") are cited in the text.

8. Jonathan Swift, "A Description of a City Shower," in *The Norton Anthology of English Literature,* ed. M. H. Abrams et al., 6th ed., vol. 1 (New York: Norton, 1993), 2009–11.

9. Charles Dickens, *Dombey and Son,* The Oxford Illustrated Dickens (Oxford: Oxford University Press, 1991), 647–48.

10. In this assumption, I align myself with William A. Cohen, who in his introduction to the collection *Filth: Dirt, Disgust, and Modern Life,* ed. William A. Cohen and Ryan Johnson (Minneapolis: University of Minnesota Press, 2005) maintains that "filth in nineteenth-century Europe . . . first and foremost signifies urban squalor and disease" (xix).

11. Geoffrey Best, *Mid-Victorian Britain, 1851–1875* (London: Weidenfeld and Nicolson, 1971), 6.

12. Roy Porter, *London: A Social History* (Cambridge, MA: Harvard University Press, 1994), 205.

13. Ibid., 208–9.

14. Best identifies these structural changes with the modernization of the capital: "a more or less conscious and deliberate adaptation of its forms to the requirements of 'modern' mid-Victorian city life" (*Mid-Victorian Britain,* 61).

15. Wohl, *Endangered Lives,* 80.

16. [Henry Morley], "A Way to Clean Rivers," *Household Words,* 10 July 1858, 79. Attributions of authorship to this and other articles from *Household Words* are derived from

Anne Lohrli, Household Words: *A Weekly Journal, 1850–1859* (Toronto: University of Toronto Press, 1973).

17. Wohl, *Endangered Lives,* 87.

18. Michael Worboys, *Spreading Germs: Disease Theories and Medical Practice in Britain, 1865–1900* (Cambridge: Cambridge University Press, 2000), 39–40.

19. Worboys, 38. See also Margaret Pelling's entry "Contagion/Germ Theory/Specificity," in *Companion Encyclopedia of the History of Medicine,* ed. W. F. Bynum and Roy Porter (London: Routledge, 1993), where she describes the sanitarians' efforts to simplify explanations of infectious diseases and their causation for political and administrative purposes (323).

20. Wohl, *Endangered Lives,* 118.

21. Ibid.

22. Ibid.; Francis Sheppard, *London 1808–1870: The Infernal Wen* (Berkeley and Los Angeles: University of California Press, 1971), 249.

23. Sheppard, *London,* 246–47.

24. Wohl, *Endangered Lives,* 125.

25. Ibid., 121.

26. Bill Luckin, *Pollution and Control: A Social History of the Thames in the Nineteenth Century* (Bristol, UK: Adam Hilger, 1986), 96.

27. Hector Gavin, *Sanitary Ramblings: Being Sketches and Illustrations of Bethnal Green, a Type of the Condition of the Metropolis and Other Large Towns,* Cass Library of Victorian Times 8 (1848; repr., London: Cass, 1971), 4.

28. George Godwin, *Town Swamps and Social Bridges,* The Victorian Library (1859; repr., Leicester: Leicester University Press, 1972), 49.

29. R. Porter, 260.

30. Sheppard, *London,* 253.

31. Parliament, *First Report of the Royal Commission on Means for the Improvement of the Health of the Metropolis,* 1847–48 (888), vol. 32, Irish University Press Series of British Parliamentary Papers, Health: General, 7 (Shannon: Irish University Press, 1970), 21.

32. S. E. Finer, *The Life and Times of Sir Edwin Chadwick* (New York: Barnes and Noble, 1970), 222.

33. Ibid., 157.

34. Gerry Kearns, "Biology, Class and the Urban Penalty," in *Urbanising Britain: Essays on Class and Community in the Nineteenth Century,* ed. Gerry Kearns and Charles W. J. Withers (Cambridge: Cambridge University Press, 1991), 12.

35. Parliament, *First Report of the Royal Commission on the State of Large Towns and Populous Districts,* 1844 (572), vol. 17, Irish University Press Series of British Parliamentary Papers, Health: General, 5 (Shannon: Irish University Press, 1970), 81.

36. Mary Douglas, *Purity and Danger: An Analysis of the Concepts of Pollution and Taboo* (1966; repr., London: Routledge, 1991), 36.

37. David Trotter, *Cooking with Mud: The Idea of Mess in Nineteenth-Century Art and Fiction* (Oxford: Oxford University Press, 2000), 20.

38. Cohen, "Introduction," xvi. See Cohen's introduction to *Filth* for a review of the theoretical literature on filth and purity (xi–xvii).

39. Charles Kingsley, "Great Cities and Their Influence for Good and Evil," in *Sanitary and Social Lectures and Essays* (London: Macmillan, 1889), 190–91.

40. Ibid., 204.

41. Late in the century, General William Booth and the Salvation Army retained the principle that material aid—or social salvation—must provide the basis for spiritual salvation among the suffering poor. But the principle apparently still required defending, judging from Booth's remarks on the established Church's response to poverty in his work, *In Darkest England and the Way Out* (1890; repr., London: International Headquarters of the Salvation Army, [1970]): "Why all this apparatus of temples and meeting-houses to save men from perdition in a world which is to come, while never a helping hand is stretched out to save them from the inferno of their present life?" (23).

42. Charles Kingsley, *Who Causes Pestilence? Four Sermons* (London: Richard Griffin, 1854), 3.

43. Graeme Davison, "The City as a Natural System: Theories of Urban Society in Early Nineteenth-Century Britain," in *The Pursuit of Urban History,* ed. Derek Fraser and Anthony Sutcliffe (London: Edward Arnold, 1983), 354; and Christopher Hamlin, "Providence and Putrefaction: Victorian Sanitarians and the Natural Theology of Health and Disease," *Victorian Studies* 28 (1985): 390–91.

44. Marc Reboul, "Charles Kingsley: The Rector in the City," in *Victorian Writers and the City,* ed. Jean-Paul Hulin and Pierre Coustillas ([Lille, France]: Université de Lille III, [1979]), 48. In "Providence and Putrefaction," Hamlin also emphasizes Kingsley's conviction that sanitary science (specifically, sewage recycling) could bring about "earthly salvation" (403).

45. Trotter, 163.

46. Davison, 362.

47. See, for instance, Wohl's pioneering study of Victorian sanitation, *Endangered Lives,* in which he emphasizes the prevailing positive attitude toward sanitary reform: "For the Victorians, public health, like so many other social reforms and endeavours, took on the form of a moral crusade" (6); "The enthusiasm with which the Victorians threw themselves into this mission was fed by a sense that they would succeed" (8).

48. In "Muddling in Bumbledom: On the Enormity of Large Sanitary Improvements in Four British Towns, 1855–1885," *Victorian Studies* 32 (1988/89), Christopher Hamlin usefully describes how historians' own expectations and ideas of history as a narrative of progressive change have influenced interpretations of the sanitary movement (55). Most historians, Hamlin contends, join with Victorian reformers in viewing improvements as desirable and inevitable and opposition to reform as socially irresponsible (60). Perhaps typical of this perspective is F. B. Smith, *The People's Health, 1830–1910* (New York: Holmes and Meier, 1979). Smith represents the early sanitary reformers as pioneers, succeeding against the odds: "It is difficult now to recapture the visionary quality of their early programme or to comprehend the dirt, decay, disease and desolation they confronted,

let alone understand the minds of their opponents, but the sanitarians' achievements, however misapplied, piecemeal and belated and, in the outcome, overestimated, bettered the life chances of every person in Victorian Britain" (195).

49. Joseph W. Childers, "The Novel and the Utilitarian," in *Novel Possibilities: Fiction and the Formation of Early Victorian Culture* (Philadelphia: University of Pennsylvania Press, 1995), 71–85; Metz, "Discovering a World"; and Mary Poovey, "Domesticity and Class Formation: Chadwick's 1842 *Sanitary Report*," in *Making a Social Body: British Cultural Formation, 1830–1864* (Chicago: University of Chicago Press, 1995), 115–31.

50. For instance, see Simon Joyce, *Capital Offenses: Geographies of Class and Crime in Victorian London* (Charlottesville: University of Virginia Press, 2003); Richard Phillips, *Mapping Men and Empire: A Geography of Adventure* (London: Routledge, 1997); and Cynthia Wall, *The Literary and Cultural Spaces of Restoration London* (Cambridge: Cambridge University Press, 1998). The exchanges between the disciplines of literature and geography have been mutually beneficial. Postpositivist geography was itself influenced by poststructuralist literary theory, with its insistence on the constitutive quality of language. Applying this insight to space allowed geographers to develop a theory of space as similarly constitutive of social experience. Literary critics have since responded to the challenge of postmodern geographical theory with studies that bring together textual, spatial, and social landscapes.

51. Henri Lefebvre, *The Production of Space,* trans. Donald Nicholson-Smith (1974; repr., Malden, MA: Blackwell, 1991), 83–84.

52. Edward W. Soja, *Postmodern Geographies: The Reassertion of Space in Critical Social Theory* (London: Verso, 1989), 79–80.

53. Soja, "The Spatiality of Social Life: Towards a Transformative Retheorisation," in *Social Relations and Spatial Structures,* ed. Derek Gregory and John Urry (London: Macmillan, 1985), 94.

54. Michel Foucault, "The Eye of Power," in *Power/Knowledge: Selected Interviews and Other Writings, 1972–1977,* ed. Colin Gordon (Brighton, UK: Harvester, 1980), 148.

55. Trevor Barnes and Derek Gregory, eds., *Reading Human Geography: The Poetics and Politics of Inquiry* (London: Arnold, 1997), 293.

56. Yi-Fu Tuan, *Topophilia: A Study of Environmental Perception, Attitudes, and Values* (1974; repr., New York: Columbia University Press, 1990), 93.

57. Soja, *Postmodern Geographies,* 130.

58. Very often the ambitious scope of works that take as their subject the city and literature precludes the investigation of urban particulars. This is true of Raymond Williams's important study *The Country and the City* (New York: Oxford, 1973), which successfully relates the English literary tradition to processes of urban and rural change. In cases where the focus is more restricted, the city is still very often conceived as an undifferentiated space. See, for instance, two very different studies treating the nineteenth-century city: Deborah Epstein Nord, *Walking the Victorian Streets: Women, Representation, and the City* (Ithaca, NY: Cornell University Press, 1995), and Julian Wolfreys, *Writing London:*

The Trace of the Urban Text from Blake to Dickens (New York: St. Martin's Press, 1998). Nord traces the figures of female spectator and spectacle across a series of texts representing urban experience, connecting their roles to ideas about Victorian social relations. Unlike Nord, Wolfreys vigorously rejects any concern with the empirical reality of the city, focusing on London strictly as imaginative construct and on its representation as a window into a modern urban consciousness.

59. Joseph McLaughlin, *Writing the Urban Jungle: Reading Empire in London from Doyle to Eliot* (Charlottesville: University Press of Virginia, 2000), 150. For other studies attuned to geographic particulars, see Lynda Nead, *Victorian Babylon: People, Streets and Images in Nineteenth-Century London* (New Haven, CT: Yale University Press, 2000), and Franco Moretti, *Atlas of the European Novel, 1800–1900* (London: Verso, 1998). Nead carefully constructs historical and visual narratives of specific sites in nineteenth-century London, such as Cremorne Gardens and Holywell Street. Although not concerned specifically with London, Moretti's book is noteworthy for its creation of literary maps based on the geographic information provided in individual novels.

60. Wohl, *Endangered Lives,* 330.

Chapter 1

The epigraph to this chapter is drawn from John Hollingshead, *Underground London* (London: Groombridge and Sons, 1862), 1.

1. Gertrude Himmelfarb, *The Idea of Poverty: England in the Early Industrial Age* (New York: Knopf, 1984), 314–22.

2. Ibid., 361.

3. Anne Humpherys, *Travels into the Poor Man's Country: The Work of Henry Mayhew* (Athens: University of Georgia Press, 1977), 81–82.

4. Henry Mayhew, *London Labour and the London Poor,* 4 vols. (1861–62; reprint, New York: Dover, 1968), 2:160–62, 386. Subsequent references are to this edition and are cited in the text.

5. Edwin Chadwick, *Report on the Sanitary Condition of the Labouring Population of Great Britain,* ed. M. W. Flinn (1842; repr., Edinburgh: Edinburgh University Press, 1965), 117.

6. Joseph William Bazalgette, *On the Main Drainage of London, and the Interception of the Sewage from the River Thames,* ed. James Forrest (London, 1865), 28; George W. Humphreys, *Main Drainage of London* (London: London County Council, 1930), 5.

7. Sheppard, *London,* 255; Wohl, *Endangered Lives,* 89.

8. Parliament, *Report of the Select Committee on the Sewers of the Metropolis,* 1823 (542), vol. 5, Irish University Press Series of British Parliamentary Papers, Urban Areas: Sanitation, 1 (Shannon: Irish University Press, 1970), 43.

9. Humphreys, 5.

10. Finer, 222–23.

11. Ibid., 326, 329, 336; Sheppard, *London,* 264–67.

12. An Act to Consolidate, and Continue in Force for Two Years and to the End of the Then Next Session of Parliament, the Metropolitan Commission of Sewers (11 and 12 Vict., cap. 112).

13. Sheppard, *London,* 273.

14. Bazalgette, 29.

15. Ibid.

16. Richard Maxwell, "Henry Mayhew and the Life of the Streets," *Journal of British Studies* 17, no. 2 (1978): 91. http://www.jstor.org.

17. Ibid., 104.

18. Chadwick, 164.

19. Ibid., 163.

20. Ibid., 125.

21. David L. Pike, *Subterranean Cities: The World beneath Paris and London, 1800–1945* (Ithaca, NY: Cornell University Press, 2005), 191.

22. Hollingshead, *Underground London,* 99.

23. Ibid.

24. Richard L. Schoenwald, "Training Urban Man: A Hypothesis about the Sanitary Movement," in *The Victorian City: Images and Realities,* ed. H. J. Dyos and Michael Wolff, vol. 2 (London: Routledge and Kegan Paul, 1973), 675.

25. H. J. Dyos, "The Victorian City in Historical Perspective," in *Exploring the Urban Past: Essays in Urban History by H. J. Dyos,* ed. David Cannadine and David Reeder (Cambridge: Cambridge University Press, 1982), 17.

26. Thomas Lovick, "Report of Mr. Lovick, Assistant Surveyor, on Flushing Operations," Metropolitan Commission of Sewers, Reports and Documents (London, 1848–49), 1.

27. John Spurgin, *Drainage of Cities: Reserving Their Sewage for Use, and Keeping Their Rivers Clean; Being Especially Applicable to the Thames* (London, 1858), 3.

28. A. B. Granville, *The Great London Question of the Day; or, Can Thames Sewage Be Converted into Gold?* (London, 1865), 11.

29. Lionel Gisborne, *Thames Improvement* (London, 1853), 8.

30. [Morley], "Way to Clean Rivers," 80.

31. Finer, 223–24.

32. Christopher Hamlin, *What Becomes of Pollution? Adversary Science and the Controversy on the Self-Purification of Rivers in Britain, 1850–1900* (New York: Garland, 1987), 25.

33. John Wiggins, *The Polluted Thames: The Most Speedy, Effectual, and Economical Mode of Cleansing Its Waters, and Getting Rid of the Sewage of London* (London, 1858), 5.

34. Robert Pulling, *Sewage Turned to Profitable Account* (London, 1875), 3.

35. J. Bannehr, *The Sewage Difficulty* (London, [1866]), 19.

36. Francis Sheppard, "The Crisis of London's Government," in *The Government of Victorian London, 1855–1889: The Metropolitan Board of Works, the Vestries, and the City Corporation,* by David Owen, ed. Roy MacLeod (Cambridge, MA: Harvard University Press, 1982), 28.

37. J[oshua] Toulmin Smith, *A Letter to the Metropolitan Sanatory Commissioners: Containing an Examination of Allegations Put forth in Support of the Proposition for Superseding, under the Name of Sanatory Improvement, All Local Representative Self-Government by a System of Centralized Patronage* (London, 1848), iv.

38. Finer, 347.

39. *Times,* 7 October 1848, 4.

40. Wiggins, 10.

41. Richard L. Schoenwald, "Town Guano and 'Social Statics,'" *Victorian Studies* 11, suppl. (1968): 706. In his psychoanalytic study of Herbert Spencer's opposition to sanitary reform, Schoenwald cites this article from the *Economist* and also notes Spencer's role as a sub-editor for the magazine at the time of the cholera epidemic.

42. "A Greater Plague than Cholera," *Economist,* 27 October 1849, 1190.

43. Herbert Spencer, "Sanitary Supervision," in *Social Statics, Abridged and Revised; Together with The Man versus the State,* vol. 11 of *The Works of Herbert Spencer* (Osnabrück, Germany: Otto Zeller, 1966), 198 (emphasis added).

44. Peter Melville Logan, *Nerves and Narratives: A Cultural History of Hysteria in Nineteenth-Century British Prose* (Berkeley: University of California Press, 1997), 164.

45. George Lewis, "Prevailing Evils Examined in Detail: I. Physical Destitution," in *Lectures on the Social and Physical Condition of the People, Especially in Large Towns* (Glasgow, [1842]), 56.

46. Joel A. Tarr, "Sewerage and the Development of the Networked City in the United States, 1850–1930," in *Technology and the Rise of the Networked City in Europe and America,* ed. Joel A. Tarr and Gabriel Dupuy (Philadelphia: Temple University Press, 1988), 159, 174.

47. [Henry Morley], "A Foe under Foot," *Household Words,* 11 December 1852, 289.

48. Ibid., 291.

49. G. Rochfort Clarke, *The Reform of the Sewers: Where Shall We Bathe? What Shall We Drink? or, Manure Wasted and Land Starved,* 2nd ed. (London, 1860), 27.

50. Ibid., 26.

51. Pike, 191.

52. S. S. Brown, *A Lay Lecture on Sanitary Matters, with a Paper on Sewer Ventilation* (London, 1873), 31.

53. G. R. Booth, *The London Sewerage Question: Some Serious Observations and Suggestions upon the Defective Plan of Sewerage Proposed by the Metropolitan Board of Works, Together with a Method for Remedying the Evil* (London, n.d.), 6.

54. Hollingshead, *Underground London,* 67.

55. Peter Stallybrass and Allon White, *The Politics and Poetics of Transgression* (Ithaca, NY: Cornell University Press, 1986), 141.

56. *Times,* 29 November 1871, 7.

57. *Times,* 28 November 1871, 9.

58. *Times,* 7 December 1871, 9.

59. Citing statistics prepared by the Metropolitan Sanitary Commission, Mayhew

notes the class-based disparity of sanitary arrangements: in the "poorer parish of St. George the Martyr, Southwark," only 10.06 percent of houses surveyed had water closets, while "in the aristocratic parish of St. James, Westminster," 65.86 percent of houses had them (*London Labour,* 2:434).

60. "The Drainage of Middle-Class Houses," *Building News,* 3 December 1869, 418.

61. H[enry] H. Collins, *On the Ill-Construction and Want of Sanitary Provisions Which Exist in the Dwellings of the Upper and Middle Classes, and Suggestions for Remedying the Same* (London, 1875), 5.

62. *Times,* 12 December 1871, 8.

63. Leonore Davidoff and Catherine Hall, *Family Fortunes: Men and Women of the English Middle Class, 1780–1850* (Chicago: University of Chicago Press, 1991), 29–33; Elizabeth Langland, *Nobody's Angels: Middle-Class Women and Domestic Ideology in Victorian Culture* (Ithaca, NY: Cornell University Press, 1995), 8–12.

64. Karen Chase and Michael Levenson, "On the Parapets of Privacy," in *A Companion to Victorian Literature and Culture,* ed. Herbert F. Tucker (Oxford: Blackwell, 1999), 433–35.

65. In her analysis of Edwin Chadwick's *Sanitary Report* of 1842, Mary Poovey argues that Chadwick deploys the domestic idea in the service of his reform agenda (*Making a Social Body,* 116–18). Although, as Poovey's work suggests, the ideologies of domesticity and sanitary reform appear mutually supportive at certain discursive moments, in practice new sanitary techniques were felt to expose the home to unprecedented dangers. Ultimately, as I argue, changes in London's sanitary landscape effected a reconception of the relation between the home and the urban environment.

66. Charles Dickens, *Great Expectations,* ed. Margaret Cardwell (Oxford: Oxford University Press, 1994), 206.

67. Ibid., 205.

68. Garrett Stewart, *Dickens and the Trials of Imagination* (Cambridge, MA: Harvard University Press, 1974), 159.

69. Lamorock Flower, *The Prince of Wales and Sanitary Reform:"An Englishman's House Is His Castle"; Not Now!! Why?* (London, 1871), 15.

70. *Times,* 7 December 1871, 9.

71. Elizabeth Wilson, *The Sphinx in the City: Urban Life, the Control of Disorder, and Women* (Berkeley: University of California Press, 1991), 27.

72. Nord, 83.

73. Ibid., 13.

74. Jasper W. Rogers, *Facts and Fallacies of the Sewerage System of London, and Other Large Towns* (London, 1857), 19–20.

75. "Sanitary Sermons," *Punch,* 13 January 1872, 15.

76. Titles from this library include Peter Hinckes Bird, *Hints on Drains, Traps, Closets, Sewer Gas, and Sewage Disposal* (Blackpool, UK, 1877); Edward T. Blake, *Sewage-Poisoning; How to Avoid It in the Simplest Way* (London, [1879]); S. S. Brown, *A Lay Lecture on Sanitary*

Matters, with a Paper on Sewer Ventilation (London, 1873); George Gordon Hoskins, *An Hour with a Sewer Rat; or, A Few Plain Hints on House Drainage and Sewer Gas* (London, 1879); Henry Masters, *An Architect's Letter about Sewer Gas and House Drainage* (London, 1876); Osborne Reynolds, *Sewer Gas, and How to Keep It out of Houses: A Handbook on House Drainage* (London, 1872); T. Pridgin Teale, *Dangers to Health: A Pictorial Guide to Domestic Sanitary Defects*, 4th ed. (London, 1883).

77. Reynolds, 6.

78. Masters, 10.

79. Hoskins, 43.

80. Masters, 5.

81. Reynolds, 15.

82. Teale, 9.

83. Benjamin Ward Richardson, *Woman as a Sanitary Reformer,* lecture delivered before the Sanitary Congress (Exeter, 1880), 7. See also S[usan] R[ugeley] P[owers], *Remarks on Woman's Work in Sanitary Reform,* Ladies' Sanitary Association, 3rd ed. (London, 1862). Powers also applies the ideology of separate spheres to the work of sanitation: "[T]he great field of sanitary labour may be considered as divided into two parts:—the amelioration of injurious external circumstances, and the reform of injurious habits and customs. Of these parts, the former may be considered as belonging principally to man—the latter, principally to woman" (5).

84. Richardson, 12.

85. Hollingshead, *Underground London,* 52.

86. It is worth noting that London had nothing comparable to the Parisian sewer tours, which began in 1867; visitors were transported in boats through the vaulted galleries underground. For the Parisian sewer tour see Donald Reid, *Paris Sewers and Sewermen: Realities and Representations* (Cambridge, MA: Harvard University Press, 1991); see also Pike, 241–44.

87. *Times,* 15 October 1874, 7.

Chapter 2

The epigraphs to this chapter are drawn from "To the Thames (After Tennyson)," *Punch,* 3 July 1858, 7; W. R. Greg, "The Special Beauty Conferred by Imperfection and Decay," *Contemporary Review* 20 (October 1872): 692.

1. For information about the Great Stink and Thames pollution more generally, I have relied on pamphlets published in and around 1858, as well as on articles from the *Builder* and the *Times* appearing in the 1850s and 1860s. Useful secondary sources include Stephen Halliday, *The Great Stink of London: Sir Joseph Bazalgette and the Cleansing of the Victorian Capital* (Phoenix Mill, UK: Sutton, 1999), which features an impressive selection of illustrations; Luckin, *Pollution and Control,* which is strong on the political context of river pollution; Dale Porter, *The Thames Embankment: Environment, Technology, and Society in*

Victorian London (Akron, OH: University of Akron Press, 1998), which situates Thames pollution and the Embankment in the context of structural and environmental events on the river; and Wohl, *Endangered Lives,* with a chapter devoted to river pollution.

2. T. S., letter to the editor, *Times,* 18 June 1858, 12.

3. "A hard-worked and nearly-stifled MP," letter to the editor, *Times,* 2 July 1858, 5.

4. In July 1858, the *Times* reported the hasty exodus of a committee from one of the meeting rooms overlooking the river: "[T]he Chancellor of the Exchequer, who, with a mass of papers in one hand and with his pocket handkerchief clutched in the other, and applied closely to his nose, with body half bent, hastened in dismay from the pestilential odour, followed closely by Sir James Graham, who seemed to be attacked by a sudden fit of expectoration; Mr. Gladstone also paid particular attention to his nose" ("The Thames on the Bank Acts," *Times,* 3 July 1858, 9). See also Halliday, 71.

5. "The Condition of the Thames," *Builder,* 3 July 1858, 449.

6. *Times,* 26 June 1858, 9.

7. For these poems and others, as well as relevant cartoons, see issues of *Punch* from June and July 1858.

8. "The Position of the Drainage Question," *Builder,* 3 July 1858, 450; "State of the Thames," *Times,* 30 June 1858, 9.

9. Luckin, 16.

10. Wiggins, 20.

11. Alfred Smee, letter to the editor, *Times,* 26 June 1858, 9.

12. Spurgin, 3.

13. "The Thames," *Sanitary Review, and Journal of Public Health* 4 (1858), 142.

14. Luckin, 17.

15. Thomas L. Wood, *London Health and London Traffic* (London, 1859), 18.

16. Wohl, *Endangered Lives,* 233–34.

17. Sheppard, *London,* 122.

18. Wohl, *Endangered Lives,* 234.

19. "Embankment of the Thames," *Times,* 5 October 1859, 12.

20. *Report on Main Drainage of the Metropolis Presented to the Metropolitan Board of Works by Messrs. Hawksley, Bidder, Bazalgette,* 1857–58 (419), vol. 48, Irish University Press Series of British Parliamentary Papers, Urban Areas: Sanitation, 4 (Shannon: Irish University Press, 1970), 42. Cited hereafter as *Report on Main Drainage.*

21. "The Condition of the Thames," *Builder,* 3 July 1858, 454.

22. [George Augustus Sala], "Powder Dick and His Train," *Household Words,* 7 May 1853, 236.

23. Lynda Nead, *Myths of Sexuality: Representations of Women in Victorian Britain* (New York: Basil Blackwell, 1988), 121.

24. Ibid., 138–41.

25. Charles Dickens, *David Copperfield,* ed. Nina Burgis (Oxford: Oxford University Press, 1982), 554.

26. Ibid., 555.

27. Susan P. Casteras, *Images of Victorian Womanhood in English Art* (London: Associated University Presses, 1987), 132; Nead, *Myths of Sexuality,* 168–69.

28. John Clubbe, ed., *Selected Poems of Thomas Hood* (Cambridge, MA: Harvard University Press, 1970), 392; Alvin Whitley, "Thomas Hood and 'The Times,'" *Times Literary Supplement,* 17 May 1957, 309.

29. Thomas Hood, "The Bridge of Sighs," in Clubbe, *Selected Poems of Thomas Hood,* 318. Illustrations of Hood's poem include E. Barnes, *The Bridge of Sighs* (1856) [painting]; John Everett Millais, illustration in *Passages from the Poems of Thomas Hood, Illustrated by the Junior Etching Club* (1858); Gustave Doré, two illustrations in *Thomas Hood, Illustrated by Gustave Doré* (1878). Works that may have been influenced by Hood's poem and that depict a woman either in the act of committing suicide or dead on the shore include George Cruikshank, "The Maniac Father and the Convict Brother Are Gone—The Poor Girl, Homeless, Friendless, Deserted, Destitute and Gin Mad Commits Self Murder," plate 8 in *The Drunkard's Children* (1848); George Frederic Watts, *Found Drowned* (c. 1848–50) [painting]; Hablot K. Browne, "The River," illustration in Charles Dickens, *David Copperfield* (August 1850); Abraham Solomon, *Drowned! Drowned!* (1860) [painting]; W. Gray, "Found," illustration in William Hayward's novel, *London by Night* (c. 1870). These additional works do not depict the act of suicide, but they do feature the river in their representations of fallen womanhood: Dante Gabriel Rossetti, *Found* (c. 1853) [painting]; Simeon Solomon, *"I am starving"* (1857) [drawing]; Augustus Egg, *Past and Present,* panel 3 (1858) [painting]. For these works and further information on the prostitute in Victorian visual art see Casteras, *Images of Victorian Womanhood;* Nead, *Myths of Sexuality;* and Julian Treuherz et al., *Hard Times: Social Realism in Victorian Art* (London: Lund Humphries, 1987).

30. "Thames Banks—Quays to Come," *Builder,* 16 July 1859, 466.

31. Ibid.

32. See "The Victoria Embankment," *Builder,* 16 July 1870, 562, for details of the physical characteristics of the Embankment as reported on the occasion of its official opening.

33. Granville, 12.

34. *Times,* 7 May 1860, 8.

35. *Report on Main Drainage,* 38.

36. The legislation approving construction of the main drainage reportedly owed as much to the location of the Houses of Parliament on the banks of the Thames as it did to public opinion, for—as noted above—members of the House suffered severely from the noxious fumes rising from the river. See Halliday, 71–76; David Owen, *The Government of Victorian London, 1855–1889: The Metropolitan Board of Works, the Vestries, and the City Corporation,* ed. Roy MacLeod (Cambridge, MA: Harvard University Press, 1982), 53–55.

37. Owen, 75.

38. *Report on Main Drainage,* 42–43.

39. Dale Porter discusses four possible options for the course of the low-level sewer presented by the Metropolitan Board of Works, including the plan to run the sewer under the foreshore of the Thames without an embankment (*Thames Embankment,* 74–75).

40. *Report on Main Drainage,* 43.

41. "A Word about the Thames Embankment," letter to the editor, *Builder*, 12 March 1870, 209.

42. David Sibley, "Outsiders in Society and Space," in *Inventing Places: Studies in Cultural Geography*, ed. Kay Anderson and Fay Gale (Sydney: Longman Cheshire, 1992), 114.

43. James Winter, *London's Teeming Streets, 1830–1914* (London: Routledge, 1993), 17–21.

44. Donald J. Olsen, *The City as a Work of Art: London, Paris, Vienna* (New Haven, CT: Yale University Press, 1986), 24.

45. "Embankment of the Thames," *Builder*, 10 February 1866, 105.

46. "The Thames Embankment, in Reference to the General Embellishment of London," *Builder*, 12 March 1864, 182.

47. "The Thames Embankment," *Times*, 21 July 1864, 8.

48. *Times*, 31 July 1860, 9.

49. *Times*, 19 March 1863, 11.

50. "London on the Thames: The Desired Embankments," *Builder*, 25 January 1862, 62.

51. Ibid.

52. Ibid.

53. "Thames Banks—Quays to Come," *Builder*, 16 July 1859, 466.

54. *Times*, 19 March 1863, 11.

55. Owen, 74.

56. Donald J. Olsen, *The Growth of Victorian London* (London: B. T. Batsford, 1976), 51–54.

57. "The Thames Embankment," *Times*, 21 July 1864, 8.

58. Angus B. Reach, *London on the Thames; or, Life Above and Below Bridge* (London, 1848), 10.

59. Ibid.

60. Ibid., 13.

61. Ibid., 13–14.

62. "Silent Highway-Men" is attributed to Edmund Yates by Ella Ann Oppenlander in *Dickens' All the Year Round: Descriptive Index and Contributor List* (Troy, NY: Whitston, 1984). All further attributions of authorship to pieces from *All the Year Round* are derived from Oppenlander.

63. [Edmund Yates], "Silent Highway-Men," *All the Year Round*, 31 October 1863, 234.

64. Ibid.

65. Ibid., 235.

66. This discussion of the picturesque is informed by Nancy K. Hill, *A Reformer's Art: Dickens' Picturesque and Grotesque Imagery* (Athens: Ohio University Press, 1981); George Landow, "Two Modes of the Picturesque," in *The Aesthetic and Critical Theories of John Ruskin* (Princeton, NJ: Princeton University Press, 1971); and Nicholas Taylor, "The Awful Sublimity of the Victorian City: Its Aesthetic and Architectural Origins," in *The Victorian City: Images and Realities*, ed. H. J. Dyos and Michael Wolff, vol. 2 (London: Routledge and Kegan Paul, 1973), 431–47.

67. Taylor, 433.

68. Jerrold refers to himself and Doré as "wanderers in search of the picturesque," and the term recurs throughout the work (Gustave Doré and Blanchard Jerrold, *London: A Pilgrimage* [1872; repr., New York: Dover, 1970], 15). Although *London: A Pilgrimage* was a collaboration and its text and images are certainly in dialogue with one another, we must also recognize where text and images diverge. In the catalogue for the exhibit *Monet's London: Artists' Reflections on the Thames, 1859–1914* (St. Petersburg: Museum of Fine Arts, St. Petersburg, Florida, 2005), Jennifer Hardin argues, "The meaning of some of Doré's illustrations runs counter to passages in Jerrold's text" (171). In her more comprehensive treatment of *London: A Pilgrimage,* Griselda Pollock suggests that Jerrold's nostalgic text and Doré's Gothic images are operating on different aesthetic registers, although this point is not central to her argument; see Pollock, "Vicarious Excitements: *London: A Pilgrimage* by Gustave Doré and Blanchard Jerrold, 1872," *New Formations* 4 (1988): 47.

69. Doré and Jerrold, 8.

70. Ibid., 21–22.

71. Ibid., 34.

72. Ibid.

73. Ibid., 36–37.

74. Pollock, 47.

75. Doré and Jerrold, 37.

76. Ibid.

77. "What to Do with the Thames Embankment," *Building News,* 12 August 1870, 112–13.

78. William Worsley, *Thames Reform: A New Plan for the Drainage of the Metropolis; Combined with Practical Suggestions for Public Convenience, Health, and Recreation* (London, 1856), 22.

79. "River Pollutions: The River Thames," *Builder,* 11 July 1868, 513.

80. Luckin, *Pollution and Control,* 146–48, and Wohl, *Endangered Lives,* 240, discuss the new pressures that the main drainage put on communities downstream from central London. In this context, they also describe the accident of the *Princess Alice* and the public outcry it excited.

81. "Population and Thoroughfares," *Building News,* 23 October 1874, 481.

82. "The Thames Embankment," *Builder,* 18 March 1882, 306.

83. "A Stranger on the Thames Embankment," letter to the editor, *Builder,* 16 October 1869, 824.

84. "The Thames Embankment," letter to the editor, *Builder,* 28 November 1868, 881.

85. "'Decency' and the Victoria Embankment," letter to the editor, *Building News,* 19 April 1872, 325.

86. "The Thames Embankment," *Times,* 16 March 1882, 10.

87. "The Thames Embankment," *Builder,* 18 March 1882, 306.

88. W. Booth, 38.

89. Literary representations of the Thames Embankment as a haunt of the homeless appear in Richard Dowling's short story collection *On the Embankment* (London, 1884)

and in Cicely Hamilton's "new woman" play *Diana of Dobson's* (1908), in *New Woman Plays,* ed. Linda Fitzsimmons and Viv Gardner (London: Methuen, 1991).

90. Olsen, *Growth,* 294.

91. Soja, "Spatiality of Social Life," 94.

92. Doré and Jerrold, 37.

Chapter 3

The epigraph to this chapter is drawn from Algernon Charles Swinburne, "Charles Dickens," *Quarterly Review* 196 (July 1902): 21.

1. Charles Dickens, *Our Mutual Friend,* ed. Stephen Gill (New York: Penguin, 1971), 56. Subsequent references are to this edition and are cited in the text.

2. Humphry House, *The Dickens World,* 2nd ed. (Oxford: Oxford University Press, 1960); Edgar Johnson, "The Great Dust-Heap," in *Charles Dickens: His Tragedy and Triumph,* vol. 2 (New York: Simon and Schuster, 1952), 1022–45; Earle Davis, *The Flint and the Flame: The Artistry of Charles Dickens* (Columbia: University of Missouri Press, 1963), 265–66.

3. In "The Dust-Heaps in *Our Mutual Friend,*" *Essays in Criticism* 23 (1973): 206–12, Harvey Peter Sucksmith outlines the points of contention in the dust-excrement debate. He reaffirms House's basic claim that dust mounds could and probably would have contained excrement and disputes Stephen Gill's later claim to the contrary. Gill's explanation in the notes to the previously cited Penguin edition of *Our Mutual Friend* (1971) derives from Henry Mayhew's careful classification of the collection of "night soil" (human waste) and "dust" (ashes) as separate activities. Gill is striving for accuracy (as was Mayhew) in an area where ambiguity seems to have been inevitable, if not embraced. As Adrian Poole puts it in the more recent Penguin edition of the novel, "In his methodical manner Mayhew tries to separate three kinds of waste (dust, street sweepings, and night-soil) . . . and the three kinds of labour involved in their removal. . . . But his distinctions keep collapsing. . . . As with the labourers, so with the matter they deal with: you cannot control what goes into the piles and heaps and pools of waste, nor can you predict what may be found in them" (Notes to *Our Mutual Friend* [New York: Penguin, 1997], 805).

4. In *Between Men: English Literature and Male Homosocial Desire* (New York: Columbia University Press, 1985), Eve Kosofsky Sedgwick reorients the dust-money line of interpretation toward its original context in Freud, that of anal eroticism: "*Our Mutual Friend* is the only English novel that everyone says is about excrement in order that they may forget it is about anality" (164). Ellen Handy, "Dust Piles and Damp Pavements: Excrement, Repression, and the Victorian City in Photography and Literature," in *Victorian Literature and the Victorian Visual Imagination,* ed. Carol T. Christ and John O. Jordan (Berkeley: University of California Press, 1995), draws on Freud's work on repression to argue the centrality of *disguised* excrement to Dickens's artistic vision (118–23).

5. Focusing on Mr. Venus's articulation of skeletons from assorted bones and Jenny Wren's creation of doll dresses from remnants of fabric, Nancy Metz argues that recla-

mation in the novel is not just a material and social act but a fundamentally imaginative one as well; see "The Artistic Reclamation of Waste in *Our Mutual Friend*," *Nineteenth-Century Fiction* 34 (1979): 68.

6. J. Hillis Miller in "The Topography of Jealousy in *Our Mutual Friend*," in *Dickens Refigured: Bodies, Desires and Other Histories,* ed. John Schad (Manchester: Manchester University Press, 1996), highlights what he calls the radical "otherness" of the river—its status as a realm outside both the social order and narrative place and time, "a region where one ceases to be oneself and may (or may not) emerge transformed" (222).

7. An important exception is Pamela K. Gilbert, "Medical Mapping: The Thames, the Body, and *Our Mutual Friend*," in *Filth: Dirt, Disgust, and Modern Life,* ed. William A. Cohen and Ryan Johnson (Minneapolis: University of Minnesota Press, 2005), 78–102. Gilbert reads the novel's representation of the Thames and the circulation of moral and material filth along the river as a response to the physician John Snow's work. During the cholera epidemic of 1854–55, Snow had linked the spread of the disease to infected water supplies drawn from the Thames. While I certainly agree with Gilbert that the Thames of the novel is a major source of contamination, I depart from her argument in seeing the river as also potentially purifying. See the fourth section of this chapter.

8. Dickens, *The Letters of Charles Dickens,* ed. Madeline House and Graham Storey, Pilgrim Edition, 12 vols. (Oxford: Oxford University Press, 1965–2002), 11:116.

9. Dickens, *Letters,* 12:268.

10. My argument about the significance of the Embankment for *Our Mutual Friend* differs considerably from that of Deirdre David, *Fictions of Resolution in Three Victorian Novels:* North and South, Our Mutual Friend, Daniel Deronda (New York: Columbia University Press, 1981), and F. S. Schwarzbach, *Dickens and the City* (London: Athlone Press, 1979). Neither David nor Schwarzbach discusses the Embankment—the physical plan, the aspirations behind it—in great detail, but David sees it as a metaphor for Dickens's novelistic project of social regeneration (53–54), and Schwarzbach similarly sees it as an important symbol of urban change for a novel that celebrates transformation (211–12). In other words, both critics align the novel and the Embankment, whereas I see them as approaching the challenge of purification in fundamentally different ways.

11. David, 55.

12. Tuan, 224.

13. David discusses at greater length Lizzie's "magical immunity from the taint of East End experience" (67–70).

14. Philip Collins, "Dickens and London," in *The Victorian City: Images and Realities,* ed. H. J. Dyos and Michael Wolff, vol. 2 (London: Routledge and Kegan Paul, 1973), 537–38; Schwarzbach, 23.

15. Charles Dickens, *Oliver Twist,* ed. Philip Horne (London: Penguin, 2002), 389; Charles Dickens, *David Copperfield,* 554; Charles Dickens, *Little Dorrit,* ed. Harvey Peter Sucksmith (Oxford: Oxford University Press, 1982), 148.

16. Charles Dickens, "Down with the Tide," in *The Uncommercial Traveller and Reprinted Pieces* (London: Oxford University Press, 1968), 528, 529.

17. Ibid., 527.

18. Charles Dickens, "On Duty with Inspector Field," in *The Uncommercial Traveller and Reprinted Pieces*, 522.

19. See Catherine Gallagher, *The Body Economic: Life, Death, and Sensation in Political Economy and the Victorian Novel* (Princeton, NJ: Princeton University Press, 2006), for a reading of this scene and what it suggests about the limits of a humanitarian economic theory that invests value in the human body (93—97).

20. Dickens, *Letters*, 9:383.

21. Dickens, *David Copperfield*, 555.

22. In *The City of Dickens* (Cambridge, MA: Harvard University Press, 1986), Alexander Welsh explains, "The problem of where bodies went in London became acute by the middle of the century" (62). Thus, the biblical association of the earthly city with death—still prevalent in the nineteenth century—had a very concrete dimension.

23. Poole, "Introduction," *Our Mutual Friend*, xv.

24. [William M. Thackeray], "Greenwich—Whitebait," *New Monthly Magazine*, ser. 2, 71 (July 1844): 420.

25. Richard Doyle, "Dining down the River," *Cornhill* 5 (January 1862): 105.

26. [Edmund Yates], "The Business of Pleasure," *All the Year Round*, 10 October 1863, 149—52.

27. Robert Allbut, *Rambles in Dickens' Land* (New York: Truslove, 1899), 116.

28. Wohl, *Endangered Lives*, 234.

29. [Charles Dickens], "A Paper-Mill," *Household Words*, 31 August 1850, 529, 531.

30. Ibid., 529—30.

31. Ibid., 530.

32. Gilbert, 94; emphasis added.

Chapter 4

The epigraph to this chapter is drawn from *Daily Telegraph*, 13 November 1874, in newspaper clippings collected by the Metropolitan Board of Works, p. 289, shelf mark MBW 1920, London Metropolitan Archives.

1. Charles Dickens, preface to *Oliver Twist*, Cheap Edition, in *Oliver Twist*, ed. Philip Horne (New York: Penguin, 2002), 461.

2. Arnold White, *The Problems of a Great City* (1886; repr., New York: Garland, 1985), 23.

3. George Sale Reaney, "Outcast London," *Fortnightly Review*, n.s., 40 (December 1886): 689.

4. Parliament, *Second Report of the Royal Commission on the State of Large Towns and Populous Districts*, 1845 (602), vol. 18, Irish University Press Series of British Parliamentary Papers, Health: General, 6 (Shannon: Irish University Press, 1970), 58.

5. Parliament, *Second Report from the Select Committee on Metropolis Improvements*, 1837—

38 (661), vol. 16, Irish University Press Series of British Parliamentary Papers, Urban Areas: Planning, 1 (Shannon: Irish University Press, 1968), 103. Cited hereafter as *Second Report on Metropolis Improvements.*

6. *Times,* 26 August 1871, 7.

7. As Winter has shown in *London's Teeming Streets,* circulatory and respiratory metaphors derived from medical discourse helped define Victorian conceptions of the healthy (or sick) city (8).

8. See H. J. Dyos, "The Objects of Street Improvement in Regency and Early Victorian London," in *Exploring the Urban Past: Essays in Urban History by H. J. Dyos,* ed. David Cannadine and David Reeder (Cambridge: Cambridge University Press, 1982), 81–86. According to Dyos, the fact that there was limited public and financial support for sweeping improvements in London may explain the tendency of street reforms to encompass sanitary concerns, and the corresponding tendency of sanitary reformers to accept street construction as a means to further their agenda (85).

9. *Second Report on Metropolis Improvements,* 93.

10. Ibid., iv.

11. Dyos, *Exploring the Urban Past,* 85.

12. Anthony S. Wohl, *The Eternal Slum* (London: Edward Arnold, 1977), 21–44.

13. Chadwick, 346.

14. Henry Jephson, *The Sanitary Evolution of London* (1907; repr., New York: Arno, 1978), 9.

15. William Denton, *Observations on the Displacement of the Poor, by Metropolitan Railways and by Other Public Improvements* (London, 1861), 10. Dyos, basing his figures on the demolition statements that railways were required to provide after 1853, determined that 76,000 persons were displaced between 1853 and 1901 by clearance schemes executed solely for railways; see "Railways and Housing in Victorian London," *The Journal of Transport History* 2 (1955): 14.

16. [Joseph Charles Parkinson], "Attila in London," *All the Year Round,* 26 May 1866, 466.

17. Ibid.

18. W[illiam] M. Torrens, "What Is to Be Done with the Slums?" *Macmillan's Magazine* 39 (April 1879): 535.

19. For more on the origins and implementation of the Cross Act, see Owen, 109–13; Gareth Stedman Jones, *Outcast London: A Study in the Relationship between Classes in Victorian Society* (New York: Pantheon, 1984), chap. 10; and J. A. Yelling, *Slums and Slum Clearance in Victorian London* (London: Allen and Unwin, 1986), 9–30. For a discussion of the Cross Act in reference to the Torrens Act and earlier housing and sanitary legislation, see Wohl, *Eternal Slum,* 92–108.

20. Yelling, 14.

21. Owen, 111; Yelling, 26.

22. Yelling, 26.

23. Jones explains that the strict rules governing most of the model dwellings prevented occupants from engaging in offensive trades, such as fur-pulling and matchbox making, in their rooms. This and other restrictions (including especially limits on the number of people allowed in a room) deterred many of London's casual laborers from seeking accommodation in such places (*Outcast London,* 184–85, 202–4).

24. Parliament, *First Report from the Royal Commission on the Housing of the Working Classes,* 1884–85 (c. 4402) (c. 4402-I), vol. 30, Irish University Press Series of British Parliamentary Papers, Urban Areas: Housing, 2 (Shannon: Irish University Press, 1970), 54. Cited hereafter as *Report on the Housing of the Working Classes.*

25. George R. Sims, *How the Poor Live and Horrible London* (1889; repr., New York: Garland, 1984), 106. "How the Poor Live" first appeared as a series of articles in the *Pictorial World* in 1883 (Wohl, *Eternal Slum,* 201).

26. Richard Assheton Cross, "Homes of the Poor in London," *Nineteenth Century* 12 (August 1882): 237.

27. Andrew Mearns, *The Bitter Cry of Outcast London,* ed. Anthony S. Wohl, The Victorian Library (1883; repr., New York: Humanities Press, 1970), 69.

28. *Daily Chronicle,* 8 February 1879, in newspaper clippings collected by the Metropolitan Board of Works, p. 291, shelf mark MBW 1921, London Metropolitan Archives. Cited hereafter as MBW newspaper.

29. "The Artisans' Dwelling Bill," *Saturday Review,* 10 May 1879, in MBW newspaper, p. 325a.

30. "How the Poor Are Housed," *Clerkenwell Press,* 24 August 1878, 3.

31. Inquests, *Times,* 19 August 1878, 11.

32. "How the Poor Are Housed," 3.

33. *Daily News,* 19 August 1878, in MBW newspaper, p. 59.

34. *Daily Telegraph,* 19 August 1878, in MBW newspaper, p. 60.

35. Cross, 231.

36. Ibid., 235.

37. Anthony S. Wohl, introduction to *The Bitter Cry of Outcast London,* by Andrew Mearns, 17–18.

38. Marquess of Salisbury (Robert Cecil), "Housing of the Working Classes," Speech to the House of Lords, 22 February 1884, *Hansard Parliamentary Debates,* 3rd series, vol. 284 (1884), col. 1686.

39. *Report on the Housing of the Working Classes,* 4.

40. Ibid., 8.

41. Ibid., 6–7.

42. "Objectionable Lodgers," *Globe,* 31 August 1878, in MBW newspaper, p. 79.

43. Sims, *How the Poor Live and Horrible London,* 115.

44. Jones, 286.

45. Peter Keating, ed., *Into Unknown England, 1866–1913: Selections from the Social Explorers* (Manchester: Manchester University Press, 1976), 19–20.

46. Jones, 281–82.

47. William Greenslade, *Degeneration, Culture and the Novel, 1880–1940* (Cambridge: Cambridge University Press, 1994), 39.

48. Jones, 127–28.

49. White, 28.

50. Wohl, *Endangered Lives,* 332.

51. Alfred Marshall, "The Housing of the London Poor: Where to House Them," *Contemporary Review* 45 (February 1884): 226.

52. Ibid., 229.

53. The potentially negative implications of degeneration theory for social activism were not lost on General William Booth. In his tract *In Darkest England and the Way Out,* he insists that there is indeed a "way out" for everyone, no matter how enfeebled or depraved. He utterly rejects degeneration as an interpretation of modern social life: "The doctrine of Heredity and the suggestion of Irresponsibility come perilously near reestablishing, on scientific bases, the awful dogma of Reprobation which has cast so terrible a shadow over the Christian Church" (55).

54. Harold E. Boulton, "The Housing of the Poor," *Fortnightly Review,* o.s., 49 (February 1888): 282.

55. Mearns, 61.

56. Sims, *How the Poor Live and Horrible London,* 43.

57. Keating, 20.

58. Jack London, *The People of the Abyss* (1902; repr., London: Pluto, 2001), 20.

59. Octavia Hill, *Homes of the London Poor* (1883; repr., London: Cass, 1970), 89.

60. London, 28.

61. C. F. G. Masterman, *From the Abyss: Of its Inhabitants by One of Them* (1902; repr., New York: Garland, 1980), 12.

62. *Report on the Housing of the Working Classes,* 37.

63. Ibid.

64. Ibid., 60.

65. Ibid.

66. Ibid.

67. *Daily News,* 14 October 1878, in MBW newspaper, p. 433.

68. George R. Sims, "Evicted London," in *Living London: Its Work and Its Play, Its Humour and Its Pathos, Its Sights and Its Scenes,* ed. George R. Sims, vol. 1 (London: Cassell, 1903), 206.

69. Ibid., 204.

70. Ibid.

71. Brooke Lambert, "The Outcast Poor: Esau's Cry," *Contemporary Review* 44 (December 1883): 917.

72. H. O. Arnold-Forster, "Common Sense and the Dwellings of the Poor: The Existing Law," *Nineteenth Century* 14 (December 1883): 941.

73. Sims, *How the Poor Live and Horrible London,* 44.

74. Matthew Beaumont, "Cacotopianism, the Paris Commune, and England's Anti-Communist Imaginary, 1870–1900," *ELH* 73 (2006): 466. http://muse.jhu.edu.

75. For a full account of the Trafalgar Square demonstration and succeeding riot, as well as the official response of the government, see Donald C. Richter, *Riotous Victorians* (Athens: Ohio University Press, 1981), 103–32.

76. "The Unemployed in London," *Times*, 9 February 1886, 6.

77. The *Times* ("Unemployed in London," 9 February 1886, 6) puts the number of those who marched into Pall Mall Street at one to two thousand, while the Parliamentary report on the riot and police response estimates this part of the crowd at three to five thousand people; see *Report of a Committee to Inquire and Report as to the Origin and Character of the Disturbances Which Took Place in the Metropolis on Monday, the 8th of February, and as to the Conduct of the Police Authorities in Relation Thereto*, 1886 (c. 4665), vol. 34, p. vi. Cited hereafter as *Report of the Disturbances*.

78. Richter, 110, 113.

79. Jones, 292–94.

80. "Riots in London," *Times*, 11 February 1886, 6.

81. Jones, 292.

82. *Report of the Disturbances*, 8.

83. Ibid.

84. Ibid., 28.

85. Jones, 295.

86. "The Police and the Mob," *Times*, 22 October 1887, 6.

87. "Our Homeless Poor—Midday in St. James's Park," *Graphic*, 17 September 1887, 302.

88. Ibid.

89. See Richter, 133–62, for an account of Bloody Sunday and events leading up to it.

90. "The No-Police Riots," *Saturday Review*, 13 February 1886, 219.

91. *Times*, 10 February 1886, 9.

92. *Times*, 18 October 1887, 9.

93. Reaney, 695.

94. Ibid.

95. H[enry] M. Hyndman, "The English Workers as They Are," *Contemporary Review* 52 (July 1887): 123.

96. Ibid., 136.

97. Hubert Bland, "The Socialist Party in Relation to Politics," *Practical Socialist* (October 1886), quoted in A. M. McBriar, *Fabian Socialism and English Politics, 1884–1918* (Cambridge: Cambridge University Press, 1966), 18.

98. G. B. Shaw, "The Transition to Social Democracy," in *Fabian Essays in Socialism* (London: Walter Scott, 1889), quoted in McBriar, *Fabian Socialism*, 19.

99. Jones, 343.

100. Samuel A. Barnett, "A Scheme for the Unemployed," *Nineteenth Century* 24 (November 1888): 753.

101. W. Booth, 33.
102. Masterman, 2.
103. Ibid., 70.
104. Ibid., 71.

Chapter 5

The epigraphs to this chapter are drawn from George Gissing, *The Nether World,* ed. Stephen Gill (Oxford: Oxford University Press, 1992), 364, 387. Subsequent references are to this edition and are cited in the text.

1. Ibid.

2. David Grylls, *The Paradox of Gissing* (London: Allen and Unwin, 1986), 39.

3. See Jacob Korg, *George Gissing: A Critical Biography* (Seattle: University of Washington Press, 1963), especially 11–13, 110–11.

4. Gissing, *The Collected Letters of George Gissing,* ed. Paul F. Mattheisen et al., 9 vols. (Athens: Ohio University Press, 1990), 3:188.

5. George Gissing, *London and the Life of Literature in Late Victorian England: The Diary of George Gissing, Novelist,* ed. Pierre Coustillas (Lewisburg, PA: Bucknell University Press, 1978), 23.

6. F[rederick] W. Farrar, "*The Nether World,*" *Contemporary Review* 56 (September 1889): 370.

7. Ibid., 377, 370–71.

8. Unsigned review of *The Nether World,* by George Gissing, *Court Journal* (27 April 1889), 590, quoted in Pierre Coustillas and Colin Partridge, eds., *Gissing: The Critical Heritage* (London: Routledge and Kegan Paul, 1972), 136.

9. Unsigned review of *The Nether World,* by George Gissing, *Whitehall Review* (4 May 1889), 19, quoted in Coustillas and Partridge, 138.

10. Introduction to *The Nether World,* by George Gissing, Colonial Edition (1890), quoted in Coustillas and Partridge, 136.

11. Ibid. For a very different contemporary assessment of Gissing (specifically, of his novel *Thyrza*) see Edith Sichel, "Two Philanthropic Novelists: Mr. Walter Besant and Mr. George Gissing," *Murray's Magazine* 3 (April 1888): 506–18.

12. Eduard Bertz, "George Gissing: Ein Real-Idealist," *Deutsche Presse* (3, 10, 17 November 1889), quoted in Coustillas and Partridge, 151–52.

13. Ibid., 152.

14. Aaron Matz, "George Gissing's Ambivalent Realism," *Nineteenth-Century Literature* 59, no. 2 (2004): 220.

15. George Gissing, "The Place of Realism in Fiction," *Humanitarian* 7, no. 1 (1895): 16.

16. Bertz, quoted in Coustillas and Partridge, 153, 154.

17. Ibid., 154.

18. Matz, 243.

19. George Orwell, "George Gissing," in *The Collected Essays, Journalism and Letters*

of George Orwell, ed. Sonia Orwell and Ian Angus, vol. 4 (New York: Harcourt, 1968), 435.

20. Ibid.

21. Stephen D. Arata, "Realism, Sympathy, and Gissing's Fictions of Failure," *Victorians Institute Journal* 23 (1995): 27–29.

22. Georg Lukács, *Writer and Critic and Other Essays,* ed. and trans. Arthur Kahn (London: Merlin Press, 1970), 16, quoted in Arata, 28.

23. Frederic Jameson, "Authentic *Ressentiment:* Generic Discontinuities and Ideologemes in the 'Experimental' Novels of George Gissing," in *The Political Unconscious: Narrative as a Socially Symbolic Act* (Ithaca, NY: Cornell University Press, 1981), 193.

24. Ibid., 196.

25. John Goode, "George Gissing's *The Nether World,*" in *Tradition and Tolerance in Nineteenth-Century Fiction: Critical Essays on Some English and American Novels,* ed. David Howard et al. (New York: Barnes and Noble, 1967), 237–39; Adrian Poole, *Gissing in Context* (London: Macmillan, 1975), 90–96.

26. Notable exceptions to this critical trend are Regenia Gagnier, *Subjectivities: A History of Self-Representation in Britain, 1832–1920* (New York: Oxford University Press, 1991); and Trotter, *Cooking with Mud.* Gagnier expresses some frustration with critical assessments of Gissing that fail to recognize how closely he comes (in her assessment) to representing a working-class perspective honestly. Comparing Gissing to Hardy, she insists, "Only the Gissing of *The Nether World* (1889) comes closer to capturing the feeling of systematic overdeterminism in working-class life, and he, like Hardy, has often been mystified by critics as describing an existential condition rather than, as Raymond Williams and Terry Eagleton have ceaselessly pointed out, social injustice" (*Subjectivities,* 108).

27. John Hollingshead, *Ragged London in 1861* (1861; repr., New York: Garland, 1985), 18.

28. *Report on the Housing of the Working Classes,* 61.

29. William Dawson, *A Mid-London Parish: Short History of the Parish of S. John's, Clerkenwell* (London: T. G. Johnson, 1885), 44–45.

30. Hollingshead, *Ragged London,* 10.

31. This and another article from the *Builder* on the housing of the London poor (published 12 and 26 March 1853) appear in a revised form in George Godwin's book-length investigation *London Shadows: A Glance at the "Homes" of the Thousands* (1854). Godwin was editor of the *Builder.*

32. *Builder,* 12 March 1853, 161.

33. Ibid.

34. Ibid.

35. Ibid., 162.

36. "The Waste Ground of New Farringdon-street," *Times,* 10 September 1857, 5.

37. *Builder,* 12 March 1853, 161; emphasis in original.

38. Dawson, 40–41.

39. Ibid., 42.

40. Hollingshead, *Ragged London,* 31.

41. J. W. Griffith to Metropolitan Board of Works, 4 November 1876, Papers of the Metropolitan Board of Works, box 1838, folder 8, London Metropolitan Archives. Cited hereafter as MBW papers.

42. Metropolitan Board of Works, *Report of Proceedings, of Enquiry into Metropolis (Pear Tree Court Clerkenwell) Improvement Scheme,* 28 March 1877, p. 71, shelf mark MBW 1877, London Metropolitan Archives.

43. Ibid., pp. 20, 9.

44. Ibid., p. 154.

45. Yelling, 26.

46. Order submitted to Parliament by J. E. Wakefield, 11 June 1877, MBW papers.

47. *Report on the Housing of the Working Classes,* 20.

48. Ibid., 38.

49. Ibid., 77.

50. John Nelson Tarn, *Five Per Cent Philanthropy: An Account of Housing in Urban Areas between 1840 and 1914* (Cambridge: Cambridge University Press, 1973), 97.

51. For Gissing's complex relationship to aestheticism, see Diana Maltz, "Practical Aesthetics and Decadent Rationale in George Gissing," *Victorian Literature and Culture* 28 (2000): 55–71.

52. Adrian Poole explains that Gissing had read Arnold White's book *The Problems of a Great City* (1886) before writing *The Nether World* (Poole, *Gissing in Context,* 85). The influence of White's discussion of the reproductive activities of the London poor is especially evident in Gissing's representation of children in the novel.

53. The epigraph, from Ernest Renan, reads as follows: "La peinture d'un fumier peut être justifiée pourvu qu'il y pousse une belle fleur; sans cela, le fumier n'est que repoussant." Stephen Gill provides the following translation in his notes to the Oxford University Press edition of the novel: "A painting of a dung-heap might be justified if a beautiful flower grew out of it; otherwise the dung-heap is merely repulsive" (Gissing, *Nether World,* 393).

54. John Goode, *George Gissing: Ideology and Fiction* (London: Vision, 1978), 92, 97.

55. Charles Booth's topographic survey of poverty in London is reproduced as *Charles Booth's Descriptive Map of London Poverty, 1889* (London: London Topographical Society, 1984), with an introduction by David A. Reeder.

56. Goode, *George Gissing,* 94.

57. Tuan, 174.

58. Trotter, 254.

Afterword

The epigraph to this chapter is drawn from G. B. Shaw, *Major Barbara,* ed. Dan H. Laurence (London: Penguin, 1960), 141.

1. Shaw, 109. Subsequent references are to this edition and are cited in the text.

2. Stanton B. Garner, "Shaw's Comedy of Disillusionment," *Modern Drama* 28, no. 4 (1985): 655.

3. Gissing, *Nether World*, 109.

4. Shaw himself, as a Fabian socialist active in local politics, was very much a participant in the renewed culture of reform.

5. Hall is quoted in Dennis Hardy, *From Garden Cities to New Towns: Campaigning for Town and Country Planning, 1899–1946* (London: E. and F. N. Spon, 1991), 5.

6. Tarn, 116.

7. Anthony Sutcliffe, *Towards the Planned City: Germany, Britain, the United States and France, 1780–1914* (New York: St. Martin's Press, 1981), 56, 63. In response to the recruiting debacle, the Inter-Departmental Committee on Physical Deterioration was created in 1903 to investigate the role town life played in the physical degeneration of its inhabitants (Sutcliffe, 71).

8. The first garden city, Letchworth, was founded in 1903. For the origins and evolution of the garden city movement, see Hardy.

9. For the suburban housing estates developed by the London County Council, see Tarn, 137–42.

10. McBriar, 190.

11. Susan D. Pennybacker, *A Vision for London, 1889–1914: Labour, Everyday Life and the LCC Experiment* (London and New York: Routledge, 1995), 11.

12. Wohl, *Eternal Slum*, 252–55.

13. Ibid., 260.

14. Tarn, 130.

15. Ibid., 129.

16. See Pennybacker for a discussion of the imperial dimensions of the London County Council's work.

17. Jon A. Peterson, *The Birth of City Planning in the United States, 1840–1917* (Baltimore: Johns Hopkins University Press, 2003), 33–38.

18. Martin V. Melosi, *The Sanitary City: Urban Infrastructure in America from Colonial Times to the Present* (Baltimore: Johns Hopkins University Press, 2000), 110.

19. Ibid., 110–12.

20. Dirk Schubert and Anthony Sutcliffe, "The 'Haussmannization' of London? The Planning and Construction of Kingsway-Aldwych, 1889–1935," *Planning Perspectives* 11 (1996): 120.

21. Ibid., 129.

22. Hermione Hobhouse, *Lost London* (Boston: Houghton Mifflin, 1972), 73.

23. For Clare Market, see Schubert and Sutcliffe, 127–28; for Holywell Street, see Nead, *Victorian Babylon*, 165.

24. Quoted in Schubert and Sutcliffe, 128.

25. G. Shaw Lefevre, "London Street Improvements," *Contemporary Review* 75 (February 1899): 212.

26. Jonathan Schneer, *London, 1900: The Imperial Metropolis* (New Haven, CT: Yale University Press, 2001), 22, 268–69 n. 10.

27. Schubert and Sutcliffe, 135–38.

28. Wilfred Whitten, *A Londoner's London* (Boston: Small Maynard and Co., 1912), 8.

29. Ibid., 9.

30. Ibid., 146.

31. Ibid., 142.

bibliography

Allbut, Robert. *Rambles in Dickens' Land*. New York: Truslove, 1899.

Arata, Stephen D. "Realism, Sympathy, and Gissing's Fictions of Failure." *Victorians Institute Journal* 23 (1995): 27–49.

Arnold-Forster, H. O. "Common Sense and the Dwellings of the Poor: The Existing Law." *Nineteenth Century* 14 (December 1883): 940–51.

Bannehr, J. *The Sewage Difficulty*. London, [1866].

Barnes, Trevor, and Derek Gregory, eds. *Reading Human Geography: The Poetics and Politics of Inquiry*. London: Arnold, 1997.

Barnett, Samuel A. "A Scheme for the Unemployed." *Nineteenth Century* 24 (November 1888): 753–63.

Bazalgette, Joseph William. *On the Main Drainage of London, and the Interception of the Sewage from the River Thames*. Edited by James Forrest. London, 1865.

Beaumont, Matthew. "Cacotopianism, the Paris Commune, and England's Anti-Communist Imaginary, 1870–1900." *ELH* 73 (2006): 465–87. http://muse.jhu.edu.

Best, Geoffrey. *Mid-Victorian Britain, 1851–1875*. London: Weidenfeld and Nicolson, 1971.

Bird, Peter Hinckes. *Hints on Drains, Traps, Closets, Sewer Gas, and Sewage Disposal*. Blackpool, UK, 1877.

Blake, Edward T. *Sewage-Poisoning; How to Avoid It in the Simplest Way*. London, [1879].

Booth, Charles. *Charles Booth's Descriptive Map of London Poverty, 1889*. Introduction by David A. Reeder. London: London Topographical Society, 1984.

Booth, G. R. *The London Sewerage Question: Some Serious Observations and Suggestions upon the Defective Plan of Sewerage Proposed by the Metropolitan Board of Works, Together with a Method for Remedying the Evil*. London, n.d.

Booth, William. *In Darkest England and the Way Out*. 1890. Reprint, London: International Headquarters of the Salvation Army, [1970].

Boulton, Harold E. "The Housing of the Poor." *Fortnightly Review*, o.s., 49 (February 1888): 279–86.

Brown, S. S. *A Lay Lecture on Sanitary Matters, with a Paper on Sewer Ventilation*. London, 1873.

Builder 11 (12 March 1853): 161–62.

Casteras, Susan P. *Images of Victorian Womanhood in English Art*. London: Associated University Presses, 1987.

Chadwick, Edwin. *Report on the Sanitary Condition of the Labouring Population of Great Britain*. Edited by M. W. Flinn. 1842. Reprint, Edinburgh: Edinburgh University Press, 1965.

Chase, Karen, and Michael Levenson. "On the Parapets of Privacy." In *A Companion to Victorian Literature and Culture,* edited by Herbert F. Tucker, 425–37. Oxford, UK: Blackwell, 1999.

Childers, Joseph W. *Novel Possibilities: Fiction and the Formation of Early Victorian Culture.* Philadelphia: University of Pennsylvania Press, 1995.

Clarke, G. Rochfort. *The Reform of the Sewers: Where Shall We Bathe? What Shall We Drink? or, Manure Wasted and Land Starved.* 2nd ed. London, 1860.

Clubbe, John, ed. *Selected Poems of Thomas Hood.* Cambridge, MA: Harvard University Press, 1970.

Cohen, William A. "Locating Filth." Introduction to Cohen and Johnson, *Filth,* vii–xxxvii.

Cohen, William A., and Ryan Johnson, eds. *Filth: Dirt, Disgust, and Modern Life.* Minneapolis: University of Minnesota Press, 2005.

Collins, H[enry] H. *On the Ill-Construction and Want of Sanitary Provisions Which Exist in the Dwellings of the Upper and Middle Classes, and Suggestions for Remedying the Same.* London, 1875.

Collins, Philip. "Dickens and London." In Dyos and Wolff, *The Victorian City,* 2:537–57.

"The Condition of the Thames." *Builder,* 3 July 1858, 449ff.

Coustillas, Pierre, and Colin Partridge, eds. *Gissing: The Critical Heritage.* London: Routledge and Kegan Paul, 1972.

Cross, Richard Assheton. "Homes of the Poor in London." *Nineteenth Century* 12 (August 1882): 231–41.

David, Deirdre. *Fictions of Resolution in Three Victorian Novels:* North and South, Our Mutual Friend, Daniel Deronda. New York: Columbia University Press, 1981.

Davidoff, Leonore, and Catherine Hall. *Family Fortunes: Men and Women of the English Middle Class, 1780–1850.* Chicago: University of Chicago Press, 1991.

Davis, Earle. *The Flint and the Flame: The Artistry of Charles Dickens.* Columbia: University of Missouri Press, 1963.

Davison, Graeme. "The City as a Natural System: Theories of Urban Society in Early Nineteenth-Century Britain." In *The Pursuit of Urban History,* edited by Derek Fraser and Anthony Sutcliffe, 349–70. London: Edward Arnold, 1983.

Dawson, William. *A Mid-London Parish: Short History of the Parish of S. John's, Clerkenwell.* London: T. G. Johnson, 1885.

"'Decency' and the Victoria Embankment." Letter to the editor. *Building News,* 19 April 1872, 325.

Denton, William. *Observations on the Displacement of the Poor, by Metropolitan Railways and by Other Public Improvements.* London, 1861.

Dickens, Charles. *David Copperfield.* Edited by Nina Burgis. Oxford: Oxford University Press, 1982.

———. *Dombey and Son.* The Oxford Illustrated Dickens. Oxford: Oxford University Press, 1991.

———. "Down with the Tide." In Dickens, *Uncommercial Traveller,* 527–36.

————. *Great Expectations.* Edited by Margaret Cardwell. Oxford: Oxford University Press, 1994.

————. *The Letters of Charles Dickens.* Edited by Madeline House and Graham Storey. Pilgrim Edition. 12 vols. Oxford: Oxford University Press, 1965–2002.

————. *Little Dorrit.* Edited by Harvey Peter Sucksmith. Oxford: Oxford University Press, 1982.

————. *Oliver Twist.* Edited by Philip Horne. London: Penguin, 2002.

————. "On Duty with Inspector Field." In Dickens, *Uncommercial Traveller,* 513–26.

————. *Our Mutual Friend.* Edited by Stephen Gill. New York: Penguin, 1971.

[————]. "A Paper-Mill." *Household Words,* 31 August 1850, 529–31.

————. Preface to *Oliver Twist,* Cheap Edition. In *Oliver Twist,* edited by Philip Horne, 461–64. New York: Penguin, 2002.

————. *The Uncommercial Traveller and Reprinted Pieces.* The Oxford Illustrated Dickens. London: Oxford University Press, 1968.

————. *The Works of Charles Dickens.* 34 vols. New York: Scribner's, 1900.

Doré, Gustave, and Blanchard Jerrold. *London: A Pilgrimage.* 1872. Reprint, New York: Dover, 1970.

Douglas, Mary. *Purity and Danger: An Analysis of the Concepts of Pollution and Taboo.* 1966. Reprint, London: Routledge, 1991.

Dowling, Richard. *On the Embankment.* London, 1884.

Doyle, Richard. "Dining down the River." *Cornhill* 5 (January 1862): 105–06.

"The Drainage of Middle-Class Houses." *Building News,* 3 December 1869, 418.

Dyos, H. J. *Exploring the Urban Past: Essays in Urban History by H. J. Dyos.* Edited by David Cannadine and David Reeder. Cambridge: Cambridge University Press, 1982.

————. "Railways and Housing in Victorian London." Pts. 1 and 2. *Journal of Transport History* 2 (1955): 11–21, 90–100.

Dyos, H. J., and Michael Wolff, eds. *The Victorian City: Images and Realities.* 2 vols. London: Routledge and Kegan Paul, 1973.

Edwards, Percy J. *History of London Street Improvements, 1855–1897.* London: London County Council, 1898.

"Embankment of the Thames." *Builder,* 10 February 1866, 105.

Farrar, F[rederick] W. "*The Nether World.*" *Contemporary Review* 56 (September 1889): 370–80.

Finer, S. E. *The Life and Times of Sir Edwin Chadwick.* New York: Barnes and Noble, 1970.

Flower, Lamorock. *The Prince of Wales and Sanitary Reform:"An Englishman's House Is His Castle"; Not Now!! Why?* London, 1871.

Foucault, Michel. "The Eye of Power." In *Power/Knowledge: Selected Interviews and Other Writings, 1972–1977,* edited by Colin Gordon, 146–65. Brighton, UK: Harvester, 1980.

Gagnier, Regenia. *Subjectivities: A History of Self-Representation in Britain, 1832–1920.* New York: Oxford University Press, 1991.

Gallagher, Catherine. *The Body Economic: Life, Death, and Sensation in Political Economy and the Victorian Novel*. Princeton, NJ: Princeton University Press, 2006.

Garner, Stanton B. "Shaw's Comedy of Disillusionment." *Modern Drama* 28, no. 4 (1985): 638–58.

Gavin, Hector. *Sanitary Ramblings: Being Sketches and Illustrations of Bethnal Green, a Type of the Condition of the Metropolis and Other Large Towns*. Cass Library of Victorian Times 8. 1848. Reprint, London: Cass, 1971.

Gilbert, Pamela K. "Medical Mapping: The Thames, the Body, and *Our Mutual Friend*." In Cohen and Johnson, *Filth*, 78–102.

Gill, Stephen. Notes to *Our Mutual Friend*, by Charles Dickens. New York: Penguin, 1971.

——. Notes to *The Nether World*, by George Gissing. Oxford: Oxford University Press, 1992.

Girdlestone, Charles. "Rich and Poor." In *Meliora, or Better Times to Come*, edited by Viscount Ingestre, 1st series, 12–23. 1853. Reprint, London: Cass, 1971.

Gisborne, Lionel. *Thames Improvement*. London, 1853.

Gissing, George. *The Collected Letters of George Gissing*. Edited by Paul F. Mattheisen, Arthur C. Young, and Pierre Coustillas. 9 vols. Athens: Ohio University Press, 1990.

——. *London and the Life of Literature in Late Victorian England: The Diary of George Gissing, Novelist*. Edited by Pierre Coustillas. Lewisburg, PA: Bucknell University Press, 1978.

——. *The Nether World*. Edited by Stephen Gill. Oxford: Oxford University Press, 1992.

——. "The Place of Realism in Fiction." *Humanitarian* 7, no. 1 (1895): 14–16.

Godwin, George. *London Shadows: A Glance at the "Homes" of the Thousands*. 1854. Reprint, New York: Garland, 1985.

——. *Town Swamps and Social Bridges*. The Victorian Library. 1859. Reprint, Leicester: Leicester University Press, 1972.

Goode, John. *George Gissing: Ideology and Fiction*. London: Vision, 1978.

——. "George Gissing's *The Nether World*." In *Tradition and Tolerance in Nineteenth-Century Fiction: Critical Essays on Some English and American Novels*, edited by David Howard, John Lucas, and John Goode, 207–41. New York: Barnes and Noble, 1967.

Granville, A. B. *The Great London Question of the Day; or, Can Thames Sewage Be Converted into Gold?* London, 1865.

"A Greater Plague than Cholera." *Economist*, 27 October 1849, 1190–91.

Greenslade, William. *Degeneration, Culture and the Novel, 1880–1940*. Cambridge: Cambridge University Press, 1994.

Greg, W. R. "The Special Beauty Conferred by Imperfection and Decay." *Contemporary Review* 20 (October 1872): 692–97.

Grylls, David. *The Paradox of Gissing*. London: Allen and Unwin, 1986.

Halliday, Stephen. *The Great Stink of London: Sir Joseph Bazalgette and the Cleansing of the Victorian Capital*. Phoenix Mill, UK: Sutton, 1999.

Hamilton, Cicely. *Diana of Dobson's*. In *New Woman Plays*, edited by Linda Fitzsimmons and Viv Gardner, 33–77. London: Methuen, 1991.

Hamlin, Christopher. "Muddling in Bumbledom: On the Enormity of Large Sanitary Improvements in Four British Towns, 1855–1885." *Victorian Studies* 32 (1988/89): 55–83.

———. "Providence and Putrefaction: Victorian Sanitarians and the Natural Theology of Health and Disease." *Victorian Studies* 28 (1985): 381–411.

———. *What Becomes of Pollution? Adversary Science and the Controversy on the Self-Purification of Rivers in Britain, 1850–1900.* New York: Garland, 1987.

Handy, Ellen. "Dust Piles and Damp Pavements: Excrement, Repression, and the Victorian City in Photography and Literature." In *Victorian Literature and the Victorian Visual Imagination,* edited by Carol T. Christ and John O. Jordan, 111–33. Berkeley: University of California Press, 1995.

Hardin, Jennifer. *Monet's London: Artists' Reflections on the Thames, 1859–1914.* St. Petersburg: Museum of Fine Arts, St. Petersburg, Florida, 2005.

Hardy, Dennis. *From Garden Cities to New Towns: Campaigning for Town and Country Planning, 1899–1946.* London: E. and F. N. Spon, 1991.

"'Here They Come!'—The Mob in St. James's Street." *Graphic,* 13 February 1886, 177.

Hill, Nancy K. *A Reformer's Art: Dickens' Picturesque and Grotesque Imagery.* Athens: Ohio University Press, 1981.

Hill, Octavia. *Homes of the London Poor.* 1883. Reprint, London: Cass, 1970.

Himmelfarb, Gertrude. *The Idea of Poverty: England in the Early Industrial Age.* New York: Knopf, 1984.

Hobhouse, Hermione. *Lost London.* Boston: Houghton Mifflin, 1972.

Hollingshead, John. *Ragged London in 1861.* 1861. Reprint, New York: Garland, 1985.

———. *Underground London.* London: Groombridge and Sons, 1862.

Hood, Thomas. "The Bridge of Sighs." In Clubbe, *Selected Poems of Thomas Hood,* 317–20.

Hoskins, George Gordon. *An Hour with a Sewer Rat; or, a Few Plain Hints on House Drainage and Sewer Gas.* London, 1879.

House, Humphry. *The Dickens World.* 2nd ed. Oxford: Oxford University Press, 1960.

"Housing of the Working Classes." House of Lords, 22 February 1884. *Hansard Parliamentary Debates,* 3rd ser., vol. 284 (1884): 1679–1710.

"How Some of the London Poor Spend the Night." *Illustrated London News,* 29 October 1887, 510.

"How the Poor Are Housed." *Clerkenwell Press,* 24 August 1878, 3.

Humpherys, Anne. *Travels into the Poor Man's Country: The Work of Henry Mayhew.* Athens: University of Georgia Press, 1977.

Humphreys, George W. *Main Drainage of London.* London: London County Council, 1930.

Hyndman, H[enry] M. "The English Workers as They Are." *Contemporary Review* 52 (July 1887): 122–36.

Jameson, Frederic. *The Political Unconscious: Narrative as a Socially Symbolic Act.* Ithaca, NY: Cornell University Press, 1981.

Jephson, Henry. *The Sanitary Evolution of London.* 1907. Reprint, New York: Arno, 1978.

Johnson, Edgar. *Charles Dickens: His Tragedy and Triumph.* 2 vols. New York: Simon and Schuster, 1952.

Jones, Gareth Stedman. *Outcast London: A Study in the Relationship between Classes in Victorian Society.* New York: Pantheon, 1984.

Joyce, Simon. *Capital Offenses: Geographies of Class and Crime in Victorian London.* Charlottesville: University Press of Virginia, 2003.

Kearns, Gerry. "Biology, Class and the Urban Penalty." In *Urbanising Britain: Essays on Class and Community in the Nineteenth Century,* edited by Gerry Kearns and Charles W. J. Withers, 12–30. Cambridge: Cambridge University Press, 1991.

Keating, Peter, ed. *Into Unknown England, 1866–1913: Selections from the Social Explorers.* Manchester: Manchester University Press, 1976.

Kingsley, Charles. "Great Cities and Their Influence for Good and Evil." In *Sanitary and Social Lectures and Essays,* 187–222. London: Macmillan, 1889.

———. *Who Causes Pestilence? Four Sermons.* London: Richard Griffin, 1854.

Korg, Jacob. *George Gissing: A Critical Biography.* Seattle: University of Washington Press, 1963.

Lambert, Brooke. "The Outcast Poor: Esau's Cry." *Contemporary Review* 44 (December 1883): 916–23.

Landow, George P. *The Aesthetic and Critical Theories of John Ruskin.* Princeton, NJ: Princeton University Press, 1971.

Langland, Elizabeth. *Nobody's Angels: Middle-Class Women and Domestic Ideology in Victorian Culture.* Ithaca, NY: Cornell University Press, 1995.

Lefebvre, Henri. *The Production of Space.* Translated by Donald Nicholson-Smith. 1974. Reprint, Malden, MA: Blackwell, 1991.

Lefevre, G. Shaw. "London Street Improvements." *Contemporary Review* 75 (February 1899): 203–17.

Lewis, George. "Prevailing Evils Examined in Detail: I. Physical Destitution." In *Lectures on the Social and Physical Condition of the People, Especially in Large Towns.* Glasgow, [1842].

Logan, Peter Melville. *Nerves and Narratives: A Cultural History of Hysteria in Nineteenth-Century British Prose.* Berkeley: University of California Press, 1997.

Lohrli, Anne. *Household Words: A Weekly Journal, 1850–1859.* Toronto: University of Toronto Press, 1973.

London, Jack. *The People of the Abyss.* 1902. Reprint, London: Pluto, 2001.

"London on the Thames: The Desired Embankments." *Builder,* 25 January 1862, 61–62.

Lovick, Thomas. "Report of Mr. Lovick, Assistant Surveyor, on Flushing Operations." Metropolitan Commission of Sewers. Reports and Documents. London, 1848–49.

Luckin, Bill. *Pollution and Control: A Social History of the Thames in the Nineteenth Century.* Bristol, UK: Adam Hilger, 1986.

Maltz, Diana. "Practical Aesthetics and Decadent Rationale in George Gissing." *Victorian Literature and Culture* 28 (2000): 55–71.

Marshall, Alfred. "The Housing of the London Poor: Where to House Them." *Contemporary Review* 45 (February 1884): 224–31.

Masterman, C. F. G. *From the Abyss: Of Its Inhabitants by One of Them.* 1902. Reprint, New York: Garland, 1980.

Masters, Henry. *An Architect's Letter about Sewer Gas and House Drainage.* London, 1876.

Matz, Aaron. "George Gissing's Ambivalent Realism." *Nineteenth-Century Literature* 59, no. 2 (2004): 212–48.

Maxwell, Richard. "Henry Mayhew and the Life of the Streets." *Journal of British Studies* 17, no. 2 (1978): 87–105. http://www.jstor.org.

Mayhew, Henry. *London Labour and the London Poor.* 4 vols. 1861–62. Reprint, New York: Dover, 1968.

McBriar, A. M. *Fabian Socialism and English Politics, 1884–1918.* Cambridge: Cambridge University Press, 1966.

McLaughlin, Joseph. *Writing the Urban Jungle: Reading Empire in London from Doyle to Eliot.* Charlottesville: University Press of Virginia, 2000.

Mearns, Andrew. *The Bitter Cry of Outcast London.* Edited by Anthony S. Wohl. The Victorian Library. 1883. Reprint, New York: Humanities Press, 1970.

Melosi, Martin V. *The Sanitary City: Urban Infrastructure in America from Colonial Times to the Present.* Baltimore: Johns Hopkins University Press, 2000.

Metropolitan Board of Works. Newspaper clippings collected by the Metropolitan Board of Works. London Metropolitan Archives.

——. Papers of the Metropolitan Board of Works. London Metropolitan Archives.

——. *Report of Proceedings, of Enquiry into Metropolis (Pear Tree Court Clerkenwell) Improvement Scheme.* 28 March 1877. London Metropolitan Archives.

Metz, Nancy Aycock. "The Artistic Reclamation of Waste in *Our Mutual Friend.*" *Nineteenth-Century Fiction* 34 (1979): 59–72.

——. "Discovering a World of Suffering: Fiction and the Rhetoric of Sanitary Reform, 1840–1860." *Nineteenth-Century Contexts* 15 (1991): 65–81.

Miller, J. Hillis. "The Topography of Jealousy in *Our Mutual Friend.*" In *Dickens Refigured: Bodies, Desires and Other Histories,* edited by John Schad, 218–35. Manchester: Manchester University Press, 1996.

Moretti, Franco. *Atlas of the European Novel, 1800–1900.* London: Verso, 1999.

[Morley, Henry]. "A Foe under Foot." *Household Words,* 11 December 1852, 289–92.

[——]. "A Way to Clean Rivers." *Household Words,* 10 July 1858, 79–82.

Nead, Lynda. *Myths of Sexuality: Representations of Women in Victorian Britain.* New York: Basil Blackwell, 1988.

——. *Victorian Babylon: People, Streets and Images in Nineteenth-Century London.* New Haven, CT: Yale University Press, 2000.

"The No-Police Riots." *Saturday Review* 61 (13 February 1886): 219–20.

Nord, Deborah Epstein. *Walking the Victorian Streets: Women, Representation, and the City.* Ithaca, NY: Cornell University Press, 1995.

O'Connor, John. *Thames Embankment from Somerset House.* 1873. Engraving by H. Adlard from painting. Guildhall Library, City of London.

Olsen, Donald J. *The City as a Work of Art: London, Paris, Vienna.* New Haven, CT: Yale University Press, 1986.

——. *The Growth of Victorian London.* London: B. T. Batsford, 1976.

Oppenlander, Ella Ann. *Dickens' All the Year Round: Descriptive Index and Contributor List.* Troy, NY: Whitston, 1984.

Orwell, George. "George Gissing." In *The Collected Essays, Journalism and Letters of George Orwell,* edited by Sonia Orwell and Ian Angus. Vol. 4. New York: Harcourt, 1968.

"Our Homeless Poor—Midday in St. James's Park." *Graphic,* 17 September 1887, 302.

Owen, David. *The Government of Victorian London, 1855–1889: The Metropolitan Board of Works, the Vestries, and the City Corporation.* With contributions by David Reeder, Donald Olsen, and Francis Sheppard. Edited by Roy MacLeod. Cambridge, MA: Harvard University Press, 1982.

[Parkinson, Joseph Charles]. "Attila in London." *All the Year Round* 15 (26 May 1866): 466–69.

Parliament. *First Report from the Royal Commission on the Housing of the Working Classes with Minutes of Evidence and Appendix, 1884–85.* 1884–85 (c. 4402) (c. 4402-I), vol. 30. Irish University Press Series of British Parliamentary Papers. Urban Areas: Housing, 2. Shannon: Irish University Press, 1970.

———. *First Report of the Royal Commission on Means for the Improvement of the Health of the Metropolis.* 1847–48 (888), vol. 32. In *Reports from the Royal Commission on the Health of the Metropolis and from the Board of Health on Sanitary Conditions and Nuisances Removal with Minutes of Evidence, 1847–1854.* Irish University Press Series of British Parliamentary Papers. Health: General, 7. Shannon: Irish University Press, 1970.

———. *First Report of the Royal Commission on the State of Large Towns and Populous Districts, with Minutes of Evidence, Appendix and Index, 1844.* 1844 (572), vol. 17. Irish University Press Series of British Parliamentary Papers. Health: General, 5. Shannon: Irish University Press, 1970.

———. *Report of a Committee to Inquire and Report as to the Origin and Character of the Disturbances Which Took Place in the Metropolis on Monday, the 8th of February, and as to the Conduct of the Police Authorities in Relation Thereto; with Minutes of Evidence and Appendix.* Presented to both Houses of Parliament by Command of Her Majesty. 1886 (c. 4665), vol. 34.

———. *Report of the Select Committee on the Sewers of the Metropolis.* 1823 (542), vol. 5. In *Report from Select Committees on the Sewers of the Metropolis and on Town Sewers with Minutes of Evidence, Appendices and Indices, 1823–1862.* Irish University Press Series of British Parliamentary Papers. Urban Areas: Sanitation, 1. Shannon: Irish University Press, 1970.

———. *Report on Main Drainage of the Metropolis Presented to the Metropolitan Board of Works by Messrs. Hawksley, Bidder, Bazalgette.* 1857–58 (419), vol. 48. In *First and Second Reports of the Royal Commission on the Sewage of Towns and Reports and Papers Relating to Sewage Disposal with Minutes of Evidence, Appendices and Indices, 1854–1861.* Irish University Press Series of British Parliamentary Papers. Urban Areas: Sanitation, 4. Shannon: Irish University Press, 1970.

———. *Second Report from the Select Committee on Metropolis Improvements.* 1837–38 (661), vol. 16. In *Reports from Select Committees on Public Walks and Metropolis Improvements with Minutes of Evidence, Appendices and Index, 1833–1838.* Irish University Press Series of British Parliamentary Papers. Urban Areas: Planning, 1. Shannon: Irish University Press, 1968.

———. *Second Report of the Royal Commission on the State of Large Towns and Populous Districts.* 1845 (602), vol. 18. Irish University Press Series of British Parliamentary Papers. Health: General, 6. Shannon: Irish University Press, 1970.

Pelling, Margaret. "Contagion/Germ Theory/Specificity." In *Companion Encyclopedia of the History of Medicine,* edited by W. F. Bynum and Roy Porter, vol. 1, 309–34. New York: Routledge, 1993.

Pennybacker, Susan D. *A Vision for London, 1889–1914: Labour, Everyday Life and the LCC Experiment.* London: Routledge, 1995.

Peterson, Jon A. *The Birth of City Planning in the United States, 1840–1917.* Baltimore: Johns Hopkins University Press, 2003.

Phillips, Richard. *Mapping Men and Empire: A Geography of Adventure.* London: Routledge, 1997.

Pike, David L. *Subterranean Cities: The World beneath Paris and London, 1800–1945.* Ithaca, NY: Cornell University Press, 2005.

Pollock, Griselda. "Vicarious Excitements: *London: A Pilgrimage* by Gustave Doré and Blanchard Jerrold, 1872." *New Formations* 4 (1988): 25–50.

Poole, Adrian. *Gissing in Context.* London: Macmillan, 1975.

———. Introduction and notes to *Our Mutual Friend,* by Charles Dickens. New York: Penguin, 1997.

Poovey, Mary. *Making a Social Body: British Cultural Formation, 1830–1864.* Chicago: University of Chicago Press, 1995.

"Population and Thoroughfares." *Building News,* 23 October 1874, 481–82.

Porter, Dale H. *The Thames Embankment: Environment, Technology, and Society in Victorian London.* Akron, OH: University of Akron Press, 1998.

Porter, Roy. *London: A Social History.* Cambridge, MA: Harvard University Press, 1994.

"The Position of the Drainage Question." *Builder,* 3 July 1858, 450.

P[owers], S[usan] R[ugeley]. *Remarks on Woman's Work in Sanitary Reform.* Ladies' Sanitary Association. 3rd ed. London, 1862.

Pulling, Robert. *Sewage Turned to Profitable Account.* London, 1875.

Reach, Angus B. *London on the Thames; or, Life Above and Below Bridge.* London, 1848.

Reaney, George Sale. "Outcast London." *Fortnightly Review,* n.s., 40 (December 1886): 687–95.

Reboul, Marc. "Charles Kingsley: The Rector in the City." In *Victorian Writers and the City,* edited by Jean-Paul Hulin and Pierre Coustillas, 41–72. [Lille]: Université de Lille III, [1979].

Reid, Donald. *Paris Sewers and Sewermen: Realities and Representations.* Cambridge, MA: Harvard University Press, 1991.

Reynolds, Osborne. *Sewer Gas, and How to Keep It Out of Houses: A Handbook on House Drainage.* London, 1872.

Richardson, Benjamin Ward. *Woman as a Sanitary Reformer.* Lecture delivered before the Sanitary Congress. Exeter, 1880.

Richter, Donald C. *Riotous Victorians.* Athens: Ohio University Press, 1981.

"River Pollutions: The River Thames." *Builder,* 11 July 1868, 513–14.

Rogers, Jasper W. *Facts and Fallacies of the Sewerage System of London, and Other Large Towns.* London, 1857.

[Sala, George Augustus]. "Powder Dick and His Train." *Household Words,* 7 May 1853, 235–40.

Salisbury, 3rd Marquess of (Robert Cecil). "Housing of the Working Classes." Speech to the House of Lords, 22 February 1884. *Hansard Parliamentary Debates,* 3rd ser., vol. 284 (1884).

"Sanitary Sermons." *Punch,* 13 January 1872, 15.

Schneer, Jonathan. *London, 1900: The Imperial Metropolis.* New Haven, CT: Yale University Press, 2001.

Schoenwald, Richard L. "Town Guano and 'Social Statics.'" *Victorian Studies* 11, suppl. (1968): 691–710.

————. "Training Urban Man: A Hypothesis about the Sanitary Movement." In Dyos and Wolff, *The Victorian City,* 2:669–92.

Schubert, Dirk, and Anthony Sutcliffe. "The 'Haussmannization' of London? The Planning and Construction of Kingsway-Aldwych, 1889–1935." *Planning Perspectives* 11 (1996): 115–44.

Schwarzbach, F. S. *Dickens and the City.* London: Athlone Press, 1979.

"Section of Thames Embankment." *Illustrated London News,* 22 June 1867, 632.

Sedgwick, Eve Kosofsky. *Between Men: English Literature and Male Homosocial Desire.* New York: Columbia University Press, 1985.

Shaw, G. B. *Major Barbara.* Edited by Dan H. Laurence. London: Penguin, 1960.

Sheppard, Francis. "The Crisis of London's Government." In Owen, *Government of Victorian London,* 23–30.

————. *London, 1808–1870: The Infernal Wen.* Berkeley: University of California Press, 1971.

Sibley, David. "Outsiders in Society and Space." In *Inventing Places: Studies in Cultural Geography,* edited by Kay Anderson and Fay Gale, 107–22. Sydney: Longman Cheshire, 1992.

Sichel, Edith. "Two Philanthropic Novelists: Mr. Walter Besant and Mr. George Gissing." *Murray's Magazine* 3 (April 1888): 506–18.

"The 'Silent Highway'-Man." *Punch,* 10 July 1858, 15.

Sims, George R. "Evicted London." In *Living London: Its Work and Its Play, Its Humour and Its Pathos, Its Sights and Its Scenes,* edited by George R. Sims, 203–9. Vol. 1. London: Cassell, 1903.

————. *How the Poor Live and Horrible London.* 1889. Reprint, New York: Garland, 1984.

Smith, F. B. *The People's Health, 1830–1910.* New York: Holmes and Meier, 1979.

Smith, J[oshua] Toulmin. *A Letter to the Metropolitan Sanatory Commissioners: Containing an Examination of Allegations Put forth in Support of the Proposition for Superseding, under the Name of Sanatory Improvement, All Local Representative Self-Government by a System of Centralized Patronage.* London, 1848.

Soja, Edward W. *Postmodern Geographies: The Reassertion of Space in Critical Social Theory.* London: Verso, 1989.

———. "The Spatiality of Social Life: Towards a Transformative Retheorisation." In *Social Relations and Spatial Structures,* edited by Derek Gregory and John Urry, 90–127. London: Macmillan, 1985.

"Some London Clearings." *All the Year Round,* n.s., 33 (26 January 1884): 226–32.

"Some London Clearings: Clerkenwell." *All the Year Round,* n.s., 34 (7 June 1884): 124–30.

"Some London Clearings: Eastcheap." *All the Year Round,* n.s., 35 (8 November 1884): 103–9.

"Some London Clearings: Soho." *All the Year Round,* n.s., 36 (13 June 1885): 309–12.

Spencer, Herbert. *Social Statics, Abridged and Revised; Together with The Man versus the State.* Vol. 11, *The Works of Herbert Spencer.* 1892. Osnabrück, Ger.: Otto Zeller, 1966.

Spurgin, John. *Drainage of Cities: Reserving Their Sewage for Use, and Keeping Their Rivers Clean; Being Especially Applicable to the Thames.* London, 1858.

Stallybrass, Peter, and Allon White. *The Politics and Poetics of Transgression.* Ithaca, NY: Cornell University Press, 1986.

Stewart, Garrett. *Dickens and the Trials of Imagination.* Cambridge, MA: Harvard University Press, 1974.

"A Stranger on the Thames Embankment." Letter to the editor. *Builder,* 16 October 1869, 823–24.

Sucksmith, Harvey Peter. "The Dust-Heaps in *Our Mutual Friend.*" *Essays in Criticism* 23 (1973): 206–12.

Sutcliffe, Anthony. *Towards the Planned City: Germany, Britain, the United States and France, 1780–1914.* New York: St. Martin's Press, 1981.

Swift, Jonathan. "A Description of a City Shower." In *The Norton Anthology of English Literature,* edited by M. H. Abrams et al., 2009–11. 6th ed. Vol. 1. New York: Norton, 1993.

Swinburne, Algernon Charles. "Charles Dickens." *Quarterly Review* 196 (July 1902): 20–39.

Tarn, John Nelson. *Five Per Cent Philanthropy: An Account of Housing in Urban Areas between 1840 and 1914.* Cambridge: Cambridge University Press, 1973.

Tarr, Joel A. "Sewerage and the Development of the Networked City in the United States, 1850–1930." In *Technology and the Rise of the Networked City in Europe and America,* edited by Joel A. Tarr and Gabriel Dupuy, 159–85. Philadelphia: Temple University Press, 1988.

Taylor, Nicholas. "The Awful Sublimity of the Victorian City: Its Aesthetic and Architectural Origins." In Dyos and Wolff, *The Victorian City,* 2:431–47.

Teale, T. Pridgin. *Dangers to Health: A Pictorial Guide to Domestic Sanitary Defects*. 4th ed. London: Churchill, 1883.

Tenniel, John. "New London." *Punch's Almanack for 1889*, 6 December 1888.

[Thackeray, William M.]. "Greenwich—Whitebait." *New Monthly Magazine*, ser. 2, 71 (July 1844): 416–21.

"The Thames." *Sanitary Review, and Journal of Public Health* 4 (1858): 142–43.

"Thames Banks—Quays to Come." *Builder*, 16 July 1859, 465–67.

"The Thames Embankment." Letter to the editor. *Builder*, 28 November 1868, 881.

"The Thames Embankment." *Builder*, 18 March 1882, 306–7.

"The Thames Embankment, in Reference to the General Embellishment of London." *Builder*, 12 March 1864, 181–82.

"The Thames Embankment Works." *Illustrated London News*, 20 August 1864, 192.

Thornbury, Walter. *Old and New London*. 6 vols. London: Cassell, Petter, and Galpin, [1872–78].

Torrens, W[illiam] M. "What Is to Be Done with the Slums?" *Macmillan's Magazine* 39 (April 1879): 533–45.

"To the Thames (After Tennyson)." *Punch*, 3 July 1858, 7.

Treuherz, Julian. *Hard Times: Social Realism in Victorian Art*. With contributions by Susan P. Casteras, Lee M. Edwards, Peter Keating, and Louis van Tilborgh. London: Lund Humphries, 1987.

Trotter, David. *Cooking with Mud: The Idea of Mess in Nineteenth-Century Art and Fiction*. Oxford: Oxford University Press, 2000.

Tuan, Yi-Fu. *Topophilia: A Study of Environmental Perception, Attitudes, and Values*. 1974. Reprint, New York: Columbia University Press, 1990.

"Utile cum dulce." *Punch*, 6 January 1872, 2.

"The Victoria Embankment." *Builder*, 16 July 1870, 562.

Wall, Cynthia. *The Literary and Cultural Spaces of Restoration London*. Cambridge: Cambridge University Press, 1998.

Welsh, Alexander. *The City of Dickens*. Cambridge, MA: Harvard University Press, 1986.

"What to Do with the Thames Embankment." *Building News*, 12 August 1870, 112–13.

White, Arnold. *The Problems of a Great City*. 1886. Reprint, New York: Garland, 1985.

Whitley, Alvin. "Thomas Hood and 'The Times.'" *Times Literary Supplement*, 17 May 1957, 309.

Whitten, Wilfred. *A Londoner's London*. Boston: Small Maynard and Co., 1912.

Wiggins, John. *The Polluted Thames. The Most Speedy, Effectual, and Economical Mode of Cleansing Its Waters, and Getting Rid of the Sewage of London*. London, 1858.

Williams, Raymond. *The Country and the City*. New York: Oxford, 1975.

Wilson, Elizabeth. *The Sphinx in the City: Urban Life, the Control of Disorder, and Women*. Berkeley: University of California Press, 1991.

Winter, James. *London's Teeming Streets, 1830–1914*. London: Routledge, 1993.

Wohl, Anthony S. *Endangered Lives: Public Health in Victorian Britain.* London: Methuen, 1983.

————. *The Eternal Slum.* London: Edward Arnold, 1977.

————. Introduction to *The Bitter Cry of Outcast London,* by Andrew Mearns. The Victorian Library. 1883. New York: Humanities Press, 1970.

Wolfreys, Julian. *Writing London: The Trace of the Urban Text from Blake to Dickens.* New York: St. Martin's, 1998.

Wood, Thomas L. *London Health and London Traffic.* London, 1859.

Worboys, Michael. *Spreading Germs: Disease Theories and Medical Practice in Britain, 1865–1900.* Cambridge: Cambridge University Press, 2000.

"A Word about the Thames Embankment." Letter to the editor. *Builder,* 12 March 1870, 209.

Worsley, William. *Thames Reform: A New Plan for the Drainage of the Metropolis; Combined with Practical Suggestions for Public Convenience, Health, and Recreation.* London, 1856.

[Yates, Edmund]. "The Business of Pleasure." *All the Year Round,* 10 October 1863, 149–52.

[————]. "Silent Highway-Men." *All the Year Round,* 31 October 1863, 234–36.

Yelling, J. A. *Slums and Slum Clearance in Victorian London.* London: Allen and Unwin, 1986.

index